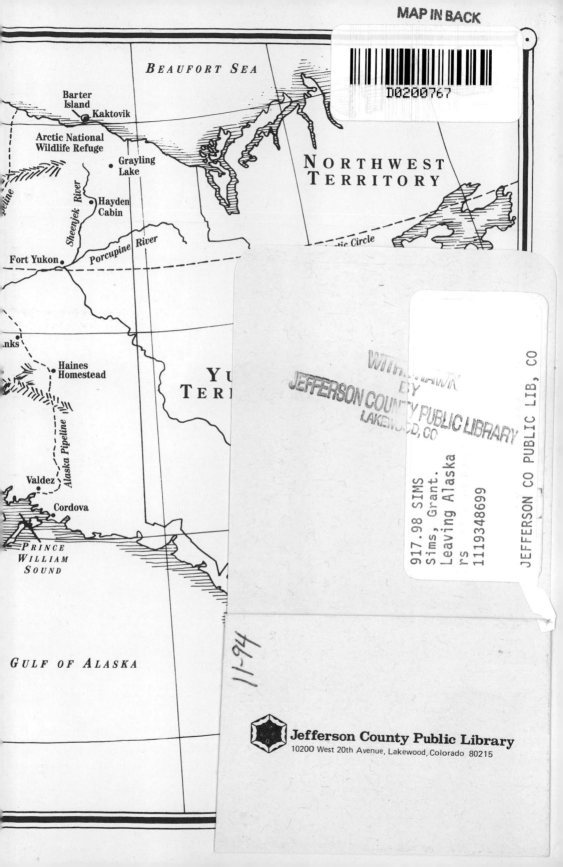

BEAUFORT SEA

Barter
Island
Kaktovik

Arctic National
Wildlife Refuge

Grayling
Lake

Sheenjek River

Hayden
Cabin

Porcupine River

Fort Yukon

NORTHWEST
TERRITORY

tic Circle

nks

Haines
Homestead

YU
TERI

Alaska Pipeline

Valdez

Cordova

PRINCE
WILLIAM
SOUND

GULF OF ALASKA

LEAVING

ALASKA

LEAVING

ALASKA

Grant Sims

THE ATLANTIC MONTHLY PRESS
NEW YORK

Portions of Chapter 3, "In All Their Rudenesses and Wilds," and of Chapter 6, "A Loss of Innocence," originally appeared in different form in *Outside* magazine as, respectively, "A Magnificent Rudeness," November 1989, and "A Clot in the Heart of the Earth," June 1989. The several epithetical and Chapter 13 quotations from John Haines are from various of his eight volumes of work, particularly "The Writer As Alaskan: Beginnings and Reflections," in *Living off the Country: Essays on Poetry and Place,* University of Michigan Press, 1981; *Stories We Listened To,* The Bench Press, 1986; *Selected Poems: 1960–1980,* Wesleyan University Press, 1982; and *New Poems: 1980–88,* Story Line Press, 1990.

Published simultaneously in Canada
Printed in the United States of America

FIRST EDITION

Library of Congress Cataloging-in-Publication Data

Sims, Grant.
Leaving Alaska / by Grant Sims.—1st ed.
ISBN 0-87113-476-4
1. Alaska—Environmental conditions. 2. Environmental
responsibility—Alaska. 3. Alaska—Description and travel. I. Title.
GE155.A4S56   1994   363.7′009798—dc20   93-43126

DESIGN BY LAURA HOUGH

The Atlantic Monthly Press
841 Broadway
New York, NY 10003

10 9 8 7 6 5 4 3 2 1

FOR MY FAMILY

Acknowledgments

I can't thank enough:

Rick Steiner, David Grimes, Dolly Garza, Roger Kaye, Stuart Pechek, Marta McWhorter, Chuck Hamel, and John Haines for patiently
submitting their private lives to my years of scrutiny.

Barry Willis for talking it all over with me first.

Anton Mueller for his editorial guidance and patience.

My wife, Joan, for the love and cheerful matronage that seem to
produce the majority of books by men.

Susannah for her faith.

Cody for his bright life.

And Alaska for causing, among ordinary people, remarkable lives.

What does it take to make a journey? A place to start from, something to leave behind.

John Haines, *Moments and Journeys*

Contents

CONTENTS

Book III: Termination Dust

BOOK I

Before the Storm

1

The Choices That Define Us

It is not, in the end, Alaska, a place where a few people can live in perpetual self-congratulation, but humankind we are talking about. What we do and say here touches everywhere the common lot of people.
—John Haines, *Living off the Country*

More than anything else about Alaska, I am haunted by flights I will always remember, and by landings I can't forget. They are the dreams and rude awakenings of my roamings through a place that I suspect has come to define my life in ways I hadn't intended. "Place makes people," says Alaska's poet laureate, John Haines; "in the end it makes everything." Alaska is the end of an America that was, the last piece of our old place. What has it made me? How has it contributed to the shaping of us all?

Alaskans fly. Over the years, if you are Alaskan, you develop an inner view, an aerial composite of the far northwest as seen from a light plane a few hundred feet up, that you can play back slowly or at light speed as the need occasions. All of us everywhere do something similar, of course; we connect ourselves to places we have been with memories that are compressions of the journeys themselves. We can visualize in less than a second the 5-mile path to Jenny Lake, or the 623 miles of road to the old family farm. Mentally, we can arrive there almost instantaneously, yet with full affection for every turn we have taken and each cottonwood we have passed. We can do that because each trip we take physically is an impregnation, a brainchild, and over the years a maturing brainchild, ever more animate with tableaus of all the times of our passing, and ever more deeply breathing—if we have been at all curious or alert—of the vapors of all that we have learned.

In the summer of 1989, on the day my inner map of Alaska became whole, I was standing on beach gravel with a friend, Stu Pechek, at Alaska's northern border looking out over the Beaufort Sea's disintegrating ice. It was the Fourth of July—the beginning of the arctic spring. The setting was new to me and disquieting, with its flat sweep of treeless coastal plain and, northward toward the pole, all ice and water, a puzzle of white pieces sliding around on a wet blackboard. We talked about it in the wary monotone of strangers:

"Formidable."

"Nothing between us and London."

"Well, ice."

"And whales." Stuart turned southward. "And 2,000 miles down to Ketchikan." He said this last more familiarly; it was a homeward look, blocked by the ragged black jut of the Brooks Range 30 miles to the south, but homeward nonetheless. We had the map inside us; we could fill it in; we knew the lay of the land between us and Fairbanks, and between us and Fort Yukon, and Valdez, and Homer, Haines, and Ketchikan. We stood side by side, not saying anything, and I realized that we were each taking in all of Alaska, all of its 586 thousand square miles, taking it all in with one swift glide of mind.

Until that day I had never flown north of the Brooks Range; the stark far northland wasn't part of my inner view. But now it was. Now I could lift from the arctic coastal plain to weave among the black and white peaks of the Brooks, and south of those treeless mountains I could pick up the tree line at Arctic Village and skim down a river, maybe the Chandalar, southward to the lake lands of the Yukon Flats, and lift again over the chalky castles of the White Mountains, drop down over the brief clutter of Fairbanks, watch my shadow flick over the tundra and spruce and boggy creeks of the hundred-mile-wide Tanana Valley, skirt the glacial mass of Mt. McKinley to climb with the upward sweep of tundra toward the icy crest of the Alaska Range, then dip to the coast at Anchorage and follow the beaches through the sun and mist, the green and gray, the thousand miles and thousand isles of Prince William Sound and the Alaskan Archipelago, to the other end.

The other end was looking good to me that day. After seven years in Alaska I was poised to leave. The trip to the farthest northern reaches, in spite of leaving me awestruck, was only a diversion, a magazine assignment. Three months earlier, 11 million gallons of oil had spilled from the ruptured hull of the oil tanker *Exxon Valdez* into Prince William Sound;

and now, owing to the editorial outrage that roiled in the wake of the spill, I had been sent to the northernmost end of the Alaska pipeline to look into the oil industry's campaign to sink exploratory wells in the Arctic National Wildlife Refuge (ANWR).

I went, but I was feeling finished with Alaska. My picture of the earth from out here on its isolated rim had become for me too stark. As a writer I felt I needed to get back into the richer, hotter current of human flow. But a business had been set in motion that would keep me here, at least for a while. It would bind me to those few special friends who, each in his own little exclave of wildness, were—even as I stood with Stuart and looked vaguely toward them—rankling against the sudden loss of innocence that big oil had brought down on them in March. We all felt laid bare, exposed, as if caught in hiding. We felt vulnerable, and over the years ahead we would each and collectively become more aware of our vulnerabilities; but, more important, we would begin to understand how this great piece of the earth had made us into its own saviors, if only we could carry far enough forward with our hardening strengths.

It is difficult, in this mostly wildless age, to explain how powerfully binding can become a union between a man or a woman and wildness itself. Most of us sense it, I think; with our canine molars we bite down on meat with a genetic nostalgia for chaos, and for the great extinct tests of our mettle that lay in solitude, in the wild.

Those among us who had still gone out, looking for peace at the heart of chaos, in the end had found our wildlands to be illusion. The *Exxon Valdez* simply poured oil on them, and they disappeared. Suddenly there was no security in seclusion. One gush of petroleum into Prince William Sound had exposed the vulnerability, and we were forced to acknowledge that all that is wild today is merely indulged. Solitude, quietude, and the pride of self-sufficiency that we thought we had earned through our union with place—all were merely matters of corporate mercy, and in one accidental corporate stroke they were stripped.

It was only later we would realize that the rage within our impotency was the seed of hope, and that this vast, vulnerable land was about to have its champions.

They didn't seem like champions to me that day. I simply thought southward toward a handful of family and friends in Fairbanks and Valdez and Cordova and Sitka, and some of them not in any town, but like myself off doing summer things in the bush. And then, with a dawning awareness that I have not had many times in my life, I began to realize that something was different. I was surprised. All the friends I thought about were in seriously bad temper; they were all finally picking sides for a good fight, and here I was about to walk away. I hadn't wanted any part of championing Alaska; I had come to think of her as a frontier museum. I wanted to go, was ready to go; but suddenly it wasn't time to leave.

I went to Alaska, as do most who go, because the far north was to me a bastion of wildness and individuality. Of her 375 million acres, fewer than half a million were settled in the sense that I had come to think of as settled. True, there had been some major environmental skirmishing over the Alaska pipeline and clear-cuts in the Tongass National Forest. But in 1980, just a little more than a year before I arrived, more than a third of the state had been set aside as wildland when Congress enacted the Alaska National Interest Lands Conservation Act. This was the land with which I wanted intimacy. She was the reservoir for my wildest dreams, and a landscape symbolic of what I felt was the natural, expansive, and unconquerable spirit to which we as a people aspire.

When I arrived in Fairbanks in the fall of 1982, I was the same age and of the same attitude as was Walt Whitman when, in *Song of Myself,* he wrote, "I, now thirty-seven years old in perfect health begin, / Hoping to cease not till death." And during those first few years, Alaska fired me right up and ceased me not to my heart's content.

In California and Montana I had been a newsman and a script writer; but I wanted to write books. And I came north recognizing that although Alaska had inspired some good books, not a lot of them had been written by people who stayed. They were written by visitors: Jack London, Robert Service, John McPhee. I figured that if I stuck around, maybe I could carve a niche. I took an editing job, and later a teaching job, at the state university in Fairbanks and settled into the rhythm of being Alaskan. I was proud of manfully weathering the brittle winters and was smitten to the point of passion by the twenty-four hours of sunlight in each summer day. I wallowed in the gluttony of weighing my trout in the same increments as sacks of potatoes. I had become a meat fisherman and a meat hunter, taking half a ton of salmon every season, and half a ton of moose when I could get it. I was both sobered and quickened by the primal forces of the hunt and comfortably domesticated by the homely rituals of putting food by. I enjoyed the novelty of danger, and of preparing not so much for trips as for survival. To my outdoor equipment I added extreme cold weather gear and a bigger, more serious first aid kit, and a bear gun and rations and an ice chest and a fish smoker. Whenever I flew, which was often, all of that equipment except the smoker went with me because I could never be sure when the weather would turn or whether the pilot would clear the trees.

After a while, being Alaskan became, I think, like being an athlete or an artist or a mystic when the White Moment (or in Zen, the state of No Mind) kicks in and only those parts of your being absolutely necessary to the activity at hand are being used. If visiting Alaska is like watching a transcendent performance, then living in Alaska, for me, was the performance itself. I felt at one with the fierceness of it. "In the woods," said Emerson, "a man casts off his years, as the snake his slough, and at what period soever of life, is always a child. In the woods is perpetual youth." In the woods my son Cody was born, and his Native godmother got together with the village elders to give him a Native name, *Ak'laat,* meaning Little Brown Bear. He was part of me, we were part of the land, we were perpetually young. I felt, happily, that life was right, and that I was adding real muscle to my disposition.

Then two things happened. I was at hand when a small boy died and on hand at the wreck of the supertanker *Exxon Valdez*. The boy's death, which was senseless and reflective of a tragically rampant alcoholism among Alaska Natives, stayed with me all the next winter, disillusioned me, and—combined with other awakenings to what we have done to the far north and its peoples—eventually induced me to take Cody and the concordant woman who'd married me, Joan, and to leave Alaska. But even as I was poised to go, the wreck out at Bligh Reef roused a much loftier human force that eventually convinced me to stay—at least for a while.

Maybe I'd known all along that trying to live a frontier life is a sort of curatorship. It's a life that doesn't speak to the future; you spend your time pressing and preserving fragments of the century before. I must have had inklings that I was dabbling in the backwaters of a romanticized past rather than properly, artistically, bucking the currents of the future. If so, I ignored them until the death of little Virgil James became the summary jolt in which all the inklings became a proclamation. It was as if, while on the Yukon River looking for Virgil's body, I woke up. Over the following long winter, realization set in like a chill to the bone, until finally I accepted that my passion for Alaska had gone cold, and that even a good dream laid down over a good place can add up to a fool's paradise. I wanted out.

Friends kept asking me why, and to soften the reply I lied. This place, I told them, is under ice for eight months a year, and in darkness for half of that. It was difficult, I told them, to reconcile my own five-year-old son's prospectively dark childhood with my own, in which the days had blinked dependably on and off 365 times a year. I wanted to spend more time fly-fishing, and I didn't want my son to grow up in a frogless land with no swimming holes. I wanted him to feel mud occasionally between his toes and a toad occasionally in his pocket, and to swing, occasionally, from a rope into water that wouldn't stop his heart.

But it went deeper than that, of course; deeper, I mean, than love of a sport deprived by long winters, and deeper than idealized childhood. Because it is easier to blame winter than to explain conviction, I didn't tell my friends that I had decided, finally, that we come to Alaska not so much for its fullness as for its emptiness, which is the complement to that place in our hearts that needs to remain empty. I had decided that I didn't want to be an Alaskan writer because the wildness that is the best part of Alaska should not have an art. *Wild* in its old Teutonic infancy meant "uncivilized, ungovernable, unartful, chaotic, beyond control." We come to Alaska to measure what we have become against the backdrop of that magnificent chaos from which we sprang. We come, in other words, because we have a passion for wildness which is precisely the same passion we have for the innocent brutality of our roots.

Then, like the millions of salmon and birds and even whales that come each year to replenish themselves, we leave; and if things have gone right we leave replenished, and that is Alaska's greatest value to the rest of the world. But that is not what we are led to believe. The Alaska we sell, and the image we buy, is blind to the sophistry and dirty dealings that have led to the nation's highest rates of suicide, alcoholism, and domestic abuse, and to the sleazy politics that have wiped out cultures, corrupted coastlines, and slaughtered entire species. In Haines, whenever a cruise ship haunts the dock, Tlingit tribal dancers in red and black and white come out to dance. They look like they're supposed to look; they affirm our image of them. So we applaud; they bow. Then they insist on being paid by the tour company in cash, and a few hours later you can find a significant percentage of them asleep in their own vomit in the gutters.

I decided that Alaska is simply a lie we continue to tell—an illusion, a sacrifice of morality for the sake of image. But Kim Heacox, a wildlands photographer I groaned to one day about how we can corrupt a place with deceptive manipulation of its image, pointed out that the deception isn't Alaska's. Deceits are human foibles, he said; Alaska's greatest value lies within itself as a geography of hope. "That's what I see when I look through a lens: hope—a model of how a smoothly functioning planet can operate."

Well, maybe. What Kim Heacox saw through his lenses was a model of how a smoothly functioning planet could operate without people. And without emotion. Geographic Alaska didn't give a jot or a tittle for humanity. To be a geography of hope, a land must be championed by the hopeful. In Kim Heacox's case, the hope projected through the lens was his own, and it was for himself, and for you and me.

I wasn't yet sure that enough of us had enough honest hope to carry the business of saving this last best place up here and, by extension, ourselves and the rest of humankind. We were a complacently greedy folk; and even now, after a record of environmental travesty that had swept from coast to coast and spilled into the oceans at both sides, we found it all too easy to swallow the Great Corporate Promise of clean technology. It had served our own rapacity well, that promise; in the chalice of a nation's convenient faith it was an elixir, subduing opposition, placating politics, consoling our despair.

Still, as a people we did take Alaska seriously. We owned her, after all. The title to more than 60 percent of Alaska was held not by the state of Alaska or by Alaska Natives, or even by the Japanese, but by our own federal government, which is to say you and me. Although that at a glance might seem a dubious dominion, it was a very real power. The votes of Outsiders had determined Alaska's current path and would determine her future. She was ours; we took her personally. She was one of our last great, simple beauties. Her people were the surrogate fierce folk for a nation, and they were our proxies at the troubled interface of humanity and nature. Their philosophical struggles with whether to make that final shift from frontier to holistic thinking was representative of our struggle. Confronting crises, they also found themselves confronting their own life roles, values, and relationships. And, through them, we confronted our own.

Until the wreck of the *Exxon Valdez* in 1989, those crises didn't get a lot of attention, and Alaska wasn't really a matter of heavy national conscience. But those 11 million gallons of oil gushing into Prince William Sound, and the swell of events in the wake of the wreck, seemed to have brought a great body of simmering conflict to a boil. Alaska became caught up in that global bellowing that seemed determined to keep the coals of conscience hot as hell until we were all convinced that it was time to give the planet a vote.

The arctic language is a strange language, and the arctic experience unfamiliar. Utah State University scholar Tom Lyon, in *This Incomperable Lande,* points out that it is this strangeness that helps the reader to see the world anew, and to confront freshly the great question of how we should live. It is a place, he says, "where the choices that define us are before us once again."

Lyon traces the history of American writing (and American thought) about the land as a slow "awakening of perception to an ecological way of seeing." And writer Barry Lopez, about the time he was in Alaska researching *Arctic Dreams,* ventured that this shifting perception might one day "provide the foundation for a reorganization of American political thought."

For a while it seemed to those of us in Alaska that the rupture of the *Exxon Valdez* and the contamination of some 3,500 miles of Alaska coastline might be enough to precipitate that shift. We knew that the oil spill had stunned the nation, jostled its mind-set, and catapulted environmental worry to new heights. *Time* magazine began a cover story on the spill with the dire observation by Samuel Johnson that "when a man knows he is to be hanged in a fortnight, it concentrates his mind wonderfully." We all felt ourselves at the steps to an environmental gallows, and we all knew that our collective greed was partly to blame. Collectively we felt loss, guilt, and anger at a corporate structure to which we pay a lot of money to satisfy our appetites without making a big mess. We were nationally contrite, nationally wounded, nationally in a huff. We were in a mood to get tough.

Instead, what happened in the wake of the *Exxon Valdez* was one of the great triumphs by corporate anesthesiology over public pain. In its year of responsibility for America's nastiest human-caused environmental disaster, the Exxon corporation set itself a new record with $4 billion in profits. And three years later, the company would get off with a $125 million settlement (one thirty-second of its profits from the spill year alone) that amounted to nothing more than a fiscal wrist slap, a minor inconvenience, the cost of which it had already passed on in advance to you and me.

I still wanted to write a book; but in collecting stories of independent lives, I had come to see that the real story was of a last frontier in which Frontier Thinking was under heavy assault. And I realized that as fervently as a story of Alaska should attach value to place, it should be a story of a homeland slipping away, and of those in it who had been able to forget a hope of that particularly strong mettle that lies at the far side of despair.

Theirs were stories worth labeling as history; and in historical perspective, Alaska was a good place in which to examine such a movement of people and place through crisis and human time. For in spite of its size, Alaska remained relatively uncluttered, and easy to move about in, from past to present, from catholic to parochial. Human influence there was still a dent, not a domination. Issues and factions were easily identified, and historical trails were still clear. It was still possible to see, there, what we expected of a democracy. Our lives flowed daily through the dynamic issues at hand.

And because Alaska set the individual into wilderness, the journey of those Alaskan few had become to me representative not only of our collective dealings with nature, but also of our ultimate confrontation, which was with ourselves.

2

The Dreamers

Vast, Titanic, inhuman Nature has got him at disadvantage, caught him alone, and pilfers him of some of his divine faculty. She does not smile on him as in the plains. She seems to say sternly, Why came ye here before your time? This ground is not prepared for you. Is it not enough that I smile in the valleys? I have never made this soil for thy feet, this air for thy breathing, these rocks for thy neighbors. I cannot pity nor fondle thee here, but forever relentlessly drive thee hence to where I am kind. Why seek me where I have not called thee? . . . Shouldst thou freeze or starve, or shudder thy life away, here is no shrine, nor altar, nor any access to my ear.
— Henry David Thoreau, *Ktaadn*

As Stu Pechek and I stood on the Beaufort shore, I felt that I had a fresher angle, a better handle, on life than I'd had in years. Thinking south from near the top of the world—considering back through time and across geography—engendered an oddness of perspective as striking to me as if I were looking at the earth and my life from space or from a deathbed.

I found myself reconnected to the old joy. It had been an odd flight to this spot—a trip a thousand miles up the Alaska Pipeline from the still-spreading slick of oil that had initially affirmed my conviction that we would keep sticking it to this place until it was just like all those other myriad disappearances that are the heaviness of our history, the irretrievable anchors of our lives. I'd thought I had finally managed to disconnect myself from a way of life that I had defined as impending tragedy. But here I was, realizing that there was still this, and it was worth so very much.

And within that quickening there was something else: an acuteness with which the lives around my life had come into focus. I had come to the edge of the world away, and with the distance all our doings down there had shrunk; they were all tiny, manageable and clear.

"It's a long way to Tipperary," Stuart said.

We walked on, killing time. The magazine assignment that had taken me there to look into oil company plans to drill in the Arctic National Wildlife Refuge was on hold. At breakfast in Kaktovik, we'd heard that the plane that was to take us out into the wilds among the 180,000 animals of the refuge caribou herd was delayed again; so when we finished eating we had walked west of the village, past a cemetery and two giant radar grids, then out across the tundra and down to the beach. The north shore of Barter Island is a narrow band of sucking muck and loose cobbles that lies between the Beaufort Sea and a muddy bluff that blocked our view of the Brooks Range to the south. For a couple of miles, we scrabbled over ice floes that had jammed up against the bluff and knew we were being foolish: somewhere close by were a polar bear sow and two cubs that frequented Kaktovik's seaside dump.

If it had been a common beach, we probably would have given it up quickly as too much work and worry, but this Beaufort shore was a rare stretch—one that probably only ourselves and the bears, and maybe a hunter or some Kaktovik lovers would walk this year. No magazine was likely to send me here again; even hot politics seldom get you to a place like this twice.

There was no surf. The water was jammed with blue-white floes that you could hear colliding softly, the long, columnar crystals of their rotting ice tinkling like glass wind chimes as they collapsed. Sea ducks chattered in the leads, and a few big-eyed spotted seals watched us from the ice. For an hour, we listened to our boots and our breath and the ice and the ducks.

About noon we climbed the bluff, up to where the tundra was greening under a cool breeze and a hot sun. To the east, beyond the narrow band of ice-floed water that separated the island from the mainland, and beyond the mildly upward sweep of the arctic coastal plain, the Brooks Range shimmered hazy blue.

The day had brightened since we'd slipped down the bluff to the ice of the sun-blocked shorefront. Stuart sat in the lee of a hillock and pulled off his daypack, his down jacket and wool cap. I did the same. Stripped to a flannel shirt under Carhartt overalls, Stuart reclined against a tussock and sighted down his legs. The vee of his feet cradled a stretch of mountains to the south of us and a little east.

I figured he was drawing a bead on his Grayling Lake cabin, 150 miles precisely thataway. His intimacy with the country between here and there was the reason I'd asked him to show me around the refuge. One spring a few years back he had landed on this island, wrestled into a 125-pound backpack, walked across the rotting sea ice to the mainland, then hiked solo for four months and 450 trailless miles up and over the Brooks Range to the village of Anuktuvuk Pass. Once, wading across a storm-swollen river, he was swept off his feet and under a ledge of auf ice, where his huge pack stuck, with him strapped to it. I'd been swept under ice myself once, briefly, and knew the terror.

So we'd shared some similar dangers and a fondness for beer on free taco night at Pike's Landing in Fairbanks, and a love of this country. But Stuart was the private type; I didn't yet know him well. In bits, I'd learned that he was a small-town Minnesota boy, the first of his family to get a college degree; he had become a government biologist, then forsook the security and turned to seasonal fishing and part-time survey work to pay for his solo forays into the wilds. Most of that wayless faring was in winter, in subzero darkness. He liked the summer sun okay, he told me once. In sunlight you relaxed and opened up. But in some ways he preferred the intimacy of the dark and cold. You survived in the cold the way a mountain climber survives, by building your shelter around yourself in layers and taking it with you, moving slowly, prudently, out at the edge of life, alone.

Most winters, he flew into Grayling Lake to spend four or five months maintaining a 150-mile trapline—the northernmost line in Alaska. "Working hard out there makes me belong," he'd say. In the couple of years we'd been friends, I still had no more than a vague idea of what he meant. But as we lay back against the breeze-dried sedge and gazed vaguely toward his cabin sanctuary, I wondered whether he, whether *we,* really pine for wildness or for simplicity—for qualities disappearing from the earth or from ourselves.

"You going in this winter?" I said.

"I hope so."

"The sanity of solitude," I said. We were both students of aloneness; we'd talked about it before. But during the winter just past, the long, cold night that I thought I had tamed had turned feral on me. I wondered aloud whether any of his winters had ever been as hard on him.

He grinned, a little sheepishly. "I didn't tell you about the butter?"

"Butter. I would remember."

"You have to understand about milk fat," he said. "Every winter I lose twenty pounds of paunch between November and March, and it would be a lot worse if it weren't for the BTUs I put on my pancakes every morning."

"BTUs?"

"Butter thermal units. Quarter of a pound every day. Forty below, hot pancakes, all that sweet cream; after a while you *live* for butter."

But a year ago January, seven one-pound blocks of it had been stolen from his food cache by a pine marten while he was away from the cabin on his trapline rounds. "Little pisser got around the tin cones I'd put on the legs of the cache. I don't know how he did it. You could see his tracks all over, like he'd taken over the minute I left.

"And somehow he got past those leg protectors and up there in the cache and pushed out a five-pound bag of chicken breasts, a loaf of Christmas bread my mom sends up special every year, and all my butter.

"At first I was just mad. Seven pounds, a quarter-pound a day, twenty-eight days; that would put me right up close to March. A month without butter. But after a while I figured, what the hey. A fellow could do that standing on his head."

It had been a long winter, he said; mostly clear, mostly dark, always cold, usually a tolerable thirty to forty below. But, a few days after the butter disappeared, a spell set in at fifty and sixty below that carried through January and the first three weeks of February—butterless, brittle, and black.

"It ate at me. He'd left this endless network of trails that fanned into the brush, and for days I followed every one. I woke up and ate pancakes without butter and went outside and followed marten tracks. I dug umpteen holes with a snowshoe. Down along the creek there were marten tracks under every cutbank. I went pawing under those banks like a dog.

"One place, I broke into a sort of cavern and thought sure I'd found it. But you know what he had in there? He had the head—just the head—from every marten I'd trapped and skinned out that winter. Every one. Dozens. Stacked like cordwood."

Stuart stopped talking. He was thinking, I supposed, about a chamber full of furless, frozen marten heads. "Ever find any butter?" I said.

"One solid-gold brick of it. Made it last six weeks." His eyes narrowed off toward the distant cabin. "I got to feeling lonely. And a lot older."

There were days, he said, that he'd be sitting on his padded Sterno can, eating or reading or fiddling with the radio, and something out the window would catch his eye, some small motion among the thick stands of white spruce toward Grayling Lake. Abruptly he would get up and grab his seven-millimeter Magnum from where it hung. He would reach the doorway in a stride and stand glaring toward the spruce.

"Nothing ever moved," he said. "Ever. Just me, bouncing off the walls and eating little tiny pats of butter."

He looked over at me and grinned. "The sanity of solitude. Way out there at wits' end."

In the sun, on the soft arctic tundra among the whispering sedge with a big white bear somewhere close at our backs, it was the right story to tell. To me, on a day when I was seeing clearly, it was a story exemplary of all those years we'd had when life in Alaska was its own justification and didn't have to have any meaning other than whatever meaning is inherent in the harmless things you do in dangerous places.

I can't say that I had a premonition that day that all our lives would change so much—were, in fact, already changing. The sense of impending loss that I felt as I lay on that island plain killing time was due, I suspect, to the change in my own life on which I was so intent. And the clarity, I suppose, was of that poignant kind that comes with the realization, when you are saying good-bye, that you have loved these years more dearly than you knew.

★ ★ ★

17

One summer week in 1983, I and my brother-in-law Tom Edmiston rode a raft down sixty miles of the Gulkana River, including a heart-stopping five minutes through its Class V Canyon Rapids, where our raft hung up on a black rock at the lip of a fall.

We got out onto the slippery outcropping and pried with our oars until the raft began to swing the right way round, then we dove back in and went over the drop. When it was over we stood ashore down below, still in the roar, watching the white foam dribble to a hiss over black depths. My hands shook. We tossed down a shot of Johnnie Walker Red.

And that's the way life in Alaska became for me: hard on the body, easy on the career, a life of bush flights and distant rivers, of glaciers and rough seas, of big fish and big bears, a life that could write itself as long as I could live it. To me, Alaska's molding philosophy was to exceed caution, and, along with the rest of the fraternity, I subscribed to it fully.

In 1989 as I loafed on Barter Island with Stu Pechek, I was coming off a stretch of years during which I and my family and friends were all full-stride Alaskans. I had a circle of friends who were prominent people in a territory 2,000 miles wide and 1,500 long. Not that being prominent in Alaska required a big portfolio, or even meant anything much to anyone other than ourselves. It was just that you had picked a place so out of the ordinary that you assumed uncommonness by association, and achieved prominence by virtue of getting by.

It made you feel good, being a definable presence in such a powerful land. I'm not talking about being a presence in capital Juneau, where politics are made, or in metropolitan Anchorage, where politicians are made, but in Alaska's nether regions, where the bush people call Anchorage Los Anchorage and say that the nicest thing about Los Anchorage is that it is so close to Alaska.

Out there, you stitched together the fabric of companionship with precarious flight and high adventure, and with commiserations that were really braggings about how you were matching up to the territory. It was an exhilarating life, in which decisions were simple, and actions uncomplicated, and the graces other than social.

I realized, as I dreamed southward from that sunny patch of arctic tundra, that travel here, as it tends to be anywhere, is as much through a network of friends as through territory, and the network creates a larger whole, so that you are in some real ways extensions of each other. In Alaska we were bonded by all those moments of being willingly feral together, and of being not yet serious. Although we were each busy doing what we had come to Alaska to do, we could at any time of night or day think out across the territory and know pretty much how the others were getting by.

Rick Steiner, for instance. A few months before I went to the Arctic, Rick's life at the other end of the Alaska pipeline in Cordova was breached by the wreck of the *Exxon Valdez,* and he was shortly transformed there into a man burdened and grim. But even as I remembered southward from the Arctic, knowing that as a biologist and fisherman he was still living from calamity to calamity in Prince William Sound, grim was not how I thought of him. I pictured him as long-strided and smiling, as I'd seen him so often when life was still as we had come here to live it.

Rick hadn't owned a comb in a decade; he didn't iron his clothes. He was an expert on salmon, herring, and halibut, as well as on ocean currents, killer whales, sea lions, and otters. He was six foot four, with a stride he said varied according to what he was running from. Before moving to Cordova, he had been the university's marine advisory agent in the Eskimo village of Kotzebue, where the locals called him *Ivalu,* which means "sinew." He looked like a skinny Viking, with unkempt blond hair and a full beard, all of it framing an almost constant smile and crinkling blue eyes.

Six years before, the University of Alaska transferred him a thousand miles south from Kotzebue to Cordova. His role as marine advisory agent—the maritime counterpart of a corn belt county farm adviser—was to learn what research needed to be done to help fishermen and, conversely, to translate research results into practical information the fishermen could use. After two years, feeling deskbound, he renegotiated his contract from twelve months to ten a year, saying that if he was not to lose touch with the community he served, he had to spend at least part of his time practicing what he preached among the hunting and gathering that has provided the precarious toehold for Alaskan survival since humanity arrived.

It worked nicely. He partnered with neighbors, fishing herring and salmon and halibut and cod, bucking seas, wallowing through swells, wading in slime, baiting hooks, pulling gear, mending nets, crewing forty-eight, sometimes sixty hours without sleep, feeling the grit of salt crystallized in his unwashed clothes, watching his paper-pushing hands crack, then callus, then crack again.

When he was a kid he crewed long months on trollers, long-liners, and gillnetters, and even had his leg crushed by a 700-pound crab pot in the Gulf of Alaska. And for two seasons when he was fresh out of school, he was an official National Marine Fisheries Service observer on the Japanese high seas gill net fleet. So the annual two months at sea these recent years had proffered nothing dramatically new but had been dramatic nonetheless. He still found great joy in muscling around on a boat, and in the eyes of his neighbors it kept his credentials current.

Rick had grown up in Washington, D.C. (his mother, Faye, was a staff assistant to seven consecutive presidents), where he, like most, tended to cluster with like-minded friends and ignore the rest of the world except what couldn't be avoided of it in newsprint. But in Kotzebue, and then in Cordova, you had to live with the whole town. When small-town politics sizzled, you couldn't afford big-town tactics. You couldn't hide, and you couldn't hit and run. You lived next door to the guy you wanted to belt. Your boat floated in the same harbor, you ate at the same places, he wanted the same woman you wanted, and, when his boat was going down, you'd grab the butt of his pants and pull him aboard, the same way he would you.

You had to work it all out; and Rick had, and he had found the rhythm and camaraderie of it so rewarding that he didn't notice the small-town embroilments when he was embroiled nearly so much as he felt their absence whenever he went away.

And finally he had fallen in love and bought a house.

From where I lay I could see across a westerly stretch of tundra a hundred yards or so to the thin line of blue where two whistling swans had mounded a nest beside a small pond. One of the swans sat like an S on the nest, and the other alternately grazed the shoreside grass and stretched up to scout, its thin neck wavering chimerically in heat waves.

I remembered Rick telling me the story about the day he realized it was time to commit. We had met in Anchorage, at a restaurant that had a glass wall on the Cook Inlet side. We were looking out across the water to the Alaska Range, sipping beer, catching each other up, and he began to talk so meticulously about what he had been doing that there was an oddness to the telling, as though he were combing the experience for clues.

And just as I would probably always hereafter picture the now peacefully napping Stu Pechek howling for butter under the northern lights, I would probably always see Rick Steiner through the window he opened into himself that day.

He had spent the summer at Egegik Bay, 300 miles west of Cordova and 700 or 800 from where I now sat with Stu, out on the north side of the Alaska Peninsula, set netting for salmon. As clearly as he told it, I could see him at the edge of the gray Bering Sea, salt water ruckling up around his bare feet as he anchored one end of the fifty-fathom net onshore, then hopped into a skiff to drag the other end 300 feet out.

I could see him feed the webbing over the gunwale, a lead-weighted line pulling the bottom edge down and small, polymer corks keeping the top afloat. And with me seeing it through his telling, he anchored the out end of the net a few degrees up current, watched the running tide push a long, smooth arc into the line of thirty little floats, then ran the skiff ashore, climbed from the beach to a low bluff, and settled in to wait.

"And as I sat at the rim watching the water, I could see Claudia from the corner of my eye, maybe fifty feet away, step into the doorway of the cabin. She was there just a few seconds. I don't know what made it perfect, but it was perfect, the way the sea was, and her just standing. I remember she was wearing some denim shorts and that maroon halter, brushing her hair, not waving or smiling, just affirming; and then she went back inside."

Something in the moment had made him realize how much he felt at home there. Habitually he told people that he was born on a small, windswept island in the North Atlantic. Long Island. It was an old joke; but thinking of it that day on the shore of the Bering Sea, it dawned on him how deeply wistful the old joke felt. He couldn't remember when he'd made it up, or even *if* he'd made it up. But he realized, there on the reach of another ocean entirely, that this scene, or the archetype of this scene, had been the backdrop to his being for as long as he could remember. This was where he had always wanted to be from, where he had always wanted to be, with a stiff onshore breeze whipping through his hair, and him tasting the salt on his tongue, looking out into an eternity of gray swells, and feeling the flat, gray sand stretching toward his bare feet from infinity right and infinity left.

The set-net site belonged to another friend, Dan Strickland, who was not fishing it that year because he wanted to stay closer to civilization with his due-to-deliver wife. Rick had offered to tend it for a split of the take. He was in the mood for a season of solitude. As to me, and to Stu Pechek, and to most of the others we knew in the far north, periodic aloneness felt necessary to him. He had become habituated, maybe even addicted, to sojourns that disconnected him from professional blather and replenished him with quietude.

But this time he'd decided, after Strickland accepted his offer, to invite along a friend. At first he wasn't sure it was the right thing to do. Oh, he and Claudia Bain had been friends and lovers for a time, but that was there, in another and very busy Cordova life. He didn't know if she would fit into his seclusions.

She did, of course. He should have known. She was an effusive, lovely, kind woman. He had begun to recognize and delight in the complements they brought to each other, he with his biologist's careful fascination with what was going on, she the new age spiritualist marveling at the energies of the earth, and, like that golden retriever pup of hers, Fritha, always wearing her heart on her sleeve.

And she was a darn fine masseuse.

That one special day Rick told me about, they'd been there a week, getting the fish camp ready, watching the motes of fishing boats move to and from the Columbia Ward Seafoods cannery at the head of Egegik Bay. If he squinted he could see the cannery and the squat, drab buildings of the Eskimo village of Egegik sprawled along the mouth of the Egegik River. A few miles out to the northwest, at Coffee Point, the big tender *Grizzly* rode at anchor, high in the water. She'd ride a lot lower later in the day, when Rick and the other set netters around the bay started queuing over to sell her their catch.

It would turn out to be an exceptional year for salmon, but even though Rick didn't yet know that, he knew, that day as he sat on the beach, that it was going to be a good season for himself. He planned to spend six or eight weeks in the small cabin with Claudia, fishing through Bristol Bay's king and red salmon seasons. Word had spread among the fishermen that the price was going to be hot, and at two-something a pound, a seven-pound red would be worth more than a barrel of North Slope crude.

If the run was as big and the prices as high as they said, the money could come to ten, twenty-five, fifty, even seventy-five thousand apiece. Sometimes a fisherman would go broke waiting to hit a banner year, but when one such season did roll around, and you were in on it, you shared a lot of smiles, felt a lot younger, didn't kick your dog. Rick Steiner had been eyeing a boat, a forty-eight-foot seiner named *The Buddy,* and if that kind of money came in this year, it would be fine; he'd put it down on *The Buddy.*

He wasn't really there for the cash, though; it was just a chance to roll up his sleeves. Usually when he did something like this it was no big deal, but this time it felt like a big deal, and for a while after he arrived, he had been puzzled by his own ebullience. This flat, treeless north shore of the Alaska Peninsula wasn't nearly so comely as was Cordova, the port he'd been calling home for the past six years.

Cordova is among Alaska's prettiest towns. It looks tucked and nestled, with its snug harbor and seaside flats and hilly roads, and the big mountains with their thickly timbered flanks of spruce and snowcapped peaks that dwarf the town. Cordova borders a paradise of wildlands and a seaful of treasures along Prince William Sound's 3,600 miles of shoreline fjords and isles and islets, river mouths and tidal flats, reefs and smooth-stone beaches where the orca wriggle clear up onshore to rub the barnacles from their glossy black hides. So why did this muddy gray beach on the Bering Sea feel so much like the place he was born to be?

And then he realized: it was the sense of release. Without knowing that he had become knotted into the gripping weft of small-town fabric, he had stepped unsuspectingly away, into this, into liberation.

* * *

Dan Strickland's spartan little cabin, Rick said, had been tacked up on the low, sandy bluff over the beach. Behind the cabin, the treeless tundra stretched southward toward green hills. The tundra was full of blossoms and birds. Fork-tailed jaegers, black and white, drifted in killer packs over the blossoming turf, where little ruddy turnstones scrunched down in the grass and mewled. Sometimes there were caribou, and occasionally a bear. A scraggly red fox was almost always in evidence on the near tundra, ranging, napping. When Rick and Claudia went down to tend the nets, the fox came and sat on the bluff at the very spot from which Rick himself kept watch. They would look up from their work and see the fox looking down, looking hungry.

I don't know what Rick's most vivid memories might be of that summer, or of that one particular poetic day that had stuck with him in such detail. But I do know the one stretch of his story—the one brief image—that struck me as finally defining my old friend with utter, if enigmatic, clarity.

The tide was three-quarters in, he told me, when a school of sockeye hit the net. From where he stood, Rick could see the silvery flashes as the fish moved swiftly in with the current, just a few yards out from shore. When the first of the heads slipped irreversibly through the mesh, the little polymer floats started to bob wildly. As Rick watched, the body of the school stacked up against those thrashing in the net. The untrapped fish recoiled, boiled at the surface, swirled aimlessly, retreated up tide. Some slipped out toward the seaward end of the web. A very few, bright as needles, stitched over the net and hurried on.

Rick felt his pulse quicken. It was primal excitement, and he felt more keenly now, as he had begun to feel during the past week, that there was a particular wonder and integrity about getting food this way. It had happened for aeons: the reds spawned, their fry fed for a year in lakes then disappeared into the Pacific, and then, two or three years later, they came back. They came back to you. They came back to the bears. To a land that was quiet and almost humanless for ten months a year, they returned as a sudden, huge, contracted pulse; and the bears, and the birds, and the people with nets all felt the intoxication, and the sensuousness, and maybe even the sacredness of what was at once this bizarre yet perfectly sensible glut.

Rick shouted. Claudia stepped to the door of the little cabin, then saw the net and came at a trot. They raced through the slick gray mud and out through the slap of wavelets that passed in good weather for a Bristol Bay surf. They pulled in the skiff, a twenty-four-footer that they kept anchored out beyond the tide line because it was more than a skiff, really, and too big to wrestle on and off the beach. Rick kicked over the Johnson outboard and swung the boat to the down-current side of the net. For a while he cowboyed the salmon, herding them into the net with the skiff. Then he cut the motor, nosed the skiff into the net, and he and Claudia began to pull the shoreward section of net over the gunwale. They could feel the throb of struggling fish, and as they worked the boat outward, pulling the net over the side as they went, the first of the season's red salmon came to hand, thumping like drumbeats against the hull.

Rick couldn't help hooting, hollering, as the fish piled up against his legs. They stared up at him bright-eyed, their flanks glistening like mercury, their backs as green as a sunlit sea. He tried to count them, but after a while he forgot about everything other than the rhythm of the work, and mastering the certain twist that freed the entangled gills from the net.

When he and Claudia were through, with the boat loaded so heavily that the waterline was almost to the gunwales, they headed together across the bay toward the tender, *Grizzly,* to off-load the fish. Rick was not a hunter, but he told me that he imagined that this feeling was not unlike what a hunter must feel. The prey had gone from quick to dead, and his own exhilaration was tempered now by the solemn recognition that all of this was, in the end, a serious business.

Yet an afterglow of elation remained. Aboard the tender, all hands were at the rail to read a sign of the season from this first set. Approaching them, "I felt like a kid with a lunker," Rick told me, "a retriever with a goose."

And a year later, and a thousand miles away, I knew that the flow and the peace that he had found were gone; and I began to hate the slick corporate sophistry that had interrupted it and was killing him even as he tried to help heal the damage down in Prince William Sound.

★ ★ ★

The chimeric swan, the one on patrol, suddenly spread its wings and cocked its neck. Maybe twenty yards in front of it, a vague patch of white and russet that I hadn't seen before scuttled quickly back, then forward, then to one side, almost as if swirling in a breeze. Through the heat waves I couldn't tell what it was until it passed through a window of clear air. It was an arctic fox. The swan rushed it once, and again, and again, and finally it retreated for good, bobbing off through the thermals and over a swale and out of sight. The swan's wings settled slowly, and it waddled over to graze closer to the nest.

It looked like a dream, and felt like the end of a dream. For so many years, I realized, we had all been dreamers. Like those of most of the rest of Western humanity, our lives had been anchored in complacency—that unfounded trust in the human powers that run the planet. But we thought that because we lived closer than most to the outer edge of human power, our lives were less complacent, less to blame, and maybe even a little more authentic and a little more pure.

If they were, there hadn't, after all, been a lot of protection for the purity of it from the foxes.

So how was Rick doing now, I wondered. How were *all* my Alaskan friends doing? We'd each stepped out of the mainstream for one reason or another, and now here it was bursting into our backwater with that same unconscionable punitiveness with which a torrential society always seems to flush itself a new bed. You see the wall of it coming, and you brace for it, knowing it's going to catch you up, knowing you're going to have to plunge back in, and wondering why you don't just flinch, duck, and run.

"Stuart," I said, "I hear bagpipes."

"I hear a plane," Stuart said, and, sure enough, the keening on the wind became a dilating drone, and in half a minute a red and white Cessna 185 purred over on a downwind toward the Kaktovik airstrip.

"Is that Ross?" I said.

Stuart shook his head. "His is green and white. That one there ought to be Roger Kaye."

Stuart had told me that our bush pilot, Don Ross, was an Alaskan legend. For two days he had also been myth. Exxon had monopolized all available fuel and fuel containers for its Prince William Sound oil spill cleanup effort. Kaktovik was out of airplane juice. Ross, according to a relayed radio message, had sucked his own cached barrels dry and had flown south over the Brooks Range to try to find more.

Mark Kelley, the photographer assigned by the magazine to the story, was frustrated by the delays. After breakfast he had paced off across the village on his own, testy and muttering. Somewhere out on the plains the caribou—*tuttu,* the Inupiat call them—had banded into that great congregation that is one of the largest herds of big mammals in the world. It is a brief phenomenon. At any hour, all 180,000 mosquito-tortured animals would bolt for the high country and within a day could be splitting into smaller and smaller bands, spreading out into a summer range the size of Montana. The weather had been impossibly beautiful, and over scrambled eggs and sausage Mark had had to listen in anguish to a *National Geographic* crew describe the shots they got by flying out in a leased helicopter that had brought in its own fuel.

After he scowled off among the Eskimos, I'd glimpsed Mark once, outside the town hall shooting Native faces with his Nikon. He'd shot my face, too, when village Mayor George Tagarook delayed this hike by collaring me for an egg race to kick off the Fourth of July festivities, but when the race was over, Mark had disappeared. Now, half a day later and a mile out of Kaktovik, the photographer's six-five frame rematerialized, draped over his tripod at the edge of the seaward bluff like a scarecrow hung on a stake. He was facing a small, lumpy man.

"Now I'm hearing bagpipes," said Stuart.

We got up and hiked the 200 yards over tundra swales toward Mark Kelley and the small man and the strange sounds.

"This is John Liestman," said Mark. "From Houston. He's a micropaleontologist. For Exxon?"

"Right," said John Liestman.

John, said Mark, was analyzing drill cores in a lab in the village. Today being the Fourth and all, he had the day off, and, the weather being what it was, had hiked out here to set a new world record for the northernmost playing of the Northumbrian smallpipes.

So we sat in the blossoming tundra on a bluff thirty feet above a mosaic of turquoise ice and listened to the thin, sweet, wind-buffeted melody of "Sweet Hesleyside" until John unlipped his reeds, carefully emptied the leather air bag, and wiped down the drone pipes with a cloth.

He disassembled the bony black pipes from the gray bag, looking like a man pulling the legs off a plucked sandhill crane.

"That was as good as a polar bear any day," said Stuart.

"I haven't had the pleasure of that particular compliment before," said John. He began to pack the lot into a small black case.

Mark capped his lens. "Is this something smallpipe players do—go for records?"

"It is," said the musician. "Last year, the newsletter had a piece about someone playing in Antarctica."

"You have a newsletter," said Mark.

"We do." John Liestman smiled modestly, thanked us, touched a forefinger to the side of his glasses in a small salute, and strode away.

Back in Kaktovik two hours later the mayor had fingered me again, this time to umpire the Fourth of July softball game on the gravel runway east of the village. We were in the third inning when Don Ross's green and white Cessna 185 scattered the outfielders.

Half an hour later we were in the air. Mark sat up front so he could open the window and take shots, but by now the unbelievable weather had been displaced by a great, roily darkness over the arctic plain. We flew west along the coastline at about 300 feet, dodging the biggest of the thunderheads and getting pelted by brief sheets of rain. Below, the Beaufort sea ice was dull gray, the tundra dull brown, and the hundreds of small thaw lakes flat black, staring up at us like sockets.

Then, fifty miles or so west of Kaktovik, we were flying through shafts of sunlight. The cloud cover thinned to cirrus. The lakes went from black to emerald, the sea ice from gray to turquoise, the tundra from soggy brown to a subtle tapestry of botanical greens, tans, reds, and yellows.

Mark perked up. He rubbernecked, and soon he was having the pilot go into the semistall that allowed him to open the window against the airstream and the sudden acceleration that kept the window pinned up under the wing. Mark leaned from the window, shooting, the motor drive on his Nikon going *Wow! Wow! Wow!*

Stuart tapped my shoulder and pointed ahead. It was a herd of maybe fifty caribou cows and calves, lounging on a grassy isthmus between two small lakes. They were not a much different color than the tundra, really, but in the evening light they stood in sharp relief against their magnified shadows, their mottled coats glowing a warm buff and white. As the plane passed overhead, a couple of resting calves struggled to their feet, but otherwise the herd seemed unconcerned.

Stuart tapped me again. This time the caribou on the furry mounds and swales ahead looked like flies swarmed on a pelt. There were thousands. From the front seat, Mark turned to me with a big grin and a clenched fist.

We landed on gravel beside the Tamayariak River, just a few miles inland from the sea. Within five minutes our gear had been dumped and the plane was gone. From here, the plain looked like a short-grass prairie somewhere in Kansas. Although it was about 8:30 P.M., the sun had simply circled up to due north without descending much, and the temperature was somewhere in the breezeless seventies.

"I can't believe it," said Mark. "No wind and no bugs."

"No caribou either," said Stuart. He had walked to a small rise so that he could see out beyond the cut of the river. As we joined him, he handed me his binoculars. From the air, the tundra had thronged with animals from horizon to horizon, but now it seemed that the plains I scanned were empty. I felt a twinge of panic, realizing that all our careful planning had been built around a silly assumption that once we got here we could simply amble like Moses into a living sea, parting caribou.

Fifteen or twenty miles southward, the Brooks Range rose heron blue, its foothills shimmering in the heat. I could see the shallow valley of the Tamayariak snaking from the hills to here, where it flowed by flat and clear and silent. I gave it the fisherman's eye and was disappointed. It was wadable, fishy-looking water, but I could see a healthy hatch of mayflies sailing the surface without a single grayling rising to the meal. There was nothing here; not a bird, not a lemming. Just desolation. I unpacked my gear, set up my tent, leafed through my Inupiat dictionary. Tamayariak, it told me, means "place where some people were lost."

But after setting up camp we went for a walk, toward the west, beyond the river, and there through the desertlike shimmering I saw a wavering brown line on the horizon. From north to west the line was unbroken, and from west to south it spilled onto the nearer tundra, materializing into an antlered forest of brown.

We split up. Carrying packs and heavy tripods, Mark and Stuart moved upstream testing the waters of the Tamayariak, looking for a place to cross. I headed downstream, the plan being that if we got part of the herd between us, one of us was going to get photos of something other than caribou buttocks. Besides, I'd noticed that the plains were dotted with snowy owls, perched on hummocks in a pattern of striking regularity, like white benchmarks, one per square half mile. One of them sat not far from our camp on the other side of the river.

In waders, I crossed the Tamayariak at a shallow tailout, then dropped to my belly and wormed up out of the riverbed toward the owl. The tundra, with its short sedge and small flowers, looked and felt like a blossoming lawn. It was firmer than I expected, and later Roger Kaye explained that this Tamayariak grass was growing on firm river delta topsoil, unlike the deeply matted, spongy stuff elsewhere on the plain, which the biologists say produces two tons of protein per acre.

I stayed on my stomach until I figured I was within camera range of the owl, then lifted my head over a clump of grass to find baleful yellow eyes pinning me like a rat. I took a couple of shots and moved closer, this time to within about thirty feet, before the owl began to shift nervously from foot to foot. I rose slowly to my knees for that one last shot before it flew, and, as I centered the bird and released the shutter, I was surprised at what I got: not fifty yards beyond the owl was a peacefully munching band of several hundred caribou.

The owl gave one bothered screech and left. I dropped to all fours and crawled to the hummock it had left. It was not a nest but a hunting perch, littered with white feathers and with owl balls, those regurgitated wads of gray fur and tiny bones.

The caribou had moved closer. There on the higher hummock I could see that what I had taken to be a band was actually a peninsula of caribou, for beyond the several hundred were several thousand. So far it seemed I was unnoticed. I scanned south for Mark and Stuart and spotted them behind their tripods about a mile away. They faced a huge mass of animals, but it was a mass which avoided them as if they were wolves. Half a mile beyond them the caribou had broken into a nervous trot, heads and tails high, veering in a wide arc toward a river crossing upstream. They hit the shallow water by the hundreds, and the sound of their churning came downstream like the roar of a waterfall.

Unintentionally, I had discovered the secret to stalking caribou. In the coming days, between episodes with tundra swans, and a lone musk ox bull, and arctic foxes, and ptarmigan that burst off croaking like flushed pheasants, we would simply do what I was doing now: lie down on the soft and sunny tundra and wait for the caribou to come. Time and again they did.

From the owl's hummock I watched my herd. It was mostly cows and new calves and yearlings, with here and there the yardlong curlings of bull antlers in velvet. One of the adolescents spotted me first. It stood wide-eyed and still, spraddling its hind legs to take a nervous pee, then slowly craned its neck from side to side as if for a better view. The cows and calves and bulls paid no attention, but within minutes the youngster was joined by another yearling, then another, until there were fifteen or twenty staring at me from a semicircle, the way the cattle of my childhood used to gather and stare when I cut across their pasture toward the bluegill hole.

Finally their heads went down. They remained nervous but began to graze, moving delicately closer. I was now in the middle of a sea of fur and grunts and those loose-boned, clicking hooves, which biologists theorize are built that way so they will spread wide when stepping into mud, then collapse into narrowness for easier withdrawal.

I felt a touch on my left leg. It was a calf, just a month of muscle on its spindly legs, sniffing my green wader. Its mother had her teeth to the grass a few yards away. As I swung my head, she swung hers to look me over once carefully, then resumed grazing. The calf's legs collapsed, and, curling into a ball, it fell asleep.

31

I was accustomed to creatures that recognized my killing power. I couldn't imagine what these might think I was, that I was not a threat lying there. Either they were very stupid or they somehow sensed that I was harmlessly long and slow and content.

Again this wide, clear space had infected me, and I was not at all sure that I was ready for this waltz with the chimera to be my last.

Like the small member of the big herd that slept beside me, I was bonded to this place by the aeons. How could I ever leave?

3

In All Their Rudenesses and Wilds

*The land! Don't you feel it? Doesn't it make you want to go out and
lift dead Indians tenderly from their graves, to steal from them—as if
it must be clinging even to their corpses—some authenticity.*
—William Carlos Williams, *In the American Grain*

Tossing from squall to squall above the Brooks Range after we left
the caribou, I wondered briefly if I hadn't reached an age for which spring
creek fly-fishing was wilderness enough. This kind of flight—we were
headed for another sphincter-puckering landing in weather that made the
plane feel like a leaf—was not as convenient a joy as imagining it all from
down on the tundra, and it was beginning to feel more like hazardous duty
than high adventure. But even now, after a decade of such expensive,
expeditionary testings of the odds, I had only to glance out the window
to remember that the beauty of the place alone still went a long way
toward justifying the risk.

We were in a steep-walled valley deep with shadows and bright with
sun shafts. The mountains, all stone, were ocher and green, yellow and
gray. "The last truly expeditionary wilderness on the continent," Roger
Kaye had told me. A few months before this trip, I'd sat in his office in
the federal building in Fairbanks, eyeing a foot-high pile of reference
materials he had stacked on his desk for me to take home and read. "That's
all research data and political argument. You won't find a trail map or trip
suggestion in the lot. This," he said, handing me a single sheet, "is what
we give to prospective visitors."

The sheet told me that an experience in the refuge "is one you must
search out for yourself" and said that perhaps more than anywhere in
America, "the Arctic National Wildlife Refuge is a place where the sense
of the unknown, of horizons unexplored, of nameless valleys, remains

alive." But be aware, it warned, that "where the wild has not been taken out of the wilderness, there are risks."

The biggest risk to me, it would turn out, would be to my own conscience and would come not from the country's precipitousness but from my teaching the youngsters I was about to meet a new and troubling way to kill. And the image that would haunt me most from this trip would be not of the massifs that seemed about to clutch our plane but of a caribou, childlike, even smaller than the one that had slept beside my leg, and dead.

But all that would come later. Right now the risk seemed less to conscience than to corpus. Don Ross had put the lurching Cessna into a sickening semistall again so that Mark Kelley could open the window to shoot, and the plane had flopped over onto one wing to do a dizzying 360. A thunderstorm was lowering a slaty curtain of rain onto peaks just to the east, and against the curtain was a perfect double rainbow. I looked straight down 500 feet to the braided froth of the Hulahula River. Its name came from neither the Inupiat Eskimos nor the Gwich'in Athabascans but from a turn-of-the-century, homesick Hawaiian whaler. The dancing river. The dancing Cessna. It was no waltz.

We were crossing back over the Brooks to the south side of the refuge to visit some friends of Stuart, the Richard Hayden family, the only family allowed to live in the refuge year-round. Hayden, his wife, and their five children were grandfathered residents whose trapping and building permits predated ANWR's refuge status. They were, according to Roger Kaye, a "cultural resource," a microcosm of the arctic subsistence life that had depended upon the caribou for some 27,000 years. The Haydens were earnestly against oil development, as were the several hundred Athabascan villagers—both Alaskan and Canadian—who shared their south slope hunting grounds.

I wondered who they were, these wild people of whom Roger had talked so affectionately. Why were they here? Roderick Nash, whose book *Wilderness and the American Mind* is a sort of ethics bible for civilized uncivilization, says that "in the final analysis, wilderness is a game everyone plays in his own way." I'd never figured out exactly what he meant by that and had often wondered whether, in stating a truism, Nash had missed the point. Wilderness might be a game only because we have made it one. At a deeper level it might be a genuine passion, and a passion is very much like a god in that, although we can never completely understand it, we can trust it to be what it is.

I didn't think you could treat passion as a game. You could treat it as an art, like fly-fishing, but not as a game. Was wildness a passion for these people we were going to see—or a game?

A hundred and fifty years ago, frontier painter George Catlin was sitting on the banks of the Teton River in what he called "melancholy contemplation." No one was running a pipeline through his passion, but they were butchering a lot of Indians, and the remaining Plains Indians were, in turn, butchering about 200,000 buffalo a year, for which they received a pint of whiskey per hide. Such, Catlin decided, was wilderness at "the desolating hands of cultivating man. Yet this interesting community, with its sports, its wildnesses, its languages, and all its manners and customs, could be perpetuated, and also the buffaloes, whose numbers would increase and supply them with food for ages and centuries to come, if a system of non-intercourse could be established and preserved."

What *if?* he wondered. What if all these things *could* be preserved "in their primitive rudeness, in a magnificent park?" What a beautiful and thrilling specimen for future ages: a nation's park, containing man and beast in all their "rudenesses and wilds."

Catlin decided that such probably wasn't going to be the case. If power was right, he figured, then the wilderness was righteously doomed. "It is not enough in this polished and extravagant age that we get from the Indian his lands and the very clothes from his back, but the food from his mouth must be stopped to add . . . to the fashionable world's luxuries."

Fifty years later, a preserve somewhat along the lines Catlin had envisioned was formed. In 1877, five years after Yellowstone became our first national park, Indians were still hunting buffalo within its borders. But cavalrymen were hunting Indians within its borders, too, and it wasn't long until that older, cruder wilderness of Catlin's day was gone.

In Alaska it was not. The arctic wildland was more akin to what Yellowstone once was than to what Yellowstone has become. Wilderness man—these people we were traveling toward—still killed to live here, and the raven remained a major deity, and many Indians did not like the presence of the desolating hands of cultivating man at all. But substitute caribou for buffalo, and oil for whiskey . . .

I wasn't sure, anymore, which wilderness was right, or even of what true wilderness consists. Maybe we were evolving to some state of being in which we would be satisfied with deer parks and angling clubs. Maybe, but we weren't there yet. Our industrial appetite for oil had evolved ahead of our genes.

Not a lot of wildland chaos crossed our desks these days, but we remembered it in our cells. Our longing for wilderness had as much to do with untamed man as with untamed land. We could deny our canine molars, but until they dropped out we remained genetically hunters. In sport and business we killed, we conquered.

The Hayden cabin was on the Sheenjek River, 100 miles or so upstream from its confluence with the Porcupine River, for which the caribou herd was named. At the Haydens', we would be 150 air miles and on the other side of some pretty formidable mountains from our camp on the Tamayariak. Nonetheless, many of the 180,000 caribou we'd seen there would be leaving their calving grounds on the arctic coastal plain, crossing the southerly passes of the Brooks Range into the Sheenjek drainage, and passing the Hayden place within a couple of weeks. The Porcupine and Sheenjek are two of several major rivers—including the Chandalar, the Christian, the Coleen, the Black, and others—that drain a vast area of northeastern Alaska and the northwestern Yukon Territory, a drainage bigger than Texas that fills a basin bigger than Vermont.

As we passed over the Brooks cordillera, I watched our shadow slide impossibly up a steep green slope that was strung with a necklace of bighorn sheep, and on up toward the black and white of a ragged wet peak and its glistening snowfield. The shadow climbed to within a couple of hundred feet of the plane, then fluttered over the spine and plummeted a couple of thousand feet into a small lake at the headwaters of the East Fork of the Chandalar River. A name from yet another place, the Chandalar. It is a bastardization of the French *gens de large,* or "nomadic people," used by Hudson's Bay Company trappers to describe the river's resident Gwich'in Indians.

All the rivers now had southerly flows. Within a few miles of the small lake, the Chandalar was joined by one tributary, then another, and then it flowed into a broad basin that was full of lakes. It was in this basin that we rejoined the tree line creeping up from the south like the green wash of a watercolor. Trees mean firewood. It is along this line that the raw food–eating Inupiat of the coastal plain are supplanted by the cooked food–eating Athabascans of the interior.

It is in this basin, too, where Eskimos from the rim of the Beaufort Sea spent the first winter of a remarkable migration. In a sort of Ice Bowl exodus triggered by a pullout of the Beaufort commercial whaling fleet in 1903, Japanese expatriate Kyosuke Yasuda talked scores of Inupiat Eskimos into packing their families and leaving their coastal home of some thirty millennia to trek up and over the Brooks Range, then a hundred miles or so down the Chandalar to the Yukon River, and another fifty miles down the Yukon to the mouth of Beaver Creek. Yasuda made two trips of two years each to collect a population for his new little trading-post village of Beaver. There, today, 275 miles from the Beaufort Sea, live several score of the immigrants' descendants. Among the Yukon's more eagle-faced Gwich'in Athabascans, they were incongruously flat-featured Inupiat, with a touch of Japanese. As for Yasuda: After fifty-one years as an American, in 1941 he was flown almost 4,000 miles south to New Mexico and placed behind barbed wire with other Japanese in a wartime internment camp. He was seventy-four.

Fifty miles down the Chandalar we touched down briefly at Arctic Village to refuel, then swung southeast another seventy miles along the Brooks Range's gentle southerly slopes to the upper Sheenjek River.

The Sheenjek is a national Wild and Scenic River. Often that designation invites unprecedented fondling by lovers of the wild and scenic, but this one is so remote that it had been left pretty much alone. The name *Sheenjek* translates to Salmon River, although its salmon run had been sparse for as long as anyone could remember. Right now I was concerned with neither its scenery nor its salmon, for the Cessna had banked into a sharp spruce-top turn as if to land, and I saw nothing below except a violence of white water and boulders.

"I don't see a strip," I said to Stuart.

"I don't either."

"This must be the wrong spot."

"I think you're right."

I was. But it is of such wrong spots that legends are made, so the pilot went in anyway. The Cessna's wheels missed the gray race of the Sheenjek by inches, then pounded down among the boulders. My head thumped the window, probably dented the ceiling, and I braced for more.

Don Ross shut her down.

I glanced sidelong at Stuart, who was glancing sidelong at me. "Pretty short landing," I said.

The pilot nodded. "Pretty short."

"Pretty big rocks," I added.

"Pretty big." He surveyed the terrain, then mildly cocked an eyebrow. "Oh," he said. "That must be the strip over there."

The Haydens, it developed, could see the landing strip from their cabin on the other side of the river. When the plane cut its engine but didn't show up on the strip, they assumed that it had bellied into the Sheenjek, and they bolted to the rescue.

The first I saw of them was a canoe slicing upstream in the shallows, its occupants purposeful and armed. When the craft rattled up onto the stones of the bar, I didn't recognize those who stepped from it as children. I saw two slung rifles and a sturdy hand resting on the grip of a forty-four, faces shadowed beneath the brims of caps, and the one in the lead with long, straight, black hair whipping in a stiff breeze.

Stuart strode past me. "It's the Three Amigos!" he boomed, and embraced the one with the long hair, the face tilting back to look at him with a broad girlish smile and coy black eyes.

These were the children of a man who had spent twenty-nine years in the Alaskan bush, sometimes letting years slip by between trips to town. His youngsters shared his grandfather rights to the southerly slopes of the Arctic National Wildlife Refuge; they'd be allowed to live out their lives here, too, if they wanted. But their children wouldn't. These three, in their teens, were the last of the ANWR line.

Their handshakes were firm, and they were immediately friendly. The eldest, Richard Junior, was quiet and carefully spoken. His thick-lensed glasses were bound to deteriorating frames with duct tape. In the days to come, he appointed himself my personal guard. Even when I tried to wander off alone, he was quietly insistent, tailing me with his bear protection, a bolt-action twenty-five aught six. Richard was also, I noticed, wearing red and white cross-country ski boots. He caught me glancing. "It doesn't matter what I wear in summer," he said. "In winter, it matters."

Fifteen-year-old Daniel was the family talker. He had a broad, spontaneous smile and spent all day, every day, usually until two or three in the morning, giving and milking information. He was also the family fisherman, and his eyes immediately latched onto my aluminum fly rod case. "Can you show me how to use that thing?"

Susan interrupted. "He'd fish till his hands fell off if he could." Her voice was deep for a girl's, and slightly abrupt. She was the take-charge sibling, the most ardent hunter and trapper of the group. I didn't know it yet, but today was her fourteenth birthday. She had just received her first marriage proposal, from a trapper's son over on another river, and it had her puzzled.

At the cabin we met Richard Hayden. He was a smallish man but powerful, with the big, leathery hands and ropes of muscles that come from thirty years in the bush and a diet of lean caribou and moose. He was forty-seven. He had blue eyes in a hawk face and wore an old red-felt crusher hat with the brim on one side pinned rakishly up to the crown. It was his summer hat, he said. Come winter, he'd wear wolverine or fox.

Right now, winter seemed a long way off. It was somewhere between 10:00 and 11:00 P.M. and—although a hundred miles inside the Arctic Circle—pushing 90 degrees. Today, Hayden said, the thermometer had topped at 106. As we shuttled our gear from river to cabin, I sweated in a T-shirt. Yet all the Haydens, I noticed, wore two long-sleeved shirts, the outer one wool. "Two pairs of pants, too," said Susan. "Because of all the blackflies and mosquitoes."

"I don't see how you can stand it."

"We jump in the river every time our clothes start to dry out."

Richard Hayden introduced his wife, Shannon, a Tlingit Indian originally from a few hundred miles southeast of here in the Yukon Territory. She had quick black eyes and a soft voice. A toddler, Duane, peeked doubtfully at us from behind her leg, and in the crook of her right arm she cradled a baby, Judi Ann, who was born in February.

"At sixty below?" I said, remembering February.

"Well, fifty-two. They say the planes can't fly below forty-five, but Roger, he came in and got me anyway." Roger Dowding was a bush pilot out of Fort Yukon, another legend.

"You had her in Fairbanks, then?"

"Had to," said Richard. "Shannon was having problems. All we've got's a little handheld two-way; can't radio out to Fort Yukon, so we relayed through a Japanese airliner flying over the pole."

He showed us around the place. Most years, it was the family's winter trapping cabin, he said. The summer place was forty miles up the tributary Koness River on the shores of Big Fish Lake. Last year, however, the Sheenjek had shifted a channel and had since been chewing at the six-foot-high bank. Richard had decided to keep his family on the river this year so that he could spend the summer moving the cabin, log by log, farther back into the woods. But when the spring flood had receded, it had left the river still forty feet from the walls, so he'd since changed his mind. Instead, he had built a split-rail fence along the high bank to keep his toddler away from the water.

The Haydens also had a "caribou camp," a ridgetop wall tent with a long view, from which they hunted for a month every fall before moving to winter quarters. And then there was the trapline cabin about twenty miles downriver, and another upriver, and then the place up at Grayling Lake. With an income of about five grand a year, this was a wilderness family with six homes.

"I wish you could see the one at Big Fish," said Shannon. "It's the nicest. It's the one we call home."

This one on the Sheenjek was nice enough. It was in a valley, in a clearing ringed by spruce trees and feathered with blossoming fireweed. The cabin was a neat log structure with a green tarp stretched tight over the roof for waterproofing. The main cabin was maybe sixteen by twenty with a loft. To one side, three small bedrooms had been added for the teenagers.

Outdoors, a log food cache perched like a rustic flight control tower on sturdy pilings about fifteen feet above the ground. The braces that connected the pilings were hung with dozens of steel leghold traps, and on the earth beneath the sheltering tower were several freight sleds, snowshoes, and half a dozen pairs of cross-country skis.

Against one side of the cabin was a small log corral, which the Haydens called the nursery. It was occupied by three pups with needle teeth and canted eyes that flashed both domestic curiosity and feral caution. The pups were half wolf. Last month, said Susan, she and Daniel had tracked a wolf to its den and crawled inside to retrieve the whelps they had named Killik, Bear, and Sheenjek. "They'll make good, strong freight dogs," said Susan.

"Like those." She looked out into the yard, where twenty-two other dogs had each been assigned its own miniature log-cabin doghouse and six-foot length of chain. Most of the hundred-pound dogs reacted with a wiggling eagerness to even such a token of attention from Susan as her pointed finger. But the four dark, long-limbed animals she singled out had backed off to the far ends of their chains and focused their yellow eyes unwaveringly on me, the stranger.

It was past midnight. Little Judi Ann was peacefully asleep, swaying in a swing suspended from the cabin's main beam. Through the mosquito netting over the door I could see down to the river, where Daniel Hayden had pieced together my fly rod and was whipping an eddy for grayling. Richard Hayden lounged on the hide-covered couch, the red crusher still cocked over one brow. He was telling his story.

Somewhere along the line, he said, the years had started to blend. "A lot of things, I couldn't tell you they happened in year ten or fifteen. But ask me about the first, I can tell you every mile I walked and every bite I took."

There were a lot of miles that year, and not enough bites. It was 1960. Alaska was a year into statehood, and Hayden was an eighteen-year-old busboy at the Kahler Hotel, across the street from the Mayo Clinic in Rochester, Minnesota. One day on break he read an article in *Outdoor Life* on how to live in the woods. A few months later he loaded his car with some camping gear and a couple of do-it-yourself trapping manuals, drove to Anchorage, sold the car, bought a rubber raft and four-horse outboard motor, a box of oatmeal, and some powdered milk, sugar, salt, and rice. He spent his last hundred dollars to have the lot of it hauled across Cook Inlet and into the trackless lowlands of the Little Susitna River.

That was in August. For the next two and a half months, waiting for snowfall and the trapping season that would bring more money, Hayden ate nothing but oatmeal and spruce grouse. He got skinny. It got cold.

The man who had freighted his gear had taken note of Hayden's meager supplies; just before freeze-up he appeared with several boxes of groceries. "I fell on 'em like a wolf on a bone. It was the only time in my life that it felt so good to get so sick."

Two weeks later he shot a moose. Then snow fell, and he took to the woods with his traps. "I didn't do too bad, I guess, for a kid wandering around looking on page twenty-three to see what to do next." By spring breakup, when he appeared at David Green Furriers in Anchorage, he had collected seven fox pelts, fifty-six muskrats, two mink, two coyote, three lynx, and two beaver. His net: $133.

Now, twenty-nine years later and 500 miles farther north, he trapped mainly marten and the occasional wolverine, along with Daniel and Susan, who were running their own hundred-mile traplines by themselves this winter. The annual take was about 150 pelts.

Richard Hayden's philosophy about trapping was simple. Nature provides a surplus, he said. "Without the trapper, the surplus dies of starvation or disease, in which case it becomes a wasted resource." Trapping is a culture, like agriculture, tree culture, or aquaculture. As a culturist, Richard had found that 150 marten was a sustainable yield, whereas 175 was too many; if harvested at that level, the area's marten population would begin to decline.

"What about wolves?" I asked. A good wolf pelt would fetch $300 or $400. Twice this evening, when the dogs outside stretched their muzzles and began to sing, I heard deep-throated answers from the not-too-distant woods. It was said that wolves would kill tethered dogs, but in this neighborhood the wolves seemed to be lovers, not fighters. Regularly, dog and wolf joined to set the Sheenjek hills echoing with song, and sometimes on moonlit winter nights, a commotion outside meant that the wolves were in among the dogs again, grinning and springing high, vaulting among the domestic cousins in a frenzied but oddly silent dog yard dance.

"I don't trap wolves," said Richard.

He had trapped one wolf by accident a few winters back. Her clamped foot was badly frostbitten. She panicked at his approach. "I didn't know how to calm her down, so I fired a pistol, and she just lay down and resigned herself to whatever was going to happen." He wrapped her in a blanket and took her home. When the foot recovered, he turned her loose. She went but soon returned and had been the family wolf-in-residence ever since. She migrated with the Haydens from home to home, ran ahead of the dog teams in winter, and fed off caribou gut piles during the fall hunt. We'd seen her earlier in the evening, a black face peering at us from behind a thick bouquet of lavender fireweed blossoms, a face decidedly feminine, almost demure.

It was two in the morning, but only the infants were asleep. Richard, Stuart, and I had been sipping brandy with our coffee. I'd set aside my notebook and was listening benignly to Richard and Stuart launch tales of bears and old miners, and of the mysterious brushmen, which I gathered were the arctic cousins of the Yeti and Sasquatch. They talked of being hurt, and spooked, and of Richard and Shannon losing a cabin to midwinter fire, and of the dangers of overflow and auf ice along the rivers, and of the specter of all they'd left behind catching up.

"In most ways the kids aren't backward, though, just different. They'd logged dozens of flights in bush planes before they ever saw a car. First time we took Susan for a car ride in Fairbanks, we went and went, and finally she said, 'When does this thing take off?' "

"Ever wonder if you did the right thing?" I asked. "Leaving?"

He shook his head no but then caught himself and looked over at Judi Ann. "Did too," he said. "After Shannon was in trouble with the baby. Not when it happened, but later." He didn't explain himself directly but started telling about an April day at the end of the long winter that seemed to have gotten to us all. I retrieved my notebook.

"I didn't pick the day," he said. "I don't know how you'd pick a day to question your life. It just sneaked up. Maybe it was a weak day, I don't know, but it was an odd one. You ever have a day when it seems like you're remembering every single detail even while it's happening, and you know you'll probably remember it for the rest of your life, and you don't know why because there's no particular reason to remember it at all?"

He looked at his right hand, clenched it. "I remember picking up that bucket."

It was first light. He carried the bucket from the cabin to the river, to the shallows where black-looking water flowed out from under thick ice and churned through a ten-foot stretch of riffle where rocks kept the water from freezing.

Before he filled the bucket, he stood a moment listening. He could hear the clack and bump of stones rolling along under the ice. The current was swelling, moving faster down there, pushing the rocks along. The snowmelt had started. It would be another five or six weeks before the ice went out completely here on the south slope of the Brooks Range, but these long, warm days of April were the beginning of its end.

He dipped the bucket full and lugged it back up the steps his middle son had chipped into the hard snow that covered the steep bank between the cabin and the river. In the yard, a few of the family's twenty-plus dogs had come out of their houses to watch, but they knew that feeding time wouldn't come until after they could smell the gruel aboil. Then they'd howl and leap against the ends of their chains as the dipper made its rounds.

Richard Hayden poured the water into a fifty-five-gallon drum from which he'd cut the top third. He sloshed the drum to mix the water with the rice, the frozen caribou fat, and the dried whitefish that he'd already put in. The drum hung on a steel rod over an open fire in such a way that he could tilt it to dole out the heated gruel.

He added a couple more chunks of spruce to the fire, then turned back toward the cabin. As he turned he saw the wolf, as black and still as a hole in the snow. She had shadowed him for two years now. Usually he had to fill her bowl someplace where he and his family couldn't watch her eat or she wouldn't come to it. Today the fact that she had come out into the open signaled her impatience, even though she was motionless there in the snow beneath the spruce. As always, she watched him with yellow eyes.

She had looked heavier than usual. It struck him suddenly that she was pregnant again. He grunted and shifted his gaze to the four half-breeds that were her pups. They were always among the first up in the morning, the last to curl into their three-by-three-foot houses at night. Richard worried about them, wondered if maybe they'd be trouble someday down the road. But Susan loved them. She was breaking them into harness and wanted to use them next winter to haul on her own trapline. Richard knew that they'd been watching him, lowering their heads and looking at him from the tops of those feral yellow eyes, but, as always when he looked directly at them, they looked away.

He walked into the cabin. Shannon was up cooking coffee and pancakes. The kids were still sleeping, the four oldest ones in the loft, the baby in the swing.

As he looked at the baby, just two months old and back from the hospital a week, he felt a wash of relief. And then he remembered his doubt.

"She was alive. When Shannon was about to lose her, I don't think I'd felt much, you know, after we radioed the liner, and prayed that the message would get through, and then waited, I must have been in shock. I don't think I felt much."

But now, he looked at Judi Ann and wondered why he had ever subjected his wife and child to that; why he had become the man responsible for maybe the most isolated family on earth. The Hayden cabin was more than a hundred miles from the nearest village, two hundred from the nearest road, four hundred from the nearest town. Richard knew of villages as isolated as they, but not families, at least not any that he had heard about. He realized now that deep inside he had thought, that day in February, that no one would come. It was in the middle of the cold snap, and no planes were supposed to fly when it was that cold. But Roger Dowding had come up from Fort Yukon anyway; he could still hear the screech of those skis on the river ice at fifty-two below.

And in April it had finally hit him. Why then? He had looked at

Shannon, who ran a spoon through her batter and dripped another pancake onto the woodstove griddle as she acknowledged his look with her eyes. "I heard a plane," she said.

Richard grunted. They heard planes several times a day, of course, but most of those were the liners crossing the pole. What Shannon really meant was that she heard a light plane, and it might be the one they were waiting to hear. The fur buyer, Ed Green, was due in any day. It had been a long winter. They needed the money, and they needed the groceries and dog rice and supplies the buyer would bring if he'd gotten the message they'd sent out with the itinerant schoolteacher. Was that why it was hitting him now? Because the cupboards were going bare?

Shannon flipped the pancake; Richard watched. "How much of that stuff you got left?"

She shrugged. "Enough."

He knew that she knew to the day and hour how much pancake flour she had left. He figured it was maybe a week's worth. He felt a moment of mild panic. He glanced around. The cabin was sixteen feet by twenty, all one room with a loft, seven bodies living and breathing inside, with him responsible for all of them plus the gang of dogs, and running out of food, and not a penny to his name.

He took a deep breath, and let it out slowly and silently, and set his jaw. Worry wouldn't bring the bacon. Besides, he knew the rhythm of things up here. He knew that the season was about to turn.

So he let the panic pass, and after that one odd day he didn't worry anymore.

The Haydens lay sprawled around the cabin's main room, listening to their wiry patriarch tell his story. Judi Ann's swing had stopped swinging, and Mark Kelley was fooling around with time exposures of her sleeping face in the dim light. "What do you think about oil?" I asked Richard, and he knew what I meant.

"If it affects us, it'll be through the caribou," he said, "and that's a complex thing, isn't it? I mean, if you lose the caribou, you lose the ways of life that have depended on them for tens of thousands of years. And you lose a whole lot beyond that: the wolves, the bears, the birds that feed their young the bugs from the caribou dung, the foxes that feed on the birds. The caribou up there are a lot more important than the oil. The only people who support it are the ones who'll get the money from it. I am unconditionally opposed to destruction for profit.''

He looked away from us listening adults as if embarrassed and gave Judi Ann's swing a gentle push without realizing that Mark's camera lens was open. Mark closed the shutter, looked at his watch, and said he thought he'd hit the sack. It was an announcement met with surprised yawps from the three teenagers. "Sleep?" said Daniel. "This is the time of day to do stuff!"

Mark took it as a joke and headed for his tent. But the kids weren't kidding. This was, Richard reminded me, a family that spent eight months a year on ice. In the twenty-four-hour daylight of the brief hot summer, they saved their chores and recreation for the cool hours. For the children, staying up all night was a natural summer rhythm. They'd been doing it all their lives.

Right now their three o'clock faces were eager. They wanted some fly-casting lessons, and Daniel wanted to take me to a slough five miles downriver, where on a breezeless night like this, grayling picked insects from the slick surface by the hundreds, and where the water was "so deep you have to frown to see the bottom." With a sigh, I fished in my daypack for my tackle vest and followed them out the door.

Sometime the next evening—I had lost track of time—we headed downriver to check two small-mesh nets in which the Haydens caught mostly suckers, which they fed to the dogs. In Fairbanks, a serious musher with two dozen dogs would spend as much as a thousand dollars a month to feed them. A thousand a month was often twice the Haydens' total income; they didn't spend much of it on dogs. Instead, they boiled up a daily gruel of trapline carcasses, moose and caribou scraps, netted fish, and rice.

The two nets were stretched about thirty feet out into the river at the mouth of a small backwater slough, one net upstream and one down.

As we approached the upstream net, it erupted into a splashing about twenty feet from shore. In spite of the small mesh, something big had been snagged.

It was a red-throated loon. When it saw us, it flapped and thrashed, then stopped struggling and rode low in the water, panting. Richard stepped into the stern of the canoe left there to check the nets. Mark climbed into the center, Stuart into the bow. As Stuart leaned into his paddle to shove off, Richard pointed toward some gear he had left ashore and said, "Susan, hand me that three-fifty-seven."

Stuart glanced up sharply but took the pistol from Susan and handed it back to Richard in the stern. Mark looked confused. I was briefly amazed, then simply aware and helplessly detached, and glad I was not in the canoe. I did not want the loon to die, but I was not here to pit my values against Richard Hayden's.

Stuart, I could tell, was troubled. He knew these people. It was their Grayling Lake cabin that he had trapped from for the past eight years. He wanted us to get along with them, to see their side of what wilderness is, and he wanted them to make a good impression on us. I had noticed that in the beginning he'd been watchful on both fronts, but lately he'd seemed relieved at the camaraderie. Right now he looked as if he thought that it was all about to go to hell.

Richard saved the moment by doing nothing. As the canoe neared the bird, I heard Mark say to Stuart, "Maybe we can . . . Maybe . . . Maybe if you grab its bill . . ." The two of them leaned simultaneously over the gunwale, and the disentangled loon was off, flying low over the water to midchannel. There it turned upstream and settled, drifting back with the current. Still watching the canoe, it cried once, that mournful wilderness lament which the bird behaviorists tell us actually is an avian challenge, a battle cry.

Richard Hayden watched, bemused, then sculled in closer to the net and started picking fish.

Fishing, I discovered, can be a deceptively guileless pastime up here; two days later, a middle-of-the-night trip with the fly rod spawned a troubling conflict. It was a conflict entirely within myself, and it began simply, with an innocent dispute about where to fish.

With their spinning gear, the Hayden kids liked to fish the small, juvenile grayling of the Sheenjek, but it was a stream too swift and murky to enjoy much with a fly rod. From the air, the nearby Koness had looked perfect: emerald clear and easily wadable.

"But there's no fish in there," Daniel told me when I suggested going. He wanted to go back to the deep slough.

But I know grayling. In a land of streams without trout, they are my therapy. I have caught and released many thousands of them, and I know that in July, the bigger rivers generally are home to such eight-inch juveniles as we'd been catching in the Sheenjek, whereas the big adult spawners spend their summers feeding in clearwater tributaries. I was up the Koness, I told Daniel, with or without him. There was a bit of grumbling, but then Richard Junior wordlessly shouldered his bear gun and followed me down the trail. Susan went because Stuart and Mark were going, and she liked the company. Daniel dragged along.

As we left the clearing, Richard Senior waved. "Keep what you catch," he said. "It's dinner."

It struck me that the Haydens were almost out of food. They were hanging on until caribou season, which was still a month away. We had brought groceries, and shared them, and they were gone. On the day we'd left Fairbanks for the coastal plain, Stuart had shipped a couple of boxes of foodstuffs to the family, but there had been a mix-up in bush-flight schedules, and now those boxes wouldn't arrive until they came in with Don Ross at the end of our trip. Daniel's reluctance to fish what he considered a fishless river was rooted in hunger. Unknowingly, I had volunteered to be today's provider. For the first time in my life I would eat what I caught or I wouldn't eat. Neither would anyone else.

But the Koness *was* perfect. It was probably the clearest river I had seen in Alaska. Its boulders and overhanging willow provided good cover for the fish, and as we crossed the first gravel bar to its bank I saw swarms of caddis flies up under the willows, and small clouds of mayflies dancing above the stream.

I tied on an elkhair caddis and started catching fish immediately, grayling that were twice the length and three times the weight of those in the Sheenjek. The saillike dorsal fin on the first grayling I caught was eight inches high—the fish must have spawned a month ago but appeared to be still in its spawning colors, its flanks a deep pearlescent gray, pectoral fins slashed with bright lavender and black, and that long dorsal fin tipped with a row of blue-circled teardrops precisely the shape and color of petals on the fireweed blossoms that lined the bank.

I hated to kill them. I hadn't killed a grayling in years. A sixteen-inch grayling is twenty, maybe twenty-five years old. It has spent perhaps two hundred months under ice. It has traveled sometimes a thousand miles a year to arctic meadows where we will never go, seeing things like tiny chironomids struggling through the surface film, and snaggletoothed pike on the hunt, and the undersides of swimming caribou. Its life is too beautiful to end.

But they were dinner. As I caught them, the children killed them with stones. They landed a couple of fish with their spinning gear, but only a couple. It was easy to see why they had considered the river fishless, for as their flashy spinners went ripping through the crystalline water, the fish simply panicked and fled.

My fly rod, they decided, was the way to go. So I stood beside them and coached their casts, and hollered strike when a grayling came innocently up for the grab. We walked back to the cabin with thirty-two fish strung on forked willow branches, and, as we went, Daniel asked me, hesitantly, if it might be possible for me to pick him out a good inexpensive outfit in Fairbanks and ship it to the bush.

It was then I realized what I had done. With my three-and-a-quarter-ounce gentleman's stick, that ultimate wand of sportsmanship, I had handed these young hunters a more effective weapon, and taught them a new way to kill.

"Sure," I said.

And when I got home I picked him out one. But fly-fishing, to me, is a ritual that we have evolved as homage to the hunt. On that innocent river it had seemed too efficient to be used for the kill. It could wipe out the Koness's grayling. Would it have offsetting value if I sent Daniel books and advice on the ethics and responsibility of stewardship? Did I have any business meddling that way?

I could never decide, and I never shipped the rod.

★ ★ ★

In the end, the image that stayed with me most from those days along the Sheenjek was a photograph.

It was only one among dozens of snapshots the wilderness kids had pulled from a shelf. It was past midnight. Daniel was frying up a big platter of fist-sized doughnuts. Richard Junior was hunkered over a table working on a remarkable portfolio of bush plane drawings. I was sitting on the couch, a wide, knee-high ledge of small logs covered with caribou hide. Light was coming dimly through mosquito netting hung over the doorway and the room's one window. Draped on thongs just outside the window, drying meat swayed in a breeze that kept puffing the slightly sour scent indoors.

Susan Hayden, black-eyed, solid, and pretty on the day after her fourteenth birthday, was passing around the photos to a medley of family narration. Of the dozens, I remember a few: one taken from the rear of a trapline sled, with snow like whipped cream and the family's black wolf bitch racing ahead of the dog team; another of Daniel and Susan standing in caribou parkas and mukluks after a day out on the trapline, seventeen frozen marten arranged in two neat lines beside them in the snow; and then a shot of half a dozen malamutes fitted with packs, each dog waddling across the fall-red tundra under forty pounds of caribou meat.

"How many caribou do you use?"

"Twenty a year, maybe a couple dozen," said Richard Senior.

"I've shot twenty-seven," said Susan.

I looked at her. "In how many years?"

"Three. I shot my first when I was ten."

Then came the disquieting photo. At first it appeared unremarkable. The three older kids were gathered around a table, smilingly preoccupied with a small, swaddled bundle. I assumed that the bundle was an infant, probably a younger Duane, the toddler sleeping above me in the cabin loft. I started to pass the photo on, but in a shift of light I saw more clearly the small pink face into which the children peered.

"That's not Duane."

The children's mother laughed, a laughter of that gentle sort you hear so often among northern Natives, a sound that is more introspective commentary than surface humor. "No," she said. "It's a baby caribou. A fetus."

I looked back at the photo. "A fetus. To eat, or what?"

"To play with. We don't eat them. They used to just play with them, you know, dress them up and talk to them, like your kids would play with dolls."

In the Arctic, chaos lives; the Haydens face it. Maybe we need them there to do it for us. The year I was there, oil developers were fond of pointing out that only 315 people had visited ANWR the year before. They, too, missed a point. The refuge was not a drawing card. It was the horizon not crossed. It was a place in the heart that needed to remain empty.

As I left the Haydens, with my promise to send Daniel a fly rod, and Richard Junior a book on bush planes, I realized I hadn't promised Susan anything. The groceries Stuart had shipped weeks ago had finally arrived with the plane that had come to take us out. Susan had raided one of the boxes and was happily chewing on a stick of candy.

"Other than red licorice," I said, "what's your favorite treat?"

Without hesitation, she grinned. "Wild meat."

4

The Beginning of the End of Illusion

*When from a long distant past nothing subsists, and after the people
are dead, after the things are broken and scattered, still, alone, more
fragile, but with more vitality, more unsubstantial, more persistent,
more faithful, the smell and taste of things remain poised a long time,
like souls, ready to remind us, waiting and hoping for their moment,
amid the ruins of all the rest; and bear unfaltering, in the tiny and
almost impalpable drop of their essence, the vast structure of recollection.*
—Marcel Proust, *Remembrance of Things Past*

Those beginnings of answers in the Arctic were to questions that had
started to shadow me a year earlier, during another trip that deepened my
sense of wrongness in Alaska, and in my life there.

Again, it was a trip that started with flight—this one a flight that was
to have been toward a simple two-week fishing junket into northern pike
country out of Fort Yukon. It wound up to be something much more
complicated. It scared me and it chilled me, and over that long, hard
winter that followed, it changed me and set me on the road out.

It began on a Friday afternoon in my office at the university, where
I'd finished trying to delegate far enough ahead that I could take the two
weeks off and was waiting for Don Peter, who was overdue. Don was to
be my guide. A middle-aged, heavy-featured Athabascan village leader
who directed a cultural program for the university, he also carried a second
business card that contained a short fisherman's prayer, asking God to
judge him big enough to keep, and the phone number of a riverboat
charter service Don operated part-time out of Fort Yukon.

At a bit before five, he came into my office and shut the door. He
was glowering, which wasn't unusual, because he and our mutual boss
didn't get along. Don was a maverick, notorious for his end runs around
paperwork. "When you work with Indians," he told me, "you got to

operate on Indian time." Indian time ticks to a pendulum that swings between doldrums and impulsive frenzy. At one village council meeting I attended, an uninspired discussion lapsed quickly into silence when a flock of several dozen Canada geese gabbled low overhead. The mayor and his council listened as the birds swirled over a small lake just outside the village. When the birds began to settle, the mayor said, "Meeting adjourned," and the room emptied fast.

In my office, Don slumped into a chair. "The son of a bitch," he said. "I spend two days buying groceries. Three pickup loads. You got to box up every damn thing, tape it all up, haul it out to the airport. You got to weigh it and charter a plane. And now the son of a bitch says he won't pay for it because I didn't do a purchase request three months ago so it could go out for bid. How you gonna do a purchase order for all that shit? Hell, you know as well as I do that a purchase order's nothing more than a written guarantee the stuff will come in a month late."

I said nothing. I knew Don Peter as a religious man, a son of the first Native Episcopalian minister in Fort Yukon. I'd never heard him swear, in fact, had never heard him string so many words together.

He stared out the window, and I saw that his eyes were flooded. He blinked, and two big tears splashed down. He wiped his eyes with the heels of his hands. "It's not that," he said. "It's a bad time, is all. I been on the river all night looking for a little kid."

A two-year-old was lost, a boy from Birch Creek, about seventy miles downriver from Fort Yukon. The parents and some other family members had gone by boat to Fort Yukon to shop. They shopped, they drank, got drunk, and headed back downriver. On the way home they spotted and shot a moose, camped overnight to butcher it, then headed on to Birch Creek. It wasn't until they were unloading the boat that they realized the child was missing.

"He fell out?"

"I don't know. They don't know. They can't even remember where they camped. We been looking for that place they butchered the moose."

"He's still missing, then."

Don nodded. "God damned booze."

"You need to get back," I said. "Look, we can cancel . . ."

"You want to help look?"

"Sure. Of course."

"Do you drink?"

"Uh, socially."

"Not when you're with me, you don't." He rose, took a deep breath, and let it out with a shuddering sigh. "We got a plane to catch."

It was a droning, twin-engine Piper Navaho that held a dozen passengers. Eleven, all Native, were already seated when I stooped to follow Don in. He took the last of the passenger seats and motioned me forward to ride as copilot. The pilot glanced, nodded, and I strapped in.

Typical of July in the interior, afternoon thundershowers had rolled in from the northeast, but now in early evening the clouds were dispersing over the Tanana Valley. We climbed out of Fairbanks, passed at 1,000 feet over the Chena River, then rose above the low hills that rim three sides of the city. I watched the shadows of clouds browse westerly across thick flanks of black spruce and warp into and out of the wispier green cleavages of aspen and birch. At 1,500 feet, above the crest of the long ridge just north of town, we passed directly over my house. I missed my four-year-old son, Cody. I didn't like to leave him. He was my last child, my great pleasure, my best cause. Whenever I left him, I was grateful and afraid, and today, someone else's lost boy made it worse.

Two days before, on Wednesday afternoon, seventeen-year-old Ramona James had called her two-year-old son, Virgil, into the family's small frame house. Except for a few spare disposable diapers that she would carry herself, she had laid out on the bed all the clothes that Virgil might need for a three-day trip. In the cramped space of a small boat on the Yukon River, little shirts and socks tended to work their way to the bottom of the clutter to be trampled in fish slime. The best way to prevent this was to have Virgil be his own suitcase. So she changed his diaper and put all the clothes on him at once. She slipped on him a pair of white socks, a pair of blue jeans, a striped T-shirt; then, over the blue jeans a pair of tan cotton pants, and over the shirt a dark green sweater. She shimmed his feet into tennis shoes, tied a food-stained bib over the sweater, stuffed his

55

arms down the sleeves of a tan Carhartt jacket. Over the jacket she put a loose blue windbreaker, pulled the hood over his shiny black hair, and tightened the drawstrings. The last item on the bed was a small yellow life jacket, borrowed, with *Rosanna Du* printed across it in block letters of indelible ink.

When Virgil saw the life jacket, he headed for the door. He had spent a lot of time on the water even at two and knew that once the hampering killjoy was on, it might not come off for days. But Ramona caught him, wrestled the jacket on and tied its strings, and sent Virgil outdoors with a gentle swat and a firm look. Then she gathered a few last things and picked up her sleeping baby, little Eddie Junior. She stepped with him to the door and called to Virgil, and to her ten-year-old niece, Yessie, who was across the dirt lane at the post office. They came, and with the three children Ramona headed down toward the creek to join her husband for the trip to Fort Yukon.

It wasn't far. With a population of about thirty varying upward to a summertime high of forty, Ramona's village of Birch Creek was the smallest of the middle Yukon's two dozen or so Native communities. It was a cluster of small log and frame houses and a post office, all on the right bank of Birch Creek some thirty-five creek miles upstream from its confluence with the Yukon River. The village site was flat, marsh-fringed, wavy with willow and studded with the subarctic's dwarfish spruce trees. The creek, which began clear and sprightly high in the White Mountains to the south, flowed slowly past the lowland village and bore the tea color that is the signature of bog-fed streams. The village soil was a mixture of black marsh peat and the same fine, gray glacial silt that flanks the Yukon all the way along its two thousand miles from northwestern Canada to the Bering Sea.

Birch Creek was established as an outpost and named 140 years ago by Hudson's Bay Company traders from Fort Yukon. The Hudson's Bay men had picked it smartly; it was located at the edge of the lake-pocked Yukon Flats, which the company considered the richest fur country in North America, and at a gathering place to which the Natives would return for each winter trapping season. It was an ancient site, not a village but simply a winter encampment. Ramona's people—the Gwich'in, or river people—had no villages. They were nomads who banded into family groups and established complicated, circuitous patterns of migration from winter shelter to a series of food sources—to the rivulet-fed ponds where blackfish swarm to spawn as soon as the ice goes out, to moose calving grounds, to certain funnel mouths of stream systems where pike gather to ambush schools of outmigrating salmon smolts, to marshy headwater lakes where the whitefish and grayling go to spawn, and where waterfowl go to nest, and to the northerly bogs where cranberries and blueberries ripen below the tundra slopes over which the caribou pass each fall—and eventually back again to winter sanctuary. The site of Birch Creek, tucked shelteringly up against the White Mountains and away from the sweep of arctic winds across the Yukon Flats, was an old overwintering camp the tribal elders called Nocotocargut, or Place Where the Water Winds Back to.

So Ramona was a child of 15,000 years of Athabascan roamings along these shores. Her ancestors believed with fervent reverence that you are what you eat, and Ramona—her flesh, her blood, her language, her spirituality—was the life that had been breathed forward from aeons of moose and mastodon, of saber-toothed tiger and raven, of the millions of mosquitoes whose genes had been forged by the blood of her ancestors, of salmon and beaver and caribou, and of the very silt of the old gray riverbed itself. The primitivism lingered in and around her, but she was only vaguely conscious of its power. The Old Way, she called it and pretty much ignored it, although it was the force that had pulled her from her mother's belly and impressed itself on her daily still. Without realizing it, she had learned as a child to think a season ahead, to know that too many August feasts might lead to January famine, to whistle in the long dark, and to laugh loudest when it snows. She had learned that the bigger the animal, the bigger the spirit, and the bigger the spirit, the more lavish the taboos, to the extent, for instance, that women were never to do anything that might come between the mortally serious business that transpired between a hunter and a bear. Women were not to listen to men talk about bears, or to touch fresh bear meat or skin, and were never to eat brown bear meat, and to eat just the hindquarters of black bear meat, but only if it was several weeks dead, and absolutely never while the women were menstruating. Girls and women did not even talk about bears directly. The women's word for bear meant "a black thing," and the old tongue was full of other feminine euphemisms, too, through which the lynx became *k'akk'aant'oya,* or "the follower," the otter became *bizeeya,* or "shiny black," and the women's word for the horribly devilish wolverine meant the even more oblique "clothing trim."

When Ramona was a little girl in the village of Minto on the north shore of the Tanana River just over the White Mountains from Birch Creek, the oil companies punched a spur road to her village from the North Slope Haul Road so trucks could off-load equipment shipped to the village barge terminal. As she grew up, Ramona took the road away from the village as often as she could. She went to Fairbanks, where neither winter nor superstition could penetrate the shopping malls. In Fairbanks, bears were bears for one and all.

She entered puberty a modern girl. The older women of Minto, who were extremely proud of those girls among her friends who observed the taboos of menstrus, told her that she should sequester herself for at least a week and should observe certain interdictions regarding food and cleanliness. But just as Ramona no longer felt need in the age of television to bolster her winter courage by whistling in the dark or laughing at the snow, she no longer saw reason in her age of enlightenment, naive as it was, to screen off a corner of the house with a blanket hung from the ceiling and to hunker behind it for a week in superstitious fear.

A couple of years later, at the age of fourteen, she was pregnant with her first child, Virgil. I don't know why she married Eddie; I can only guess that she loved him, a man eighteen years older and probably as sure of himself as a thirty-two-year-old Native man could be with one foot deep in the current of a culture almost dead and the other in the lapping shallows of a white sea. I do know that the marriage turned Ramona, probably both of them, oddly and ominously in a direction opposite from the one Ramona had unconsciously taken during her childhood. They did not follow the road that led to a future among the white man's shopping malls. They followed instead the old Gwich'in road, the river road, to the tiny village that remains today among the most isolated in Alaska. For Ramona and at least one of her children, it was a tragic move.

When anthropologist Richard Nelson was living among and studying the Koyukon people—the Athabascans along another Yukon tributary some 500 miles to the west—in the 1970s, he theorized that the single characteristic dominating the subsistence economies of the Alaska interior is instability. The reasons, he said, were simply the spotty distribution and wildly fluctuating population levels of the fish and game on which the people depend. The Athabascans, he said, have to travel widely, with some skill and high hopes.

About the time that Nelson was living along the Koyukuk River, another anthropologist studying Native children in Alaska observed that the critical busyness and positive attitude necessary to survival were also crucial to mental and emotional health. In *Children of Crisis,* Robert Coles noted that Eskimo children, for instance, generally prefer winter over summer. Because it is instilled in them from birth that happiness and harmony are most important during the dead of winter, they relish "the short days in which a lot has to get done; the long nights that bring complete rest; the delightfully close quarters of family living."

Conversely, Native children tend to be bored during the summer, bored and a little nervous. "It is strange, the lethargy and even dour edginess young Eskimos can demonstrate when the world appears so delightfully beckoning," wrote Coles. In the arctic summers of plenty, there is no need to do things precisely or quickly. Time lags, becomes a weight. The Arctic's twenty-four hours of daylight take their toll on sleep. Throughout the far north, I have seen village children playing outdoors at two or three o'clock in the morning and sleeping restlessly through afternoon heat that often approaches 100 degrees. They are wary of summer, with its bears, its hordes of mosquitoes, its treacherous floods. The result, felt Coles, "is a cumulative weariness of both a physiological and psychological nature. Will the warm weather take away, drain, or sap, in some manner undo, the resilience, drive, and ingenuity that are inevitably associated with severely cold weather?"

In Ramona's case, I don't think it was warm weather that did it but rather the white man's life of amenity that not only is the social counterpart to warm weather but also extends the easy life to a year-round way. In Minto, survival assured, Ramona never learned skill as necessity, busyness as therapy, or happiness as weapon. In marrying Eddie and moving to Birch Creek, Ramona was headed back into the dim world of a past for which she had not accepted custodianship. She was unarmed; she did not know how to deal with the boredom of ease and had forgotten how to laugh at the snow."

Three years later she was a drunk. Although pretty and still slim, she had the soft-muscled, loose-skinned look of a sedentary woman and the small potbelly and dull eyes of a drinker. She and Eddie were two of those responsible for some stunning statistics among Alaska's 80,000 Natives—an alcoholism rate approaching 80 percent in many villages, a suicide rate among young Alaska Native men sixteen times the national average, a fetal alcohol syndrome rate among Native newborns two and a half times the national average, and a crime rate among Natives twice the average of that of the state as a whole. In its A People in Peril series published two months after the day Ramona stepped into Eddie's boat with her children for that July trip to Fort Yukon, the *Anchorage Daily News* reported that although Natives composed only 5 percent of the population of Anchorage, they accounted for 40 percent of all the city's fatal accidents, 27 percent of all those being treated for alcohol or drug abuse, 22 percent of all violent deaths, and 16 percent of all rape victims.

In Fairbanks, the only "white man's town" in Gwich'in territory, the statistics weren't, and aren't, much different. Interior Natives go to Fairbanks to shop, to socialize, to drink; and because many of the villages are dry by tribal law, the drinkers among them tend to visit Fairbanks even more often, until finally they stay. You see them, collapsed from the bottom of their society into the bottom of our own, clustered in the bars of downtown's Second Avenue or, in warm weather, sprawled in grass along the banks of the Chena River. As early as the 1940s, Will Rogers described Fairbanks as the biggest bar in America; and Joe McGinniss, researching his *Going to Extremes* in the late 1970s, saw the city as "a town of Teamsters and drunkards and pimps," festering beneath a layer of contaminated ice fog that he termed "a blanket of frozen filth." All in all, he wrote, "this was not a part of the world or the universe that man was intended to inhabit."

Fairbanks is where Ramona and Eddie headed to party when they could, but they didn't have the money to take the flight often. Eddie's only income came from occasional odd jobs and from a few furs, from unemployment and welfare benefits, and from the several hundred dollars a year he got in dividend checks as a member of Doyon, Ltd.—one of the thirteen regional Native corporations established to administer the $964.5 million and 40 million acres of lands distributed under the federal Alaska Native Claims Settlement Act of 1971.

The money was enough, at any rate, for Eddie to maintain a snow machine and a boat. In the winter, Fort Yukon was only twenty-seven miles away, and you could get there in an hour or so when the trail was packed. You could go just about any time you got the urge. But during the summer there was no way to get over that boggy trail, and it was a lot longer to Fort Yukon by riverboat, a 150-mile round trip that you had to plan for. On this particular trip, the whole family was going because Eddie planned to spend a couple of days at the family fish camp on the Yukon to haul in some king salmon for winter. He wanted Ramona along to gut and split and dry the fish.

Eddie's boat was a good one, a twenty-foot, flat-bottomed johnboat like most people use on the rivers up here, with a windscreen and steering pedestal built toward rear-center so that Eddie could stand up to navigate. He shoved it away from the landing shortly before noon and began the slow, winding run along which the creek took maybe thirty-five miles to cover the fifteen straight-line miles to the Yukon River. His fish camp was on the Yukon a few miles above the confluence, and Fort Yukon was maybe thirty-five miles upriver from the camp.

They overnighted at the camp and caught some fish. Sometime Saturday afternoon, according to Eddie, they decided to make the run up to Fort Yukon to buy groceries.

Don Peter was at his brother Jim's fish camp that afternoon, helping tend a fish wheel on the left bank of the Yukon. They'd just heard a couple of king salmon thump into the holding box, and Don had walked down the bank to carry the fish to camp when he saw a johnboat weaving oddly down current, Eddie James at the helm. The boat slowed as if to come in, the two men exchanged a greeting, and Don waved to Ramona and the children. Then he waved Eddie disgustedly on. With Don Peter's reputation as an antialcohol crusader, there was no need to explain why. "They were drunk out of their gourds," Don said. "I was surprised, because I thought Eddie had cleaned up. He hadn't been drinking for a long time."

The Jameses made it the remaining twenty miles to Fort Yukon. They bought groceries, then they drank. Among Alaska's 249 bush communities, Fort Yukon is one of only seventeen in which liquor can be bought legally, and one of only three with a community liquor store. That's not to say that the other villages don't get alcohol; they do, and a lot of it, through mail-order sales, booze-buying trips to cities, and—in the seventy-two villages that are either dry or have banned liquor imports— through a lively bootlegging network. In Fort Yukon, those who drink do so at an average rate of about a gallon a week, or about 12,000 gallons a year. Some drink less, of course, and the heavy drinkers swig more. Probably no one knows how much Ramona and Eddie drank in Fort Yukon that Saturday night in July, and witnesses interviewed later by Alaska State Trooper Roger Maynard varied in their reports of how much they bought to drink on Sunday. But they were all agreed that Ramona was still drunk Sunday morning, and the estimates of how much they bought at the community liquor store ranged upward to three cases of beer and a fifth of Calvert whiskey.

Lorraine Englishoe, who was at the Fort Yukon boat landing when the Jameses left about midnight Sunday, said that Ramona was "pretty well loaded" and staggering rubberly. Eddie didn't appear to be drunk, she said, but Alfred Peter, the thirty-six-year-old family friend who Eddie had rousted out of bed to help him pilot the boat back downriver, said that the two men shared about half the bottle of Calvert before they shoved off from Fort Yukon, then nursed both Calvert and beer downriver. In the boat, Ramona slept a lot and drank a little, Alfred said. "She didn't need to drink much, because she was already wasted."

Eighteen miles downriver, fifty-one-year-old Virginia Johnson lay sleeping with her husband, Elliott, inside a wall tent at the couple's left-bank fish camp. She awakened when she heard a boat whine in and grind up onto the gravel shore. She rose, left Elliott sleeping in the tent, and went outside to find two lean men, Eddie and Alfred, along with little Virgil, staggering up the steep bank in the Arctic's bright, low morning sun. It was 2:00 A.M.

"When they came in, they didn't even know where they'd come to," she told Trooper Maynard. The men told her they wanted to build a fire and make some tea, "but they had a hard time making a fire, the way they were stumbling around."

Virginia stayed up to help. She talked to the kids, went down to the boat to make sure that Ramona and the baby, curled up together in the bow asleep, were warm. While the men and children had their tea, she tried to talk them into staying. "You'll be sorry if something happens," she said she told them, "but they talked back and left anyway."

"That little boy didn't want to go with them," she told Maynard. "He cried and tried to stay with me, and kept untying that lifesaver."

The men shoved off. Alfred Peter took the helm, revved the outboard, swerved wildly out toward the main current, then grounded suddenly on a sandbar. Eddie James stuck a leg out, pushed off the sandbar, and Alfred gunned the motor again. This time the boat made it to the main current, the bow swung downstream, and Alfred raced the motor even faster to get the boat up on step. Little Virgil sat far forward in the bow, facing ahead, his hands on the gunwales bracing against the slap. The sun, rising like it does in the north at that time of year, was swinging slowly toward the east, slanting its rays through the spruce and alder along the far shore. There was no wind. The Yukon looked glassy silver. The boat was gone, although Virginia could still hear it. She shook her head, then turned back to the wall tent to rejoin Elliott.

Some forty miles below Fort Yukon, according to Alfred Peter, he turned the helm back over to Eddie James. Alfred had navigated the Yukon's tricky, braided channels near the mouth of the Chandalar River, had pulled into the James fish camp to pick up gear left there two days before, then had made the short run on downstream to an idle current at the mouth of Birch Creek. He was exhausted. He went forward to share a blanket with little Virgil, who was asleep.

About an hour later he awoke when he sensed that the boat had stopped. He rose on an elbow to look back toward the stern at Eddie, who was intently watching the left shoreline and was fumbling with one hand through a pile of gear for the rifle he kept back by the steering pedestal.

Alfred peeked over the gunwale. He spotted the moose, jerked instinctively when the rifle boomed, and saw the moose go down. Ramona and the children were instantly awake, startled and confused. Eddie started the motor again and nosed the boat to the muddy shoreline.

They all got out, and the two men began the hours-long process of butchering the half-ton animal. They were nervous, because it was an illegal kill, but Ramona lugged a couple of six-packs of beer up from the boat, and soon they were mellow, sweating over the hot carcass, which sent rolls of steam up into the morning chill.

By one o'clock or so they had stashed the meat in the boat under canvas and were under way again, Alfred and Ramona and the children sleeping again, Eddie almost dozing at the helm, the motor droning as the boat swept right, left, right, left through the dark water and the tight, monotonous curves of the meandering creek. From the site of the moose kill, it was about twenty air miles to the village of Birch Creek. But along the winding waterway, which snaked back on itself in oxbows that often swept around almost full circle, the distance was at least twice that far.

Ramona remembered Virgil waking once, squirming and whimpering in the life jacket, and tugging at its ties, until she told Alfred, who was lying next to him, to "just let him take it off for a little while."

About halfway home, Eddie swung the boat to shore to refill the emptying tank with gasoline and to mix in the outboard oil additive. It was a familiar stopping place, where beavers had built a dam partway across the creek, creating a deep, slowly swirling eddy just below. The water was deep right to shore there, so you didn't have to worry about rocks or muck or weeds. Eddie mixed the gas, restarted the motor, backed the boat into the main current, and headed upstream for the final two-hour leg home.

It's not clear, either from Trooper Maynard's report or from the hearsay that was rampant up and down the river while I was on the Yukon, just where the Jameses were when they noticed that Virgil was missing. Some of the Natives I talked with said that the boat was back in the village of Birch Creek, and that Eddie had roused his sleeping passengers from beneath the jumble of blankets in the bow and started to unload the boat when Ramona began to call for her son. Both Eddie and Ramona, however, said that it was before they got to the village, and that they had searched for their son for several hours before Eddie took his passengers home and went off to search again. Wherever it was, it was too late. The frantic and sobering anguish that Eddie James must have felt as he sped time and again through the creek's frustrating oxbows is only hinted at in the words of a still-drunk Ramona, talking into a tape recorder held by Trooper Roger Maynard. "Soon as we find out Virgil was gone, why Eddie, he just screamed and threw that beer right out of the boat."

The pilot set a course thirty degrees northeast for the 150-mile flight to Fort Yukon. The route ahead—up the Chatanika River valley and over the White Mountains—was smeared with the gray brush strokes of rain squalls. For 50 miles or so the pilot was able to dodge them, but up among the highest white peaks the cumulonimbus were jammed in tight, and finally he had no choice but to plow through.

Rain peppered the windshield, lightning flashed, the Piper bucked. I couldn't see anything ahead, but down off my right shoulder the range's disconcerting limestone tusks pierced up through the rain and fell away into misty chasms. Among the fifty or so chunks of the earth's crust that have fused together to form Alaska, this was among the first, a seventy-mile-long piece of limestone off some oceanic rim that rafted up from the tropics on a sea of magma and docked here some 200 million years ago. So white it looks snowy whether it is wet or wintry or dry, it is a plate that has buckled up into a cordillera of spires that look like the pale ghosts of the higher, darker, granite Arrigetch Peaks, 275 miles northwest in the Brooks Range. Arrigetch, reported Robert Marshall in 1931, is a local Inupiat name meaning "fingers extended."

I had flown here before; on a clear day a pilot had pointed out to me that although these stone hands were smaller and softer than those in the Brooks, there was one particularly dangerous mountain ahead. It was Lime Peak, rising right where the thunderheads form in a colliding swirl of mountain and valley air, a big, sky-grabbing fist like one last mile-high reach by the mountains before they fall away to the riverine plain. The pilot who showed me Lime Peak had banked his plane to circle, pointing out splats of metal, the wreckage of half a dozen other planes that hadn't made it.

That is the way I think when I am flying. Being in the air has always been a historic, life-changing experience for me, and I have never been able to understand my fellow passengers' cheery obliviousness to the drama. Right then, for instance, I was the only person aboard other than the pilot who knew that he was lost.

He had said damn, and now he said shit, which as every aviation accident investigator knows is the most frequently heard last expletive on flight recorders. He had a chart out, spread over his right knee. His compass was useless, gyrating to extremes even farther afield than the usual thirty-degree declination that was due to the sharp angle between here and the magnetic pole, and he was trying through his earphones to get a fix by radio. I couldn't hear what he was hearing, of course, and had to guess by his actions whether he was having any success. I guessed he wasn't. I supposed by the miles, and by the violence of the thunderhead into which we had flown, that we were somewhere near Lime Peak. The plane's altimeter registered us 600 feet shy of the summit. If we were on course, that would be okay; we would pass to the south of the mountain. But I had no idea whether we were on course and was pretty sure that neither did he. He kept looking down off his left shoulder as if searching for landmarks. Just climb, jerk, climb, I prayed; and finally he banked the plane sharply south and pulled it into a trembling ascent that got us above everything.

It was about 8:00 P.M. The sun was behind us in the west but still above the mountains and the clouds, and in its oblique clarification, the tops of the cumulonimbus were cottony, the sky deep blue. You could see 150 miles north to the Brooks Range, and 150 miles south to the Alaska Range, and right beneath us the pile of clouds against the rim of the White Mountains, giving way to the expanse of the Yukon Flats. You couldn't see the river, though. Along through here the Yukon flows close against the mountains, and on that day it was under the same heavy cloud cover that had stacked against the hills. So the pilot snaked his way downstream at 6,000 feet, looking for an opening, until finally he spotted one about the size of a football field and dropped the Piper whining through. We cruised just above the treetops, over the river in the rain, missed Fort Yukon (which was up a slough off to the right behind the trees) on the first pass, then spotted the towers of a defunct Distant Early Warning (DEW-line) system radar installation, and circled back and landed. Don Peter opened his eyes.

★ ★ ★

At the river end of the runway we hopped into an old turquoise Dodge pickup. It was my first trip to Fort Yukon, and I didn't see much of it on the initial pass. I had mainly an impression of logs and dogs as Don drove fast, kicking up a wake of dust along dirt streets lined sparsely with spruce, alder, and small weathered homes. We met kids and mothers with kids, some walking, but most of them kicking up dust of their own, driving fast on the three-wheeled all-terrain vehicles that, along with winter's snow machines, have mechanized transportation in all Alaska villages. We were headed to Don's cousin's place, he said, to pick up a couple of empty fifty-five-gallon drums so that he could fill them with gasoline for his boat.

We pulled into a driveway that led around to the backside of a dusty white frame house. It was a cluttered backyard that backed up to several other cluttered backyards, all unfenced but separated loosely by a few stunted spruce trees and some clumps of willow. Most of the clutter was machinery, the operable and discarded parts of snow machines, three-wheelers, outboard motors, and household appliances.

Piles of lumber were stacked around a platform that looked like a rear deck, and on this deck sat Don's cousin, plucking ducks. Two lay plucked on the boards, beside a pile of ten or twelve unplucked mallards and black ducks, both drakes and hens. It wasn't duck season; it was, in fact, the tail end of nesting season. I supposed that the Natives had some sort of subsistence right to hunt any time of year, but it didn't seem right. Alaska's waterfowl molt in June and can't fly until after the nesting season is over, in middle or late July, when both the adults and their offspring complete the growth of new primary feathers for the long flight south. Don Peter's cousin had been shooting sitting ducks.

The cousin's name was Harry Thomas. He was in his midfifties, a little older than Don, but trimmer. He was gray at the temples and looked like an Athabascan chief: erect and square-jawed, with a straight, substantial nose and a drooping fold over the outer corner of each eye that lent him a perpetual expression of concern. Like most who come to Alaska, I had expected round-faced, flat-nosed Eskimos with the slanting epicanthic fold over the inner corner of each eye that pulls the eye into a Mongolian slit. Eskimos there are, of course, about 50,000 of them, scattered along

15,000 miles of coastal shoreline and river deltas at the far western and northern fringes of the state. The interior, though, is the land of the state's 30,000 Athabascans, who anthropologists say are close cousins to the Southwest's Apache and Navaho. In Alaska, their territory is bigger than Texas; and, as it spreads into Canada, the arctic Athabascan realm becomes bigger than Alaska itself. Only a few thousand among the 30,000 live along the middle Yukon, as a subgroup which calls itself the Gwich'in, or river people. The Gwich'in territory, at about 150 by 600 miles, is bigger than Idaho, slightly smaller than Wyoming.

The Athabascans represent Alaska's oldest remaining culture, dating back to several thousand years before the first Eskimos and Aleuts began their migrations down the arctic coast. Physical anthropologists are still wrestling with ideas about how the New World might have been settled by migrations eastward from Asia across the Bering Land Bridge, but the most commonly accepted guess supported by archaeological finds and linguistic analysis is the three-migration theory. In that scenario, the American Indians (the Amerind, or Algonquian peoples) came across first between 23,000 and 35,000 years ago and dispersed southward through North and South America. Their only remains discovered to date in the far north are a few bone tools. One splinter of caribou bone known as the Old Crow flesher (discovered near the village of Old Crow, just 150 air miles up the Porcupine River from Fort Yukon) is an obviously man-shaped tool that has been carbon-dated at 30,000 years. Anthropologists don't know, however, whether it was fashioned when the bone was fresh or made from a bone already thousands of years old. Even older bone fragments, some of them carbon-dated at 50,000 years, have been found in the same area; but the question is whether their crudely tooled appearance is really the result of human touch or of predator teeth.

At any rate, the basin that includes Fort Yukon is where people settled in America first, and in my opinion they picked the best of the far north. I don't know if it is the oldest among the fifty or so chunks of land that drifted to here from elsewhere to lock onto the continent, but it is the chunk that has been here the longest. It has lost more of its rough edges and has been longer a part of the continental rhythm. Its valleys tend to shallow U's rather than sharp V's; its rivers are gentle, meandering down easy gradients. America's first people came directly to it almost as if they knew. I suspect that in a way they did. Their route lay along an almost straight line from the old Bering Land Bridge, eastward 650 miles along the southerly foothills of the Brooks Range to here. Even today you can read the signs, as they must have been able to read them, revealing the land in ever kindlier profiles as you move eastward, 200 miles up the valley of the Kobuk River, 100 miles across the headwater valleys of the Koyukuk River, then 50 miles across a low range of hills into the lake land of the Yukon Flats, and finally another 150 miles northeastward beyond Fort Yukon, up the valley of the Porcupine River into Canada. It is a four-hour flight of 800 air miles for me, half again that far in overland miles for them; but either way, today as then, each chunk of miles announces more caribou, deeper humus, heavier forests, and smaller, more manageable rivers.

I'm prejudiced by not being a coastal person at heart, but, even with prejudice aside, the interior seems to me Alaska at its most humane. It is half gentle hill country and half lowland, with a latticework of rivers and thousands of lakes, a country thick with timber, rich in fish and game. In summertime, with temperatures normally in the seventies and eighties, it is a land comfortable to travel, easy to harvest.

Yet it is as seasonally bitter as it is seasonally kind. The snow that falls in October is still here in May. In winter the sun doesn't get up between November and April, and the temperature never rises above freezing. Traveling these river lands during the summer I can imagine that it would, most years, be easy enough to put enough by to last through a half year of darkness and cold. But over the long haul, there would be summers when the salmon didn't come, autumns when the swarming caribou herds were in cyclic decline or maybe just passed by, in their annual migration, too far to the north. Even today the Gwich'in's remnant legends are heavy with killer winters and summertime quests by young men searching up and down the rivers among bones, looking for a nomadic camp with one young wifely woman left.

Those first fold, the Algonquians who became many of the "Indian" tribes of the Lower 48, Mexico, and South America, were smart to move on. The puzzling bones they left behind are less a mystery than why some among the second wave of immigrants, the Athabascans, decided to stay. At its best, Alaska is a fierce land in winter. Every mile southward is a mile into easier country. The theory that holds for me the best explanation of why the Gwich'in didn't keep heading south has to do with the Wisconsin Climax of North America's last glacial period. According to the glacial timetable, the first wave of immigrants—including the Algonquian Amerinds and some of the earliest Athabascans—would have migrated south before about 35,000 years ago. Then the glacial gates closed behind them. Most of Alaska and extreme northwestern Canada were never glaciated, so Athabascan peoples could have kept migrating freely across the Bering Land Bridge and as far as 800 miles eastward into the upper Yukon and Porcupine rivers. Beyond that, the way was blocked by ice for 2,500 miles to the east, 2,000 miles to the south. And it stayed blocked for some 20,000 years, reopening about 14,000 years ago. By then, the Gwich'in had been established in the upper Yukon and Porcupine drainages for 15,000 years or so, and the inclination to move south would have been dampened by a culture long established to match the arctic land. Besides, the Wisconsin ice field melted generally from south to north, and the new territories opened by its recession were quickly claimed by tribes among those natives who had wound up on the southerly side of the field before it closed. By the time a habitable corridor opened south of the Gwich'in, they would have found that territory already occupied. In legend, the Gwich'in repeatedly refer to themselves as locked into a homeland vast yet harshly boundaried by the warlike caribou people to the north and the equally aggressive bear people to the south. The Middle People, they called themselves.

And middle people they remained, between lost yesterdays and unfamiliar tomorrows, Ramona James slowly killing herself and letting her child die, and Harry Thomas blasting away at families of flightless ducks with an old bow hunter's sense of urgent freedom, but at a time when a bird less in July no longer means a meal less in December.

Harry, when I met him, wore a brown leather English touring cap, which he pushed back farther on his head with the back of one bloody hand as Don Peter and I stepped from the truck. A big black Labrador dog lay at his feet. It ignored Don but got up when it saw me, its hackles rising, and stepped stiff-legged in my direction until Harry grunted sharply and it lay back down.

"I can't shake your hand," said Harry when we were introduced, "but I can give you a duck to pluck." He handed me one solemnly, but Don took it away and tossed it back onto the small pile of ducks. "Help us load some barrels," he said. "We need gas."

"They found 'im," said Harry.

Don just looked at him.

"Up on the creek," said Harry.

"Dead?"

Harry nodded. "Paul Shewfelt and Earl. Said they'd gone by that place a dozen times, and Paul decided to swing in and look at a little muddy lump up onshore, and it was him, curled up in a ball."

"Where they got that moose?"

"No, on up the creek."

"How'd he get there?"

"I don't know."

"How'd he get up onshore without a life jacket unless they stopped?"

Harry examined the duck he'd been plucking. Then he stood. From beneath the deck he pulled a newspaper from a stack of newspapers and walked over to a lidless fifty-five-gallon drum. He shredded and wadded the paper into the drum, touched a match to it, then turned the duck in the flame to singe off its pinfeathers.

"They said there were footprints all up and down the shoreline there. Just his, nobody else's. They said he'd been chewed to pieces by the bugs. They said it looked like he would go out and stand in the water to get out of the bugs, then get cold and go curl up onshore. They said it looked like he'd done that several times; there were these little round places in the sand."

Don said nothing. He walked to the rear of the backyard lot, stood looking off through the willow and spruce, toward the river. Harry's dog got up and walked out toward Don. Harry sat back down on the deck and handed me another duck. And when I had finished plucking it and was wadding up paper for another barrel fire, Don came back.

"You want to go fishing tomorrow?" he said to Harry.

"Whereabouts?"

"I don't know. Pike country. Maybe some sheefish."

"Up the Porcupine," said Harry. "There's some sheefish up there."

"How far up?"

Harry looked at me. "He don't spend enough time around here anymore to know how to go fishing by himself."

"You don't have to go," said Don. He watched me set my singed duck beside the three others that had been plucked. I was wondering why Harry hadn't gutted the birds when he shot them; was wondering, in fact, whether he was going to gut them at all. Harry was about to hand me another duck when Don caught my eye. "Let's load a couple of barrels," he said.

Harry got up to help. "I don't want to have to be embarrassed for you when you come back without many fish," he said. "I don't want to see you embarrass yourself in front of this man. What time do you want to go?"

"Not too early," said Don.

"Good. I need to get the walls up on this place." He motioned toward a stack of three two-by-four frames covered with plywood. They were about twelve feet long and eight feet high, and I could see a window hole cut into the one on the top of the stack. I looked again at Harry's deck and could see now that it was a floor, an addition to his house. The rear of the house would form one wall, and Harry had prefabricated the other three to raise into place. "I been waiting for some good muscle to come along," Harry said. He looked at me. "You need to warm up pretty good before you get out on that cold river to go fishing."

We didn't talk about the dead boy any more that day, or the next day, or the next. But the things we did talk about were affected by the incident often, and at those times I could see the rage rise hard and black into Don Peter's eyes.

The first time it happened was later that same evening, in a conversation with a young Native waiter at the Gwich'in Zhee Lodge. From Harry Thomas's place we had driven a mile out of town to the community fuel tanks to gas up, then stopped for dinner. The Gee-Zee Lodge, as the locals called it, was a handsome and huge log inn and restaurant built by the local Native corporation of which Don Peter was currently president. It was a corporate investment, designed to the specifications of a vision filled with tourists and Native conferences. But in mid-July 1988, the dinner rush consisted of just Don Peter and myself. The waiter, a very big, strong kid who could have bent the two of us into pretzels, made cheerful small talk in the slow, soft-voiced way of most Alaska Natives. Until the food arrived. Then he remained, silent and looking awkwardly worried, at Don's elbow.

"Got a problem?" Don finally asked without looking at him.

The waiter tried to smile. "Well, yeah."

"So?"

"Well . . . The judge says I have to go to jail for thirty days unless I can get someone to sign custody of me for a while."

"What'd you do?"

"Speeding."

"Pretty stiff for speeding."

"I don't have a license."

"Pretty stiff for that, too," Don said.

I was trying to be polite, focusing intently on my plate, but now I glanced up in time to see that fierce glitter in Don's eyes as he raised them to the young waiter. "Was there alcohol?"

"Alcohol," said the waiter dumbly.

"You were drinking," said Don.

"Well, I had a couple of beers."

Don slammed his fork onto his plate hard enough to chip it and swung around to face the waiter fully. "Sit down!" he said. And when the boy sat, Don leaned far over his plate toward him and said, "I'll help you once. Don't drink. If you ever fuck up with alcohol again, you better not get close enough to me to see me coming."

He stared at the boy for half a minute. Then he leaned back, picked up his fork and knife, and began to carve at his steak. "Been up the Porcupine lately?"

"Two days ago."

"How far?"

"We came down from Rampart."

"See any sheefish up there?"

"Sheefish," said the boy as dumbly as he had said alcohol. He blinked. "There was some big fish rolling up around the mouth of the Sheenjek."

"Not salmon?"

"No, too bright; like a dime."

Don nodded, took a bite of steak. "Which judge?" he said.

As a kid, I got silently cranky with my dad if he didn't have me out on the water by daybreak, and even now I don't sleep much before a fishing trip. But in July in the Arctic with twenty-four hours of light on the water, it doesn't make much difference when a fisherman rises or dozes. Several times a summer I glance at my watch at streamside to discover it's 2:00 or 3:00 A.M. There's a boyish, goofy feel to it, as if I've somehow fished outside the bounds of natural law and human regulation, into a twilight—which is the fly fisherman's favorite hour—that might go on forever. Even at that—even though I know there is no crack of dawn to launch me—I've never gotten used to not having a beginning hour. In Fort Yukon, on July 15, I wandered out of Don Peter's house a little after 4:00 A.M. to occupy my angling energy otherwise.

I walked toward the river. The air was warm and still and heavy with those same riparian scents of life and decay, of wet mud and fecund algae, that are the hallmark odors of summery lowlands everywhere. It was a mile or so to the Yukon along silty dirt roads, some straight and wide as lanes, some twisted and narrow like alleys, and strewn with toys and bones and yard litter. Most of the houses were log. Most had whitening moose antlers nailed on somewhere, or just tossed up on the roofs. Most of the yards were junky by suburban standards, cluttered with three-wheelers and snow machines and parts of machines, and with wooden winter sleds, and with warped plywood tables where fish were gutted and split, and with tall, A-shaped drying racks. Some of the racks were fifteen or twenty feet high, of lashed spruce, willow, and alder poles, and many of them were draped with sheets of translucent Visqueen to keep the smoke in and some of the bugs out. King salmon, split down the middle except for a hinge of skin at the tail, hung on the racks flesh side out. The flesh had been scored, the scores widening as the fish dried, the peach-colored flesh darkening with the cure to strips of rich maroon.

Most of the yards had dogs, and most of the dogs were chained, and most of the chained dogs were big, silent huskies with the sort of unfathomable, wolfish eyes that make a person appreciate good steel. But around one bend I came upon a dog asleep in the road. A boy and a girl of five or six were seated in the dirt just beyond the dog, and when they stopped what they were doing to stare at me, the dog pricked its ears, swung its head, came quickly to its feet. Its hackles rose, its head lowered, and it looked at me out of the tops of its eyes.

"Hi." I said it as placatingly as I could.

The kids said nothing; the dog growled. I figured I'd sidle off the way I'd come. But then something touched the back of my right thigh, and I glanced off my shoulder to see another dog, hackle for rising hackle the twin of the one in the road. Its nose was against my leg. It sniffed, glanced balefully up, then sniffed another spot. I decided not to look at that dog.

"Listen," I said softly to the kids in the road, "I'll give you twenty dollars for one of those fish." I pointed at the fish with my eyes. "Over there."

The kids looked at each other. Then the boy hopped to his feet and sprinted for the front door of a log house. He left the door open when he went in. He was gone forever. Then a man in his twenties came squinting to the door, barefoot and wearing Levi's, pulling on a plaid flannel shirt. He stood in the doorway looking at me, buttoning a couple of buttons. Then he stepped slowly out.

Both dogs transformed. They wiggled and slunk over to meet him, their tails tucked, ears down. One of them was so beside itself as he approached that it peed and rolled over on its back.

He ignored them. When he got close to me, his eyes fastened on my wristwatch. "What the hell time is it?"

I looked. "Four twenty."

He looked around at the sky, blinking. He ran his tongue over his teeth, his lips bulging under a Fu Manchu sort of mustache that drooped meanly over the corners of his mouth. Without looking at me, he asked, "Who the hell are you?"

I told him my name, which I knew would mean nothing, and quickly added that I was a friend of Don Peter, here to do some fishing with him.

"Don Peter," he said.

"I couldn't sleep. I was just going to walk down and take a look at his boat."

The man nodded slightly. "New boat. Too big. Looks like a gas hog." Now he looked at me. "Where you going to fish?"

"I'm not sure. Up the Porcupine, I think."

He nodded. "Too damn early to go fishing, that's for sure."

"Yeah; sorry if I woke you."

He glanced toward the drying racks set back among the alder between his house and the next. "I heard you want to buy some fish."

"Right. Well, to tell the truth, it was for the dogs."

His eyebrows went up. He looked back over his shoulder. "These dogs?"

"Right."

"You want to pay me twenty dollars to feed my dogs?" He grinned briefly. "You didn't have to wait till four; you could have come by at three."

"Actually, I just thought the fish might keep them from tearing my legs off."

"These dogs?"

I shrugged lamely.

"I don't think so," he said. "But you never know." He looked over toward the drying racks. "You going to come back by here?"

"Unless there's an easier way."

"Some fish might not be a bad idea," he said.

Chewing a strip of smoked salmon, I hit the river some ways downstream from the landing, at the community liquor store. It was a small building, just a cement floor with windowless corrugated aluminum siding. Its plain backside faced the main road, so I didn't know it was a store until I walked around it intending to cut across a grassy, reedy flat to where I could see boats docked along the bank of a slough. But at what I thought would be the rear of the building, I discovered an entryway and a broken plastic liquor store sign.

The entry consisted of heavy double doors, with the outer door made of steel bars welded into a mesh heavy as a prison gate. Not far from the doors, out in the grass of the flats, squatted the rusted skeleton of a station wagon, a fifties model, I think, with no tires or windows. The driver's door stood open, and inside on the front seat a man and a woman slept leaning against each other. A few yards from the open door, three more men sat somnolently on their heels around a small fire.

One of the men looked up. He stared at me, then grinned broadly and rocked unsteadily to his feet. "Hey, there's the man that bought our hootch!"

I guess I had, sort of. After Don and I ate at the Gee-Zee Lodge, he took me to a pan game. I still couldn't tell you exactly what a pan game is, except that it is played with several decks of cards and moves so incomprehensibly fast that in dollar increments I dropped forty dollars in five minutes. Don had told me that the game is an Athabascan tradition, that all the villages have pan houses, and that some pan regulars are such fanatics that there is invariably violence if booze is present. "It is a strict rule that no one can enter a pan house if he has had even one drink," he told me. "It is a religious law."

This man, who had a thin, houndish face with sagging eyes and missing front teeth, was one of those who had raked in my dollars. If he had spent them, it wasn't at the community liquor store, which had closed some hours before the pan game started. As do most villages, though, Fort Yukon has bootleggers, and, as this fellow was about to tell me, the broken-down station wagon was *the* place for after-hours drinkers to score a buy.

"You got to pay through the nose, though," he said. "Twelve dollars a six-pack for beer"—it was normally five—"thirty-five for whiskey." He eyed the big brown paper bag I was carrying, which held four or five pounds of smoked salmon. "You got anything to drink in there?"

Such is the setting of Fort Yukon's single biggest source of income.

With a population of about 750 and an annual budget of about half a million dollars, the city depends on its liquor profits for some $125,000 a year. Don Peter and other local teetotalers led a bitter but successful campaign to close the store in 1985, but the main result was to put less food on Fort Yukon tables and more money into bootlegged alcohol. The Yukon River between Fort Yukon and road's end at Circle, seventy miles upstream, became known as Booze Alley. In addition, Fort Yukon's income from other sources began to drop as well. City fathers started to realize just how much their community's reputation as a hub for shoppers from more remote villages—Chalkyitsik, Venetie, Arctic Village, Beaver, Stevens Village, and Birch Creek—depended on it being a source of liquor as well as groceries. Within months, the matter was back on the ballot, and the store reopened early in 1986. During the eighteen months between the reopening and my arrival, incidences of stabbings, child abuse, domestic violence, and newborns with fetal alcohol syndrome all rose sharply. Half a dozen drunk Natives had been flown to hospitalization in Fairbanks with serious cases of frostbite, and five more went to the same place as hit-and-run victims of drunken snow machine drivers. On New Year's Day, one drunk slammed his snow machine into little Virgil James's twenty-six-year-old cousin Jimmy at about fifty miles an hour, killing Jimmy James outright.

I walked on down to the landing to listen to the clunking boats and watch the water. Like these people, I care next to nothing for mountaintops, measuring the quality of wildness by its water. I've never understood the hiker's habit of following the highest ridge to the tallest peak. A slope is a watershed, but the top of a mountain is the end of its usefulness, neither nourishing life nor facilitating it. Wildness in terms of mountaintops is merely the chaotic geology of magmatic caprice. Although we have come to associate wildlife with mountains, in reality our national parks and preserves are among the unkindest of our lands, the least suitable for both beast and man. It was we ourselves who pushed the lowland grizzly, the prairie wolf, the wetland deer and elk into the high alien hills, and, oddly, within a generation or two we began to think of them all as belonging way up there. Most do not; for most, mountaintops are lands of exile.

Conversely, wildlife depends on water, funnels to it, feeds from it, springs from it, makes its paths within it or beside it. A man's view of wildness from water is intimate, his activity participatory. In water wilds, life is rich, daring, precarious, fleeting. It pants and lusts and cowers and screams. It bursts forth, celebrates, prepares. To be at ease at waterside, you have to be comfortable with all that is fresh, all that lingers, and all that decays, and with the simultaneous scents of life and death.

Gwich'in: People of the river. Me, too.

5

The Terrible Meek

Courage is the price that life exacts for granting peace. The soul that knows it not, knows no release from little things; knows not the livid loneliness of fear, nor mountain heights where bitter joy can hear the sound of wings.

—Amelia Earhart Putnam, "Courage"

Not that it didn't have its moments, but when all was said and done, I was as unsettled by the way the trip ended as by the way it had begun.

From the Fort Yukon waterfront I walked back toward Don's place. The loose dogs were gone. I passed an old woman, who smiled and nodded, but otherwise the village hadn't stirred much in three hours. When I got to Don's yard I heard voices, though, and walked around to the side of the house thinking one of the voices was his.

It wasn't. The front entrance to another house was there, just thirty feet or so from the side of Don's place, and a young couple stood just outside the front door. The woman was very pretty. She was tall and had long black hair and black eyes. She held a toddler, cocked on her hip. She held her chin high and was facing a man whose back was to me, a stocky man who was shorter than she. Just as I took it all in, the man threw a quick punch that popped into the woman's cheek and snapped her head back. She didn't seem surprised; she simply stared at the man, eyes smoldering. Then, over his shoulder, she saw me. I was sorry; I didn't mean to be watching, but it was too late, and when her eyes shifted to me, he turned and saw me, too. He was caught; his expression went sullen. He looked back at her, just briefly, then strode toward a black Chevy pickup. I was inside Don's house by the time the pickup's engine turned over. Don was up. A pound of sliced bacon was beginning to sizzle in one frying pan, and he was cracking a dozen eggs into another.

★ ★ ★

A few hours later we were on the river, although every hour of fishing seemed to require four or five hours of roaring up or down some channel in Don's new boat, and another two or three hours of stopping at someone's fish camp to visit. But if it wasn't to be angling, it would be an education, for if on one level the trip was nothing more than me pitching in for the gas while two middle-aged men cruised the old neighborhood in a Cadillac, on another level it was a personal tour of the middle Yukon's past half century, and the heights and depths of its Gwich'in dreams and hells.

The fishing itself wasn't much. For a while I thought it might be. Even though we left Fort Yukon under a baking sun, which is generally a poor time to fish, I could see the rich orange flanks of king salmon swirling at the confluence of the Porcupine and the Yukon, and could see fat grayling rising in the glassy shallows as we skimmed up the Porcupine. And where tributaries trickled in through reeds and horsetails, I could see pike hanging like submarines when the sun rays were angled right, and could sometimes see a pike's slicing wake as it made a quick, deliberate hunt through the shallows.

I wanted to fish for all of those fish, and tentatively pointed some of them out, but Don Peter shrugged them off, so I settled back to enjoy the tea-colored Porcupine, which we could follow, if we were so inclined, 450 miles northeast into Canada beyond the Northwest Territories village of Old Crow. Don's shrugs, I supposed, had meant that there were better fish ahead.

Before we ever wet a line, Don cut the motor and drifted to the north shore so that we could watch three black bears.

"You want to shoot one?"

Don wasn't looking at me. He was sighting through a scope mounted on a 30.06 rifle, watching the sow and two half-grown cubs graze among fresh grass shoots on a sandbar maybe seventy-five yards upstream from us and on the far side of the river. I wasn't sure that his question was meant for me but suspected it was. I didn't want to shoot a bear.

"I don't think the season's open for me," I said.

He handed me the rifle. "Even for white guys it's open. You can kill three a year. If you want, you can kill all three of those bears right there."

I passed the rifle on to Harry. "I'd rather fish," I said.

Harry braced the rifle on the gunwale and looked through the scope. "Maybe we should get one of them," he said. He looked at me. "So that this man can have something to eat when you don't catch him any fish."

"He'll get his fish," Don said.

"We been passing up fish all afternoon," said Harry.

"Not sheefish; he wants sheefish."

Harry looked back through the scope. He snapped the rifle off safety and fingered the trigger. "I wouldn't mind taking one of those little ones," he said. "More tender, less work."

"You got to know where the sheefish are," said Don, "by how much the water has dropped, and how cold it is." He reached over the gunwale and brushed his fingers into the river. Harry, his cheek still on the rifle stock, rolled an eye toward Don but said nothing.

"When it's low and sort of warm in the middle of July, they'll all be up at the mouth of the Sheenjek," said Don.

Abruptly, Harry set the rifle down on a pile of sleeping bags. "You're full of it," he said. Then he said, "What makes you think they're up there?"

Don picked up the rifle. "You don't go telling all your secrets to every Harry dick," he said.

Don slipped the rifle back into its soft case, zipped the case, and peered upriver like a captain. "I don't know if we can get this boat up that far in this low water," he said.

"That's a pretty good excuse. You know so much about sheefish, why don't you know that?"

"I grew up with sheefish, but I just got this boat two weeks ago."

Don climbed back into the driver's seat. I stepped out of the stern, shoved off, then swung back aboard. As the big motor caught, the two black bear cubs rose simultaneously on their hind legs to look at us. They stood only a moment, glossy black against new green, then dropped to all fours and followed their mother into the thick stand of willow shoreward.

"Maybe we should have got one of them," said Harry.

Some hours later we stood in tall grass on the shore of a stream Don called Shit Creek. It was a garden of a place, with clear water and dustless greenery, and quiet in the enclosing way that quietness presses in when you first get away from a steady source of noise. We had left the low, powerful rush of the Yukon and wound for more than an hour up a channel that snaked between reeds and occasionally widened into a pond or small lake. Don had finally cut the motor and had me tie the bowline to the whitened branches of a dead spruce that leaned from the bank into the water.

We were at an elbow of the stream, just where it left a pond. "Right there's where old Edward caught that great big one," said Harry, pointing toward the deep inside the elbow. "Forty-nine pounds?" He looked at Don. "Fifty-nine?"

"Big as a leg," Don said.

The outside curve of the elbow was lined with reeds and the buttery bursts of water lily blossoms. The stream's current was almost impercepti-ble. Its flow was clear, but both the channel and the pond were so deep that the water looked black. We were in the Yukon Flats, somewhere north of the Yukon River, and somewhere east of the Christian River. Spruce and aspen grew so thickly along the banks that Shit Creek, if such it was, looked like a slick corridor through a vast wood. But I had flown over this country and knew that if I were looking down on me I would see mostly these marshy lakes and meandering streams. The spruce and aspen were just narrow belts of trees lining the creeks that connect the lakes. From the air it is deceptively innocent-looking country, 12,600 square miles of bright grassy green. It is also, however, a wetland maze, laced by thousands of miles of interconnecting waterways that flow among tens of thousands of lakes. People have wandered until they died in here; but from where I stood casting for pike with Don Peter and Harry Thomas, this piece of the Yukon Flats looked and felt like just an intimate little glen.

It was the second day into our excursion, and the first good fishing we'd had. The day before, up on the Porcupine, we had found the sheefish, porpoising at the mouth of the Sheenjek as bright as dimes, just like the waiter at the Gee-Zee Lodge had said. But Don had passed them by on the upstream leg of the trip. He'd passed them, he said, because he wanted to see if his new boat could make it up a certain stretch of shallows, and he couldn't be comfortable fishing if he was nervous about those shallows. I asked him why he wanted to test the shallows anyway. "To find out if we can get to Rampart," he said. Rampart was a tiny border settlement a hundred miles upstream.

"What's in Rampart?" I asked.

"Friends."

We didn't make it up the shallows. The jet unit on the big Mercury outboard sucked up gravel and stalled the motor, not once but on each of the several runs Don tried up a wide, riffly sweep of the Porcupine. We went back down and tried the sheefish, but they were no longer rolling at the mouth of the Sheenjek. I cast for them while Don and Harry dozed in the boat. I didn't raise a fish.

But now, in this unnamed creek, we had caught ten northern pike between us in half an hour. *Iltin,* Harry called them. The biggest so far was about two feet long and weighed maybe five pounds. But they were fun on a fly rod, and, with his story of old Edward's big fish, Harry had talked some high potential into the black water.

Don was already bored. "It's like they tell us new corporate Natives: you got to go for the high cost-benefit ratio. When you stop getting a fish on every cast, it's time to move on."

"Or time to eat," said Harry.

Don thought about that. He wandered up the bank and began to collect firewood.

Suddenly, because of a shift in light or maybe a shift of position down in the depths themselves, I saw a long, shadowy form hanging among the branches of a submerged spruce snag. I was sure it was a pike, a good foot longer than any we had caught so far. I cast. The fly was heavy, a three-inch-long Stu Apt tarpon fly tied on a big stainless steel hook. There is nothing graceful in casting such a fly; you have to use a strong rod, and a line heavy enough to uncoil from the rod like a horsewhip. The fly slaps down hard on the water and sinks fast, but however ungainly the falling and fluttering, pike like it. It looks, I suppose, bloody and gutty and like a flailing victim.

Thirty feet out, the red and yellow fly sank toward the pike. I couldn't let it tumble all the way to the fish because of the submerged branches, so when it was a yard or so under the surface, I gave the line a fast strip back toward me that pulled the billowing feathers suddenly sleek. The fly darted through a shaft of sunlight, then faltered. I stripped again.

The fish struck, a dark torpedo that engulfed the fly and kept coming, then veered right. I jerked the rod to set the hook, felt the weight, watched the fish go abruptly vertical, slice into the air, fall back in with a kabloosh. Then it held at the surface, thrashing.

Like a cheetah, the pike is built for the fast predatory dash; when hooked, it fights hard for half a minute at best, then stops running. I have come to doubt that the fight exhausts the pike; it is more as if it has turned at bay. You have to tow it in, and it comes with belligerent headshakes like a roped alligator, the aggressive eyes looking more interested now in attacking than in getting away.

I slid the fish up onto the grass. It thumped once and lay glaring.

"Not big as a leg," said Harry, "but not bad."

"Ten, twelve pounds," said Don. "Maybe fifteen."

The fly wasn't too far back in the pike's mouth; I slipped it free with a pair of needle-nosed pliers. "Want to keep this one?"

Harry looked at Don, shook his head. "We got enough of those little ones," he said.

I bent over the pike, looked into its eyes. In trout, when I catch them, I see wildness, and sometimes a spark of what I take to be desperation. In the brass-eyed pike, the expression seems nothing less than deliberate balefulness, a time-biding malignancy; given time, the pike will get you. It is a look of which the memory alone was enough to scare me once, and turn me back toward shore during a swim. I had hiked half a day over hot muskeg through clouds of mosquitoes and blackflies. I was sweaty, desperately itchy. I stripped naked, swam out into the black waters of a small tundra lake not unlike this one. When I paused a hundred feet offshore, I saw several V wakes cutting toward me from the shoreline reeds. The wakes split water to within about ten feet of me, then stopped, the fish holding in a semicircle. I couldn't see them; I had no idea exactly where or how big they were. I was suddenly aware of the small personal worm that dangled beneath me, and I remembered clearly an A. J. McClane description I had memorized as a boy: "With baleful eyes and underslung jaw, the pike comes grimly to the feast." With a tug of panic, I rolled onto my back and made for shore.

This ten-pounder from Shit Creek I nudged with my toe, sliding him into shallow water among the reeds. His gills worked healthily enough, but he made no move to leave.

"I think we ought to eat some of those little ones right now," said Don. His fire had caught. He stepped back into the boat to rummage up a frying pan, some plates, some butter. I wanted to fish more but figured I should help, so I walked over to where Harry was picking out three of the small pike that we had laid in the shade under damp grass. Using a short length of spruce log as a table, he sliced one fish from vent to gullet, pulled out the intestines, and cut them off. Then he tossed the fish into the grass.

"I'll fillet it," I said, and bent to pick it up. My brother-in-law Tom had shown me how, with a couple of deft cuts, you can slice around the Y-bones that are the reason a lot of people shun pike.

But Harry shook his head. "Too bony," he said; "just leave it lie."

I stood, confused. "But you gutted it."

From the pike's offal Harry had cut a foot-long length of white intestine and the biscuit-sized liver. He walked to the stream, holding them up for me to see. "Lunch," he said, and knelt to rinse them.

"Fish guts," said Don Peter. He had thrown a quarter pound of butter into an old skillet and was watching it melt over the flame. Harry returned to the spruce log and sliced the intestine lengthwise so that it became a flat, white sheet a foot long, about four inches wide, and something less than a quarter of an inch thick. From the sheet, he cut strips an inch wide, four long. They looked like strips of squid.

"See what I'm doing?" he said.

"Yeah. I do."

"The young ones like this are tender. On the big ones, the belly gets too thick, too tough." He finished carving the intestine and reached for the liver. "You slice this up too, as thin as you can." He looked up at me. "We need two more fish."

"I'll do one," I said. I picked up a pike, carried it to the stream, held it under water, and cut it open. Submerging pike bowels, I've found, helps screen their odor, which can be bad enough to gag a maggot.

"Fish guts?" I said.

"Fish guts," said Don. "Hurry up; the butter will scorch."

With baleful eyes and reluctant jaw, I went grimly to the feast.

We fished for days in that ambling way. Don Peter and Harry Thomas were euphoric. For a time I felt intrusive, but then I began to realize that they appreciated me for giving them an excuse. They were caught up in one of life's more pleasant exercises, two old friends with a chance to guide a stranger through their private histories and old innocences, and in reverie to hold an audience captive for a week.

It was an expedition more social than I had anticipated. In June and July, the human population along the Yukon spreads out. Athabascan villages of old were little more than winter cloisters anyway, and for many interior Natives that's still the way it is: Summer is a time for family groups to break from the social mass and head by boat to the personal territories in which they will spend the four fair months of harvest. As we cruised the Yukon and its tributaries, I began to get a sense of measured realms. There was a certain rhythm to the spaces between the boats we met, and to the miles between columns of campfire smoke, where family knots of up to a dozen people were tucked back behind the dark green walls of shoreline spruce. As if it would be rude to pass, we stopped at all these camps and shared the river news.

No one, as far as I know, has done a detailed study of the subsistence harvest patterns of Gwich'in family groups. But anthropologists Richard Nelson, Kathleen Mautner, and Ray Bane did conduct such a study in the late 1970s among the Gwich'in's downstream neighbors, the Koyukon peoples of Hughes, Huslia, Allakaket, Alatna, Bettles, and Anaktuvik Pass. I am certain, from traveling with the Gwich'in and in a limited way duplicating Bane's technique of asking people to pinpoint on topographic maps the specific sites where they fished, hunted, trapped, harvested berries, and cut firewood, that the Gwich'in's subsistence patterns have been very much like those of their Koyukon neighbors.

The anthropologists found that a Koyukon family's "subsistence use area" might encompass 500 square miles or more along a waterway or within a network of waterways, and that in taking advantage of what Bane described as the "hidden resource mosaics" of the land, a family might meander among a dozen or so campsites during the course of a year. Some of the camps would be sheltered housekeeping sites, some merely way stations. Some would be fish camps, some hunting or trapping camps, and others berry-harvest camps (usually located on tundra ridges to double as caribou lookout sites).

When I think of subsistence, I think of fishing, hunting, and gathering. The terms are an oversimplification. Hunting, for example, is a significantly different activity for each animal. When the Gwich'in point to a spot on one of my topo maps, they never label it "hunting camp." Rather, it's "caribou camp" or "bear camp." Hunting bears is different from hunting caribou. Hunting moose is different from hunting sheep. Hunting waterfowl is different from hunting grouse or ptarmigan, which in turn is different from hunting rabbits, which is child's play compared with hunting wolves, wolverines, or lynx. To hunting, add the differences between trapping for various furbearers (beavers require underwater sets, wolf sets require ingenious camouflage), the differences between fishing for various species (nets, several types of fish traps, spears, and hook and line are all used), and harvesting berries, grasses, barks, wild rhubarb and onions and other plants, and the picture of subsistence life begins to fill in as astonishingly diverse. And all that fishing, hunting, and gathering doesn't include the housekeeping chores—the bird plucking, carcass skinning, meat curing, fish jerking, hide tanning, skin sewing, equipment maintenance, dog husbandry, parenting, counseling, doctoring, taxpaying, and corporate politicking that have to be done after the fish are caught, the game shot, and the berries picked. Subsistence is not, as I once thought, poverty. Subsistence is spending some of your evenings at home to kick off the hide-tanning process by rubbing the ground-up, acidic brains of some dead animal into the flesh side of the same animal's hide. Subsistence is not poverty, but it is different from wealth. It is more active, and constant, and closer to the bone, and it doesn't hide from death.

Rivers, I discovered on the Yukon, carry different meanings for me than for the Gwich'in of interior Alaska. I go to all rivers just to study the water and cast a line. Fishing is my single practical excuse for visiting any river; beyond it, the water quickly becomes for me holy, symbolic, and barometric. My rivers have names like Wind and Big Two-Hearted. I get soulful about them, and regularly have religious experiences on their banks. Evolution is motion, and rivers are evolutionary locomotion, just as quick and slow as all of life, and just as changeable, mutable, fluid, variable, alterable, transient, inconsistent, and fickle. The currents of rivers cloud and clear in precise measurement of the storms and shinings of civilization.

But the childhood families of Don Peter and Harry Thomas were pragmatic. They were at the dying end of a civilization in which all meaning and truth lay in the meat and the berry. Their river (in Gwich'in, *Youcan* simply means "big river") was highway and larder. In asking old-timers to name sites along tributaries of the Koyukuk (which also means "big river"), anthropologist Ray Bane was given hundreds of such names, almost all of them reflecting the specifics of the environment rather than its motifs. Thus *K'its'izeeyh Hu* is "Area Where Bear Is Customarily Caught in the Den," and *Saakkaay Naalnonh Dinh* is "Place Where Children Died." In all the place naming I've seen, Athabascans never wax poetic, although some of the literal naming, such as *K'it'olt'on Da'oyh Da Kkokk'a*—"Spring Where Fish Stay Still to Catch Other Fish"—is descriptive to the point of poetry. One scruffy but poetic little knoll I remember in particular is *Gguh Tl'itlt'o Khokk'a,* or "Nape of the Rabbit Neck Hill."

I decided when the fishing was over to charter a boat upriver 70 miles from Fort Yukon to Circle, and hitch a ride the remaining 150 miles to Fairbanks.

"Why don't you just fly?" Don Peter asked.

"I haven't seen that part of the river yet," I said.

He shrugged. "Well, I can't do it. I got a board meeting tonight, and then I have to fly up to Venetie."

"I could take him in your boat," said Harry.

"The hell you say. Nobody messes with my boat until after I put a good big bang in it."

"Maybe Danny then," said Harry.

Don grunted, scowled, shrugged, reached over to grab the red throttle knob. "Maybe," he said.

From the mouth of the Chandalar River, Don put about for Fort Yukon. It was a thirty- or forty-mile run, and we had most of a day for it, but Don started the trip fast, kicking the boat up on step and shoving the throttle wide, the boat skimming, slapping, pounding up through the wide sweeps of current. Spray from the drumming hull arched back to our faces in a rhythmic wash. Ducks, mostly mallards, jumped up surprised; beavers veered, nosing their rafts of willow cuttings shoreward. A blue heron scrunched at our passing, all beak and shoulder blades.

At first the later morning sky was blue and hot, but several fires were burning in the area—the lightning-ignited fires that can smolder for months, even years, among the deep mosses and caribou lichens of the tundra and the boreal woods. As we wound south the sky palled with smoke. After a while I pulled up the hood of my windbreaker, turned my back to the spray, and watched the river play out like a rope from the stern. On clear-water rivers like the Porcupine or the Chandalar, water slides beneath the hull cleanly, but on rivers clouded with glacial silt, like the Yukon, you can hear the frictional hiss of the stone talc as it strips paint or aluminum, molecule by molecule, from the hull.

Forty-five minutes into the trip Don cut the motor, and I turned around to see what was up. We were beside a fish wheel that bobbed along midchannel on its raft of logs. Don nodded toward two inch-thick ropes that trailed from the raft's downstream side near the stern of the boat.

"Pull in those lines," he said to me. He wanted them hauled, I imagined, so that they wouldn't snarl his prop. The only way I could see to reach them was to step aboard the raft, so I did that, and as I coiled the lines, Don nosed his boat into the platform like a tug, nudging it toward shore.

The fish wheel creaked in the current like a derelict Ferris wheel. Its platform—maybe ten feet by fifteen—supported a scaffolding that in turn supported two appositive scoops made of lashed and nailed and bolted together spruce poles and alder branches. Each of the alder scoops, or baskets, was about five feet by ten, and built at a slant so that any fish it picked up as the current drove it around would slide into a wooden chute that emptied into a wooden fish box. Because they were drifting with the current rather than resisting it, the baskets weren't turning when I stepped aboard; they were cocked at an angle of repose, rocking slightly. I made the mistake of ignoring them. As Don began to nose the raft shoreward, the baskets caught the current. "Hey!" I heard Harry yell, and his voice became a tunneled sound that droned on beyond the heavy thunk at the back of my head.

I was out only for a second. I realized that I had dropped to one knee. I was dully surprised, both at being down on a knee and at the impact that had driven me there. Then Harry was at my side, his arm across my back, his hand gripping my armpit. "It almost dumped you in the fish bucket," he said. "Them women would have thought they had a world record. Split you open, hang you in the smokehouse."

The raft crunched aground on a gravel shore, and while Don pinned it there with his boat, Harry took one of the two heavy lines that I had hauled aboard, walked up the bank, and began to tie the line to the whitened root of a washed-up spruce trunk. I walked the other line in a vee up the bank away from Harry and wrapped it around the trunk of a live alder.

Don killed his motor, tied the boat's bowline to the raft, and stepped across the logs to shore. "My cousin's wheel," he said.

"Where's your cousin?"

Don eyed the river. "Ten, twelve mile upstream, I suppose." He went up the bank to look at the lines, to see if they had been cut or had broken. But the ends of the lines were still bound with a careful whip finish. "Just pulled free," he guessed and walked back down to the platform to check its lashings. While he stood on it, poking here and prying there, the creaking fish wheel harvested a salmon, then another. Their heavy bodies thunked into the fish box. They flopped, beating drumlike against the wood. I went over to look at them. They had traveled maybe a thousand miles upstream from the Bering Sea's Norton Sound to here, losing a third or more of their body weight along the way. From sea-fresh, fat, and silvery, they had grown lean and had "colored up some," as the upstream fishermen say, their flanks becoming as orange as the meat their thinning skin covered.

Don's lean, gray cousin, Jim Peter, came downriver in his boat. He tied it up next to Don's. He nodded to his cousin, then walked up the bank fast to look at the ends of the lines. He came back shaking his head. The wheel dumped another salmon into the box beside me, and he came over to look.

"How long it take to get them three?"

"About ten minutes."

Don and Harry walked over. "You want to tow this thing back up?" Don asked.

"It's fishing pretty good here," said Jim. "Maybe we'll just leave it for a while." He looked at me, a man he had never seen before, and said, "What do you think?"

"I don't know," I said. "I don't even know why all the fish wheels I've seen have been on this side of the river."

"Because we fish for kings on this side," said Jim. "Later on, we fish for silvers on the other side."

"Ah." I looked at the far shore, which looked pretty much like the one on which we stood. I was used to reading rivers, but this opaque one revealed little. It seemed to be just one broad sweep of current in which I could detect no clue as to why one species of salmon should habitually run up its south bank and another its north. "Why's that?" I said.

"Because the kings come up this side, silvers come up that side."

Harry looked at the sixty or seventy pounds of salmon in the fish box. "That's a nice mother fish," he said. "I wouldn't mind taking that one home."

Jim slid his hand beneath the hen salmon's gills, hoisted her from the box, and carried her to Don's boat. Then he returned to the box, picked up the two male fish, and tossed them into the boat beside the first.

"If you're going to ask for something, cousin," he said, "ask for enough."

Another fifteen minutes upriver, Don eased his boat over to the base of a fifteen-foot bluff along the opposite shore. A crude dock of freshly cut alder trunks lay flush against the bank, and from the dock a stairway had been carved into the earth of the bluff and was railed with a waist-high restraint of spruce poles. There was no other boat at the dock, but I could see that the site was occupied by the set net that arced out from the bank into the river just downstream from the dock. One of the floats that held the net kept bobbing under, a sign that there was at least one salmon in the net. Don killed the motor, motioned for me to tie the bowline to the dock, and then grabbed one of the buck salmon from the floor of his boat. The three of us went up the stairs.

"Who lives here?" I said.

"Nephew," said Don.

It was the steepest bank we had climbed, but otherwise the fish camp was typical of the others we had visited along the way, with its white canvas wall tents and tarpaulin awnings, and the A-frame of a fish drying rack. All the camps I had been in were clean—this one no less so—and each had its own familial variations on the campsite themes that have evolved among the people of the river for some 15,000 years. The evolution is evident not so much in the materials—most of those, with the exceptions of stone and wood, have changed—but in the subtleties of practical location and efficient design. This particular camp, like most, was set on high ground, mainly because—as the natives have known for aeons and scientists have known for a decade—most of the interior's mosquitoes never rise more than a dozen feet off the forest or tundra floor. Unlike most of the camps I'd seen, however—on both this river and others—this one had been pitched in a dense, viewless stand of black spruce. As we walked in among the trees, they closed away the rush of the river. From behind a canvas tarp that had been strung up as a wall, blue smoke rose slowly and spread into a canopy among the spruce boughs. It was breeze-less, hushed.

As we followed the skirting path along the canvas wall, a very small and pudgy boy wandered around the end of the canvas and stopped. He had a nail in his mouth, working it like a toothpick until he saw us. Then the nail and his black eyes froze. The eyes showed no surprise, just a veiled flatness. They locked on me, only for a moment; then the boy melted back behind the canvas wall.

A woman was bent over a pan washing dishes, watching with a guarded look as we came around the canvas. She relaxed when she saw Don, her eyes brushed past me, and she smiled at Harry. I hadn't recognized the toddler but would have remembered the woman even without the bruise that now darkened the brown skin over her left cheek. She was the young neighbor of Don's, the tallish, handsome woman whose husband, I supposed, threw a fist into her face on that morning we left Fort Yukon.

Her name was Virginia. She was a good camp keeper. The place was spotless. The earthen floor of the site was cleared, probably by generations of use, of the foot-deep layer of mosses that blanketed the surrounding forest floor. The earth was packed and damp, so that dust wouldn't rise. There was a white canvas wall tent to which the flaps were presently closed. There was a homemade table and chairs, wooden shelves stocked with food and utensils, a fireplace with a level grill that supported the steaming dishpan over which Virginia continued to work as she talked with Don. Between the table and the tent, a small baby lay sleeping in a hammock strung between two trees and covered with mosquito netting. Facing the fireplace beyond the dining area was a sort of conversation pit, an open ∪ of benches made by nailing one-by-twelves to sections of spruce trunk about eighteen inches high. Twenty yards farther back into the woods was a smokehouse, maybe six feet by ten, both walled and roofed with corrugated tin. There was a fish-dressing table beside the smokehouse, and another few yards beyond the table were walls of a log cabin, a beginning that looked as if it had been begun for some years.

I stood beside Harry in the conversation pit, watching him try to coax the nail from the boy's mouth.

"Kyle," said Virginia softly. "Spit it out."

He did, immediately, and looked at it there in the dirt with a wistful pout.

Don wanted to see Virginia's husband, Danny.

"He's upriver," she said.

"How long?"

"I don't know."

Don shrugged and settled onto a wooden bench beside the fireplace. He picked a cup from a rack of clean dishes, poured some coffee, handed it to Harry, and reached for another cup.

"Grant?" he said.

"Thanks." I took the coffee and asked Virginia a couple of tentative questions. She responded with the toddler's name, and the baby's (Duane), and with how many king salmon a day the family got from the set net below camp (five or six). She answered unshyly enough but was reluctant to meet my eyes. When she did, her own eyes smoldered. It didn't seem to be hostility so much as a secretiveness, and maybe it was only in my imagination that her expression acknowledged the mutual discomfort that stemmed from my having seen her take the blow, and her knowing that I saw.

I asked her how she smoked the fish.

"I need to do that one you brought," she said. She looked toward the smokehouse, then began to walk over that way, and I followed.

"There's not much to know," she said. She stopped just outside the door, at the plywood fish-dressing table where Don had dumped his gift salmon when we came into the camp. She reached for a knife that lay on a two-by-four high enough up the smokehouse wall that it would be out of a child's reach.

"Do you brine it before you smoke it?" I asked.

"Some, but mostly I just cold-smoke it."

"It keeps okay that way?"

She looked at me. "Yeah, sure."

Neatly, she eviscerated the king salmon. With the knife, she separated the heart, the liver, and the salmon's two, one-pound sperm sacks. The intestines and gills went into a bucket. Most Natives along the Yukon still use the ulu—a knife better described as a curved blade about six inches long and three inches wide, with a bone or wood handle on top of the blade rather than at one end of it. The knife Virginia used, however, was more typical of knives seen among commercial fishermen, with a long, thin blade at one end and a spoon at the other for scraping out the kidney matter that lies along the underside of the spine.

Virginia cut the head from the fish and tossed the head into the bucket. Then she deftly filleted the spine and ribs away from the body, slicing down the center of the fish until the two halves were held together only by a strip of skin at the tail. She turned the fish meat-side out and made several scouring cuts across the meat of each flank to provide the drying air and smoke better access to the meat.

With half a smile, she held the fish for me to see, the meat about the same orange as an arctic poppy, glistening with its own oil. She glanced once toward the baby in the hammock and toward where Kyle played

with Harry, then opened the low door to the smokehouse and ducked in.
I followed.

The smokehouse was simply a tin shack with a dirt floor and a ceiling
about twelve feet high. Poles of alder or aspen spanned from wall to wall
like chicken roosts, from about chest height to near the ceiling. Salmon
were draped skin-side out over most of the poles in various stages of
drying. A ladder leaned against one wall to reach the high poles. On the
floor, a small pile of ashes smoldered at the center of a ring of stones.

"How many do you dry every year?" I asked.

"I don't know, a few hundred."

Her back to me, Virginia draped the new salmon over one of the low
poles. She looked at several of the fish nearby, squeezing each slightly as
if to test it for doneness. She lifted one from its rack and turned toward
me, beginning to extend the fish, saying, "If you—" when her eyes
shifted, startled, afraid, toward the smokehouse door.

I looked. It was the same stocky man I had seen that morning a few
days back. I supposed he was Danny. His eyes, as he shifted them from
Virginia to me, were grim.

"Hey, nephew," said Don, squeezing into the smokehouse. He
moved to stand between Danny and me. "This man needs a ride back up
to Circle." He looked at me. "You pay the gas, and, what—a hundred
dollars?"

"Sure," I said.

Don looked at his nephew. "It's a good chance to go to Circle."

Danny walked out. Don shrugged at me with his eyebrows, then
followed his nephew. Virginia looked at the floor. I left.

I spent my last afternoon in Fort Yukon bouncing around town from
chore to chore with Don in the old turquoise pickup. The eighty-eight-
year-old Episcopal church—of which his father was the first Native rec-
tor—seemed to be sort of an anchor point for him. "Let's cool off," he
would say, and three times that afternoon he swung the truck into the
churchyard. We would walk in, where, true, it was cooler, the floorboards
echoing under our boots, the sanctuary dim behind stained-glass windows.

Don would tell me some more about Fort Yukon's Episcopal history while he looked around at the empty wooden pews and the icons and the altar. A Bible cover at the entry and an ornate altar cloth were both made of moosehide tanned to a creamy white by Don's mother and some other women of the village, who had then ornamented it with tens of thousands of Czechoslovakian glass seed beads in typical Athabascan floral patterns as a communal offering of thanks at the end of the First World War. On our visits Don touched the altar cloth lightly, then pointed to an uneven light brown stain that ran the length of the cloth about a third of the way up from its fringed bottom. "Watermark. From the flood of 'forty-nine."

Then we went to the airport and he was gone, off to his board meetings. I drove the old truck back to his house and hung out there, listening to tapes of Native music, waiting for Danny to come tell me he was ready to go. Danny had decided to take the money. I was to head upriver with him, and with Tony, another of Don Peter's nephews, and—though I didn't yet know it—with the gap-toothed, sour-breathed man I had seen at the pan game and at the old station wagon outside the liquor store. It was a five-hour run from Fort Yukon to road's end at Circle. Tony Peter, a student headed back to some summer activity at the university, had left his pickup truck in Circle and would give me a ride home.

I took a shower, then fell asleep in Don's front-room easy chair. And I awoke, some time later, with a performer named Sundance pledging to keep her lover's memories fed "with his feather from the eagle's bed" and a hand lightly running its fingers over the hair of my right forearm. It felt good; then I was startled.

It was a Gwich'in girl, six or seven. "Hello," I said.

"My name is Sandra Ann Skogstadt," she said. She was still running her fingers over my arm, where the summer sun had bleached the hair gold. "How did you get the yellow like that?"

"Sunshine turns it that way," I said.

"Not mine."

"The sun does different things to different people."

"What does it do to me?"

"You're a pretty young lady; it must make you pretty."

She grinned, ran her fingers down the arm one more time, then gripped my own fingers firmly and gave two quick tugs. "I'm supposed to get you," she said. "Danny's ready to go."

Well, almost ready, Danny said. He needed the hundred dollars in advance, or at least half of it, so he could buy enough gas in Fort Yukon for the round trip. He could buy it at the Native corporation prices here, but they really stuck you for it in Circle.

I gave him two fifties, and he left in his truck, saying he'd be back in an hour to pick me up. It was 5:30.

"You want some dinner?" Sandra Ann stood at the sill of Virginia's kitchen door. Virginia was dimly visible inside, at her drainboard. I saw her glance quickly, then look away when she saw me. I remembered the expression on Danny's face when he'd walked into the fish camp smoke-house.

"No thanks, sunshine," I said. She wore blue jeans and a green T-shirt; her hair was neatly banded into two perky ponytails. Her face fell when I said no. I wanted to make her smile, wanted to make the woman behind her smile, but I was still trying to think of something I could say when Sandra Ann turned inside and closed the door. She reminded me of my own daughters, older now, how at seven they could put a lump in my throat with a glance.

But these daughters here were none of my business.

Even at a little after 5:30, the temperature was between eighty and ninety. I wandered down to the house where I had bought smoked fish the week before. Two dogs were there, lying in dusty shade against a wall near the front door. I decided not to try that door. There was smoke curling from the smokehouse and some sounds from over there, so I went that way. The dogs stared, and their heads swung with me as I walked past the log home and over to the smokehouse, but they didn't get up.

The smokehouse was busy. A plywood fence, or windbreak, about four feet high led from a rear door of the home to the smokehouse, and then, in a semicircle, enclosed an area outside the smokehouse so that I couldn't see the people until I walked around the end of the barrier. Eight people sat or stood inside the enclosure. Two old women and a younger woman stood working with a big bin full of king salmon, and three young men—the one nearest me had fish scales dried on his Levi's, so I assumed it was their catch the women were processing—sat drinking beer at an old Formica-covered dinette table in the shade of the fence. Two children, the small boy and girl I had met the week before, sprawled with toys in the dirt, farther along the fence toward the rear door of their home. The younger woman was inside the Visqueen tent, hanging split salmon on the pole drying racks. The two old women stood among buzzing flies and yellow jackets, splitting salmon with ulu knives.

One of the old women glanced up, saw me, and brightened with an immediate, deeply wrinkled smile, which prompted all three of the men to swing their heads my way. Their faces, expressive until then, reacted to me with a simultaneous wash of dumbness. I felt a twinge of guilt at interrupting them and was slightly appalled that these blank masks, these poker faces, were just for me. One of the men was the one I had bought salmon from the week before. I smiled back at the old woman, nodded to the man I had met. He didn't return the smile but leaned back in his chair to a more confident position, a sort of negotiator's sprawl. "You want more fish?"

"If I can get more," I said.

"How much more?" He reached down beside the table to pull another beer from an ice chest. The wet, clacking slosh sounded cold and delicious.

I found a twenty-dollar bill in my Levi's. "Not much. One side? Maybe a beer?"

He popped open the can he held, leaned forward to hand it to me, and got another for himself. He nodded toward the table's remaining chair, a rickety one made of chrome rods and marbled red plastic uphol-stery. I squeezed between the table and the fence to sit.

The man said something in Gwich'in to one of the older women, who smiled at me as he spoke to her. I recognized the word for fish, *luk,* repeated a couple of times, the *l* a voiceless fricative making the word sound like a cross between *tluck* and *cluck*. I also caught *luk choo,* king salmon, and *drah,* the word for fish drying rack.

I told them my name and drank the cold beer. The smiling old woman brought fish in a brown paper bag and set it on the table. "No

ts'ah," she said. No fly eggs. The men got friendlier, asked me where I was
from and what I did, and in response began to talk about some of the
village students attending the university. All three of them had nephews
or nieces or cousins going there, and I knew a few, had even worked with
a couple of them in the magazine article writing courses I taught at night.

Then I leaned back to drain my beer and looked straight up into the
face of a man leaning over the fence. In a way that jolted me I recognized
him: Jim File, a fundamentalist missionary whose wife used to baby-sit my
sister's kids in the North Pole.

"There are better things to do on a Sunday than drink beer," he said.
"Are you Christians? Do you believe in Christ?"

Jim File was a joyless man. Not long after I came to Alaska my sister
had told me about him, and I'd gotten excited about his story—of a man
who for decades had each summer bundled up a few clothes, a bit of food,
and a cheap rubber raft, had them and himself flown into the headwaters
of the Kuskokwim River, and spent two or three months ministering to
villages and family fish camps as he floated the 500 or 600 miles downstream. I had envisioned the tiny raft bobbing through America's last true
wilderness, a vessel of faith among grizzlies, and I'd thought that Jim File's
story would probably be a good one. I scheduled an interview. He met me
without a smile and told me that, unless I agreed to tell a story that
glorified God, he wasn't interested in hearing my questions. I told him that
the story would be his, and that whether it glorified God would be up to
him. He agreed, doubtfully, to a few replies. I asked him what the country
was like along the upper Kuskokwim.

"I don't pay any attention," he said.

"But . . . is it tundra? Timber?"

"I told you: I don't pay any attention."

"How about—"

"What?"

"You really can't tell me whether it's tundra or timber? As many
times—"

"Timber. Partly timber, partly tundra."

"What about the feeling? The solitude."

"I'm never alone. You have to understand this: I don't go on these
trips to have a good time. I don't go to look at the country or to appreciate

the solitude. I go to deliver God's word. That is all I go for, and it requires all my attention. I don't pay any attention to anything else."

The headwaters of the Kuskokwim were almost 500 miles to the southwest. Here in Fort Yukon, Jim File was out of his territory. His was a tainting presence. He turned the Natives immediately sullen. He made me feel guilty about a cold beer on a hot evening. He disrupted a fellowship, corrupted a camaraderie.

"Go away," said the man who owned the house, the fence, the fish, and the beer.

"We have another service in half an hour," said Jim File. "At six. You are all welcome. You should all come." He proffered some tracts over the fence. No one took them. He dropped them on a table, in front of me. I glanced at them, and when I looked up again Jim File was gone.

"You want another beer?"

"Yes, but I can't," I said. "If you come to Fairbanks, give me a call. I owe you one."

"Okay, White Eyes. See you in church."

Danny came back at six-thirty. He was sipping a Budweiser and had jammed a case of Bud among the gas cans in the back of his pickup. I had all my gear packed except for a light windbreaker and a Ruger .44 magnum pistol that hung draped over a dining-room chair in a shoulder holster. I had forgotten to repack the pistol. I had borrowed it to bring along as a bear gun but hadn't even taken it out of my duffel until I was rummaging for clean clothes after the shower. I hesitated, thinking about burrowing the gun down inside the big blue waterproof duffel so that it wouldn't get banged around in the boat; then I did the easiest thing. I slipped the shoulder holster on. And, slightly embarrassed, I put on the light brown windbreaker and zipped it up halfway.

I slung the duffel, my camera case, two rod cases, and a tackle box into the truck, then swung into the bed myself because there were two other men riding up front: Tony Peter and the gap-toothed man, who kept turning around to grin at me. Finally he slid open the truck's rear window, and I picked my way forward through the gear to lean against the cab and talk.

"It's a good day," he said. "Blew the smoke away; you notice that?"

I hadn't. The sky was blue with grazing clouds. The pall that had hung over the river for the past week was gone.

"Maybe they got the fires out," I said.

"Nah. Radio says there's still thirteen." He looked at the sky. "Good breeze is all."

Twenty minutes later we were on the water, and Danny nosed his boat toward Circle, some sixty miles up the tan and blue current. It was pushing ninety degrees. The aluminum gunwales of the boat were almost as hot to the touch as was the steel bed of the black pickup. Danny's was a bare-bones craft, one of the flat green many. Pilots of these low boats have to stand in order to see enough of the river ahead to navigate; most owners have built a steering pedestal with a windscreen near the stern, so that in rough weather or wind they'll have a vantage, a grip, and a shield. Danny's had none of the above. He sat on the rear of the boat's three bench seats, his hand on the throttle of the thirty-five-horse outboard, his feet wedged between two red gas tanks, his red Giants baseball cap turned backward to keep the wind from flipping it off. I sat in the next seat forward beside Tony. My gear sat on the floor between me and the front bench, where the gap-toothed man sat generally grinning.

The case of beer down by my feet looked good. I hadn't had a beer during the days I was with Don Peter, and he had warned me against letting Danny take alcohol. "He gets mean; he beats his wife. Mean. Don't let him take beer."

But for a five-hour run upriver on a hot evening, beer sounded like just the right thing. When we were ten minutes out of town, I was the first to reach for it, glancing back at Danny for permission. He nodded. "Me, too," he said; and from the bow the gap-toothed man said, "You bet."

Nothing smells as rich as a river in the sun. I drank beer and was lulled by the sunny richness of the river, and by the flat-bottomed boat sliding right, left, around the river bends. Then the gap-toothed man in front of me leaned forward, came up gripping a twelve-gauge shotgun, and touched off a quick blast toward two pintails that were skimming into flight ahead of the boat and toward the left shore.

The pintails, both slender, white-necked drakes, lifted off into a steep climb, apparently untouched. The gap-toothed man shot twice more as the birds wheeled and disappeared behind trees.

The shooter smiled back at me after his misses. He slipped new shells into the clip of the old gun, pumped one shell into the chamber, and laid the gun across his knees. He finished the beer that he had stuck between his legs while he was shooting and reached over toward the case of beers for another. It worried me. Now we were drinking and driving and shooting.

For a while, the gap-toothed man held his shots to an arc to the left of the boat, where the swinging barrel wouldn't pass across the rest of us. He shot at some mergansers, some scoters, some more pintails, some mallards, a great blue heron, a couple of low-skimming, whirling flocks of snipe, a beaver, and a muskrat. So far as I could tell, he hit nothing except possibly the muskrat, which Danny swung the boat back around to search for, but it was gone.

Then, as we rounded a bend, a flight of cinnamon teal came directly at us and then over us, flying low. The shooter followed the small ducks with his gun, the barrel swinging around toward the stern until it was pointed just over my head. I leaned to one side. I could see the man's eyes shift from the ducks to me. He lowered the barrel briefly across my chest as he swung it away. He lifted his cheek from the gunstock and grinned.

And a few minutes later, as we slid through a slow right turn close to the left-hand shore, he trained his barrel on a snowshoe hare that had ventured out from the thick underbrush. The rabbit froze when it saw us, and, as we made the slow turn through the bend, the barrel stayed trained on the rabbit until I was between the shooter and the hare, and the barrel was trained on me.

I leaned aside, as I had before, and, as he had before, he swung the barrel with my lean, left it there for a moment, then lifted his cheek and grinned.

"Don't do that again," I said.

He cupped a hand behind one ear and shook his head—he couldn't hear me over the motor—then swung around to face the bow.

I leaned to within inches of his left ear. "Don't do that again!"

He flinched and twisted around. It was the first time he had looked at me that he didn't smile. He said nothing, just looked, his eyes narrowing, hardening, until he swung around to face forward once again. Don Peter's nephew Tony was watching. His expression was neutral; I don't think he could hear us over the motor; I don't think he knew what was going on. I glanced to my right, at Danny, who had probably seen it all but who now was looking stoically ahead, his chin high, craning for extra elevation.

For ten or fifteen minutes, Gaptooth drank another beer and passed up shots, and I saw nothing of him but the army green back of his old fatigue jacket and his black hair whipping back from beneath his red baseball cap. I relaxed. As we rounded bend after southerly bend, I felt the sun slide from left to right, right to left, across the back of my neck.

Then Gaptooth straightened. He stood, lifting the shotgun into the crook of his left arm. I leaned to my left and sighted ahead down the gunwale but could see nothing unusual, just water and trees. I looked at Danny. His expression hadn't changed, but he had raised himself to one knee, apparently to see better ahead.

So I did the same, and saw what they were looking at, although I didn't know what it was. It was a flatness above the water, like an island, or gravel bar, but oddly animate and shimmering, like a flock of black and white sheep seen through heat waves.

Danny cut the motor to idle. "Sack lunches," he said. The gaptoothed man turned to grin at him. Tony glanced at the man with the gun, at Danny, and then at me, looking, I thought, a little worried.

"You ready?" said Danny to the gap-toothed man.

Gaptooth sat back down and began grabbing handfuls of twelvegauge shells from a grimed blue daypack and stuffing them into the pockets of his fatigue jacket. Danny opened the throttle wide. The boat surged and began to chatter over the ripples in the current.

Sack lunches. Flightless geese. I'd watched some men hunt them once, down in the Minto Flats, herding the Canada geese to land, mostly ignoring the older nesters and going for the young ones, catching them among the tall island grass of the basin lakeland, splitting the skin of goose breasts with fingers, and reaching inside to tear the breast meat free. That was all they kept. From the couple of hundred geese that would have more than filled their boat, they went away with a burlap sack full of breasts.

The shimmering low island ahead of us was a raft of molting Canada geese. They couldn't quite fly yet but had become restless and had banded together, social, gabbling, drifting downstream to the breezy big river to get away, I supposed, from the hordes of mosquitoes in the marshy, windless lakelands.

The river was a quarter of a mile wide here, and the raft of geese was half that wide and long, their thousands of bodies packed into a solid throng of black over white over gray. They looked like a crowd of touring clergymen. As we skipped toward them I could begin to hear their conversation, the undertone of fluty prattle, the occasional trumpeting honk.

The gap-toothed man raised himself to one knee, wedging himself into the angle where the seat met the hull. Ahead of him I could see the individual geese now, their craning necks and identically concerned expressions rising and falling on the swells of current, an undulant carpet of white-chinned black faces that looked to me now less like clergymen than like schoolchildren, uncomprehendingly alert, not unfriendly.

Danny's boat plowed into them at twenty-five or thirty knots, and the shotgun boomed once, twice, three times, four, five times before the gap-toothed man had to stop to reload.

I could smell the geese. They had a barnyard, downy sort of odor. Danny cut back on the throttle so that the boat drifted, idling, while the shooter nervously clicked shells into the chamber of the old pump shotgun.

The geese were scattering wildly in all directions, a few of them honking but most of them thrashing across the water in mute panic. Some scrambled onto the near shore and disappeared quickly into shoreline reeds, or into thick stands of tall grass, or even higher up on the bank into coppices of willow. Some remained in the water, diving and surfacing, trying to hide in the opaque current. Some were trying to swim upstream. Their necks were stretched out, their black toes splashed and paddling fast over the surface, flightless wings pumping, losing gray and white feathers that settled convex side down onto the water and turtleshelled around on the surface.

Danny had his eye on a drifting dead goose and kicked the throttle up a bit to get over to it. I don't know how many died. I know that when it was all over he had picked up only two. I didn't see him get the second one, because I was occupied by the gap-toothed man, who had pumped off more than a dozen shots as quickly as he could reload, then swung the barrel around past my face. I think the first pass was accidental. I saw in his look the sudden recognition of what he had done, then he turned to look for another target, and a few seconds later he chose a goose off the stern of the boat and began a swing that would pass the barrel across my chest.

I was scared. I had known it would happen, and, without really making a decision to do it, I had unzipped my windbreaker and pulled the borrowed Ruger out of the holster that hung under my left armpit. I leaned my left elbow on my left knee and used my left hand to cradle and steady my other hand. My right hand shook badly; my grip on the heavy Ruger felt numb. I leveled the revolver as best I could on the gap-toothed man's face as it swung around at the other end of his shotgun. My heart was thrumming, my ears roared, I felt dizzy and suddenly sick. But I was convinced that he would pull the trigger sooner or later if I let him keep swinging his gun across me.

Curiously, what impressed me most about the whole episode later was what I have come to remember as its moment of truth. It wasn't when I decided to do what I did, or when our eyes locked in what Barry Lopez describes as the conversation of death between predator and prey. It wasn't the showdown. Rather, it was a brief occurrence just before the show-down, when the gap-toothed man stopped the swing of his shotgun barrel, and I knew that I had been right.

I killed a golden retriever once, a favorite dog, with a similar sort of swing. I was on a high bank kneeling in tall grass, pulling ahead of a mallard that was winging low along a creek below. Concentrating on the duck, I swung the barrel, pulled the trigger, and the dog was dead. My three-year-old daughter was with me; it could have been her. I got rid of the gun, but of course it wasn't the gun's fault. You don't take a shot like that. You don't lead a target toward the unknown. You have to know what's ahead of the swing, because you're never going to see it in time to stop yourself from pulling the trigger if you've already begun the squeeze.

But the gap-toothed man did see ahead of his swing. He saw the revolver. He should have been looking down the barrel of his gun, concentrating on the goose. But he wasn't; his eye was leading his own gun, looking for me. I was the target. I didn't know much about this man, other than that he drank and smiled and had given me one sullen look, but I knew the moment that his shotgun barrel stopped that he had come looking for me with a gun. When his eye shifted to look directly at me, I knew that he hated me and would kill me if he could.

The outboard motor was idling. We were drifting. It seemed very quiet on the river. I said, "Don't swing that gun over here." My voice sounded thin and weak.

He said, "What?"

The Ruger I held was the expensive model, the stainless steel six-shooter that has a double action so you can pull the hammer back to a cocked position. I had a fleeting, ridiculous urge to do just that, but it passed quickly. Vaguely, as the urge passed, I realized that for safety's sake I was carrying the Ruger without a cartridge in the chamber under the hammer. I felt heavy. My mouth felt as dry as the inside of a stone. It was difficult to concentrate. I kept telling myself that if he really did try to shoot me, I would have to do it. I would have to shoot him first.

"What the hell are you doing?" he said.

I was tired. "Just put it away," I said.

He glanced toward Danny. Danny didn't say anything but might have given him a look or a motion; I don't know, my eyes were locked onto the eyes of the gap-toothed man. He shrugged. He worked his lips, sucking the front of his upper lip into the toothless gap. He ran his eyes over me once and swung back around to face the bow. He bent forward to slip the shotgun into the old soft case that I supposed he had taken it out of. He left the case unzipped, the butt of the walnut stock sticking out.

I looked over at Danny. He was unsmiling, watching me with flat black eyes. He had picked up a second goose; two of them lay at his feet.

"Kind of a hot day," he said. He smiled briefly, twisted the throttle, and shifted his eyes to the river.

There were two beers left. I opened them both and handed him one.

★ ★ ★

That autumn, at home, I could feel the darkness coming, and the cold; and I could feel it in my bones that I had had my last good year up here. It had been two months, almost three, since I was up on the Yukon River, and both little Virgil James and the gap-toothed man with the shotgun had stuck with me. I couldn't shake the feeling that there was something morosely symbolic about the way that particular death and our particular lives had funneled to that particular shore. At night in bed I could still smell mud and fish and beer, and that downy barnyard scent of terrified geese.

The trouble was, beyond the terrible tragedy that a child's death by preventable accident always represents, I didn't know what it was about that time on the river that represented something so very wrong, and I didn't know why it made me almost terrified to face the coming freeze. I sat at my second-story desk on University Hill, looking out at the later-rising, earlier-setting sun, feeling that its briefer slide every day across the southern horizon over the Alaska Range was an ominous countdown. I felt like I'd been interrupted midstride of a very nice life, a life that had been like a loose-jointed stroll down one of those easy, grassy slopes that make your legs feel longer than they are. I didn't know why, but for the first time since I came to Alaska, I had begun to feel that it was not home, and that it held no future, and that its eight-month winter was an alienscape that I did not want to see again.

Why, I don't know. It hadn't been that way before, not since I'd nosed my pickup into Fairbanks just ahead of that first winter almost a decade ago. I knew it would be cold, and that my truck would have to be doctored with thin oil and an engine block heater. I didn't know it would be so dark, and had no idea when I came here that, starting just 120 miles north at the Arctic Circle, the sun disappeared entirely for periods that increased with latitude until, at the North Pole, the night was precisely six months long.

In that first plunge into the brittle heart of Alaska's night, I found a frontier I hadn't expected, as obscure and mysterious as an ocean bottom. I watched its stars and the ripples of its northern lights the way I would contemplate a sea, with the marveling of ignorance, and a little fear.

For all those first years, the fear had been nothing more than the delicious kind, which does no harm but heightens your excitement as you explore away your initial want of confidence. During my second Alaskan winter, I even began to sense the beauty of the long night beyond its intimidation, through Neal Brown, a scientist who had moved north *because* of the darkness. Brown's particular passion was the solar wind, and how it blows high-speed electrons into collisions with earthly nitrogen and oxygen on the crown of the revolving earth. The resulting explosion of light—white, green, and violet—settles over the polar regions like a shimmering necklace. Aurora borealis translates literally as "dawn of the north." In Fairbanks, on an average of 240 nights a year, the midnight sky is lit by the breath of an absent sun.

Like other deserts, Brown reminded me, the arctic desert punishes endurance but rewards observation. Long suffering gets you through the winter, but what works best to make the dark more than a test of endurance is the cheerful earnestness of enthusiasts on night maneuvers. Biologists are dazzled by wakeful wolves and sleeping bears. Awed geophysicists watch the earth yield to flexing muscles of ice. At thirty below, Nunamiut Eskimo villagers above the Arctic Circle at Anaktuvuk Pass crunch into the short, dim day to tally grouse and chickadees and ravens for the Audubon Society's annual Christmas Bird Count.

For some winters I was comfortable with the long night but even then was amazed to learn one day that my interminable arctic darkness was no longer than anyone else's. I had surmised that the poles received the most darkness on earth. But I hadn't done my solar math. Just as do the poles, every place on earth receives six months of sunlight and six of darkness. Seasonally, the ends of the globe get less light, but over a year, the total of light at any point on earth equals that at any other point. Such is the night of intellect. Physically and emotionally, a night several months long looks a lot bigger than the twelve-hour equatorial one. Come summer, of course, there is no darkness in Fairbanks. In July, you are on the go until you drop. (Many's the "night" I cast a fly on twilit waters from dusk to dawn, my eyes red-rimmed with a madness at the opposite extreme from cabin fever.) But the winter light is oblique, and the winter sun is a sorcerer. Rising and setting during a lunch hour, it slips its rays to earth at tricky low angles, ricocheting through layers of high and low pressure, bending with atmospheric concavities and convexities.

The broad Tanana Valley outside my window was one of the more notorious places on earth for those phenomena that only a low tricky sun can perform. On the brief days, looking out my window I saw the stubby rainbows called sun dogs within the solar halo, and arctic mirages, and light rings, and an occasional green flash at dawn or dusk. And sometimes there were castles in the air, the fata morgana, namesakes of King Arthur's sorceress-sister, who built the fabled Avalon in the mist. My castles were the peaks of the Alaska Range. Some winters ago I glanced out my window to see distant Mt. McKinley multiplied by three: right side up, upside down, right side up.

In spite of the magic days and explosions of lights, most Alaskans I know do tend toward panic up here, particularly when we plunge into January after the hearth light of the holidays. After that flash of cheer at Christmas, you are left with a bunch of bright lights to snuff and a realization that winter's worst is yet to come. But until that shortening autumn after two weeks on the Yukon, I had found comfort along with my family and neighbors in making a job of the move from autumn to spring. When we got out our boots and our layers of polypropylene and goose down and fur to insulate against the lightless cold, the clothes, until now, had felt like professional gear, equipment for a diver's insulation against the breathless wet. In our descent, the days had come and gone like snapshots until we were left at the bottom of a sea of night. At ten of an evening after teaching a late class, you walked home acutely aware that the university's wooded trails were right at the edge of the astounding, shifting tides of deep space. The aurora rippled and shone like swept and swirling colonies of small, social, biophosphorescent things. Almost always the woods were windless; dead calm, dead quiet, the dry snow crunching, squeaking underfoot. It was so absolutely still that if there was a meteor shower, and if you stopped on a frozen pond or meadow to watch, you could hear distant sonic booms as the heavy metal thumped into the Alaska sky.

And you felt so primitive under the winter moon. It would examine you sometimes for weeks, expectant of your prayers, knowing, circling, narrowing, dilating, taking a month to blink, taking so long to leave that you found yourself dreaming gratefully, almost desperately, about those moonless summer days.

And all that had worked until now. For a while I told myself that I was just sick of the cold, of a decade's accumulation of eight-month winters, but I knew there was more. That trip down the Yukon had swept not only the year but my life to an early chill, and had sucked me toward darkness all too soon.

BOOK II

A Sea Change

6

A Loss of Innocence

Things fall apart; the center cannot hold;
. . . The blood-dimmed tide is loosed, and everywhere
The ceremony of innocence is drowned.
       —William Butler Yeats, "The Second Coming"

On Good Friday afternoon, 1989, I got a call from *Outside* magazine editor John Rasmus, who wanted me to head down to Valdez to look at the damage done by the wreck of the supertanker *Exxon Valdez*.

The 360-mile drive was the liveliest thing I'd done all winter. When the call came, I had been on ice for six months. All the untimely endings along the Yukon had sent me into winter lugubrious, and by March the cold seemed to have frozen all my resistances into resignations. But as I dodged frost heaves south, the muddied and rotting municipal snow gave way to clean drifts under a blue sky, and my higher spirit poked its nose out of a stale hole.

On the radio, reports of the spill were sketchy. It seemed to be bigger news that day down in Chicago, where Rasmus had picked it up and where they were comparing it with Alaska's Good Friday of twenty-five years ago to the day, when big chunks of Southcentral Alaska had shuddered and crumbled in an earthquake that demolished the port town of Valdez and lowered its waterfront by six feet.

Alaskans were accustomed to hearing about spills. One of the radio reports said there'd been more than a thousand in the eleven years the Alaska pipeline had been in operation. That's almost two a week. Most of them were minor leaks along the pipeline. Just a few dozen had been in the water—at the loading dock in Valdez or from the tankers themselves. Still, a few had caused some anxious hours. Just the month before there had been a pretty big one somewhere along the line, 20,000 gallons or so.

The Alyeska Pipeline Service Company had been announcing its successful cleanup of that one just hours before this one happened.

The *Outside* editor, of course, was on target. This spill was the big one. A couple of days from now I would circle the huge tanker in a tugboat and hear the story: At midnight in a flat, calm sea, the *Exxon Valdez* had missed a deepwater dogleg in the shipping lanes twenty-five miles south of Valdez and wandered into shallow water with fifty million gallons of oil in her hold and a possibly tipsy skipper in command. Or not in command, it seemed, for the later report would be that the ship was steered onto an incorrect course after the captain, with a disputed amount of booze under his belt, had gone belowdecks after turning command of his 987-foot ship over to a third mate.

At 12:40 A.M., the ship lurched. She had snagged a rock pinnacle about fifty feet below the surface. In the wheelhouse, a crew minus their captain tried frantically to correct the course but couldn't override the automatic pilot. Impaled, the ship fishtailed around the rock fulcrum, then shuddered and ground to a halt as her stern rode up onto a submerged shelf on Bligh Reef. To me she looked like an embarrassed whale, stranded there massively gray and bleeding.

Bligh Reef: In 1910, the passenger steamship *Olympia* ran aground in foul weather there, and there it perched for a decade—a landmark, a warning, and a popular deck for local tea parties on nice afternoons. Otherwise, the rocks had never before been much of a problem. A few fishing boats had smacked the shoal lightly or snagged a net while chasing salmon or herring, but their skippers knew where it was, knew the risk.

The reef juts like a bad underbite off the northern shore of Bligh Island in Alaska's Prince William Sound. It was a place of clear water, of sea birds and sea mammals. Otters lolled around it, dove down into it for crabs and shellfish. Sea lions careened among its barnacles, chasing herring or salmon, and sometimes a family pod among the sound's 115 killer whales peeled in after the sea lions. You couldn't see the reef, of course; you had to imagine the submerged jetty of its teeth slung out from the island. When I first came around that dogleg in the shipping lane as a passenger on a tugboat after the spill, the scene struck me as alarmingly peaceful. On the low slopes of the island, meadows lay greening between patches of melting snow. The tension was in the stillness, as if the *Exxon*

116

Valdez and the island were frozen in a terrible moment of interruption between winter and spring.

Captain Joseph Hazelwood wouldn't lose his ship to the reef, but then again neither did Captain William Bligh, for whom the island and its rocks were named. Captain James Cook logged the name when he anchored his leaking *Resolution* off the isle in 1778 during his quest for a northwest passage. Bligh, the same who twelve years later was set adrift by Fletcher Christian and the crew of the *Bounty,* never actually made it to Alaska but had served as navigator of the *Resolution* during its previous voyage. Both Bligh and Cook sailed on to their own tragedies, the former to mutiny, the latter to a knife in the back. Their stories were examined a few years later by the poets Samuel Taylor Coleridge and William Wordsworth, who perused the sea captains' journals and brainstormed the composition of "The Rime of the Ancient Mariner" during a hiking trip through the English countryside. At the core of all tragedy, they decided during their walk, is the one mistake that places a man beyond redemption.

Whether because of misjudgment or alcoholism, Hazelwood had made the mistake, and now the tragedy—ultimately more than 10 million gallons of it in the form of thick North Slope crude—was transfusing the arteries of Prince William Sound. When Officer Michael Fox of the Alaska Division of Fish and Wildlife Protection came grimly aboard to ask what in God's name had happened, Hazelwood's face was slack.

"I think you're looking at it," he said.

To visitors, Prince William Sound is only occasionally a friendly place. Its 3,500 miles of ragged shoreline, its ring of icy alps, its frigid seas, are as dangerous as they are lovely. Until now, we have gone there not so much because we wanted to rub elbows with beachcombing grizzlies or swim in water that could kill us in minutes but because it was one of earth's few remaining harbors of innocence. It was a bastion of clean water and misty island distances, of breaching killer whales and loafing otters, of primal memory and red-eyed loons.

The place has the look and feel of a Shangri-la. It's hard to get to, deceptively serene, secretly rich. Around its 15,000 square miles, the spruce-flanked, ice-tipped Chugach Mountains are sliced by more than a thousand streams and rivers, and about 150 glaciers. And out beyond the shoreline and in the fjords, some 200 islands sprawl among hundreds of additional islets, sea stacks, rocks, and reefs.

About 15 million salmon—kings, silvers, sockeyes, and pinks—return to Prince William Sound each year, through waters that also produce millions of tons of halibut, herring, and cod, and a bounty of rockfish, crabs, shrimp, and clams. In April, the waters along a hundred miles of shoreline here, another hundred there, turn milky white with milt released by male herring as schools of more than a million fish each swirl into the sound to spawn. At the same time, half a million migratory birds are whirling into the sound to join 3,000 resident bald eagles, plus an estimated 10,000 sea otters, 10,000 harbor seals, and seven species of whales.

Together with timber and copper, they are resources over which wars have been fought and peoples wiped out. Eight resident clans of Chugach Eskimos and their neighboring enemies the Tlingits had bickered for aeons over control of fur and fish exports to interior Athabascan tribes before Vitus Bering became, in 1741, the first sailor from a world power to anchor a ship in Prince William Sound. Bering had been sent by Peter the Great to look for new lands from which Russia might replace Siberia's diminishing fur supply in the lucrative Chinese market. But Bering was indifferent to what riches the land he'd found might hold. He had stretched his voyage of discovery to the limits of supply and endurance; and when he anchored his *St. Peter* off Kayak Island, it was only to take on water so he could beat for home.

The cantankerous and excitable ship's scientist, George Steller, threw a fit when Bering gave him a time limit of ten hours ashore. "All this to fetch some American water to Asia?" he said in disgust. "Some great undertaking: ten years for the preparations, and ten hours for the work itself!" Ashore, Steller had time only to collect some plants and direct a cossack to shoot a few birds (including a dusky blue jay he greatly admired and which now carries his name), and to try to talk the crew into collecting water from some fresh springs he had found rather than the handy stagnant pools they were using. Their refusal was to prove fatal to their captain and most of themselves.

Bering's men killed a few sea otters, but only for use as gambling stakes. It would be left to later Russians to import Aleut hunters from the north to stalk the sound's furbearers to the brink of extinction. And after the Russians and Aleuts would come the Yankee whalers to decimate the whales and spread enough smallpox among the resident Natives to reduce their population by half. And then came the gold seekers and copper miners; and then the revolution of the tin can, which precipitated the construction of dozens of salmon canneries and the great Star Fleet, in which tens of thousands of mostly Chinese workers were shipped up from Seattle each season as cannery slave labor.

In those days—the twenties through the fifties—the salmon were caught with wooden fences that angled out from shore near the mouths of spawning streams. The salmon were turned by the fences into a maze of wooden stakes and nets from which there was no escape. Rival cannery workers fought fish trap wars over the best trap sites. Trap tenders not uncommonly disappeared. Others were lured to floating brothels, where they were entertained while their fish were brailed into the holds of competing company boats.

And the men were as merciless with other competition as they were with each other. "When I was in high school, we used to get a dollar a flipper for sea lions," an old fellow was soon to tell me at dockside in Cordova. "They'd haul out right there. By the hundreds." From the end of the small boat harbor dock, he'd point to Spike Island, just outside the harbor's breakwater. "We'd sneak over at night. When we'd start in to shoot, all hell would break loose. They'd bark and yell, and then the wolves would start in up on Mt. Eyak, and over on Mt. Eccles; and in the dead of night it would wake up every single soul this side of the lake.

"I feel bad about it sometimes," he would say. "But I didn't in those days. We were small-time enough to compete with nature then. Hell, now we're too big for our own good. We're so big even *we* don't stand a chance."

To the 6,000 folk who live along the sound and like to point out that the value of an average king salmon is six times that of a barrel of oil, today's salmon fisheries are worth about $120 million a year. But Chuck Hamel, an oil industry gadfly I was to meet at the site of the spill, put the figure into different perspective by comparing it with the value of oil shipped through the sound. "Do your math," he said. "Since the pipeline opened in 'seventy-eight, the fish have been worth about a billion dollars. The profits alone of pipeline oil during that same period have been about $45 billion. That's fifty times as much, and that's *net*, no pun intended.

"The total value of pipe oil would be what? A trillion? A thousand times as much as fish? Something like that. And even that's not why we let them take these asinine risks with single-hull tankers. We let them do it because we're addicted to oil. A trillion dollars and death to the planet is the going price right now for North Slope crude because it's the biggest drug deal in town."

Within two weeks of Good Friday, black sludge would plug a length of shoreline equal to the length of the California coast. Mammals would die at a rate of about 1,000 a day; birds, 10,000 a day. We suppose, from our vantage a few years down the road, that the clogged ecosystem will recover. But its innocence is lost, a victim of our complacent greed.

In talking with some of the 600 fishermen who plied the waters of the sound out of Valdez and nearby Cordova—and with some of the shoreline's other 5,400 Native and white villagers—it seemed to me that the hardest on them all was that corruption of virginity. What you and I had visited, they had nurtured. They fought the pipeline, they fought the terminal and the supertanker traffic, and they sued, time and again, to fight the practices that had allowed dozens of lesser spills and leakages into the sound over the past eleven years.

Sixty miles south of Fairbanks I slowed at John Haines's homestead, trying to convince myself to stop by if I saw any sign that he was home.

Even after several years in Haines's neighborhood, I hadn't yet met him; I was a little afraid to. He was the best poet Alaska had produced, and in my opinion the best essayist. I'd read, hungrily, everything he had written and had found it trenchant with sense of place. Like Haines, I felt myself waking each morning filled with awe, with silence, with the land. But he was anchored in it; I wasn't. He was inextricably a part of Alaska, and I didn't know that I would ever be. He was of a mind that a place should breed and shape its artists, and I wasn't sure that this particular place should shape any modern art at all. I wanted to talk to him about my feeling that Alaska's highest value might lie in its chaos, and that art by definition violates chaos; but I had never defined that feeling well enough within myself to be able to articulate it, particularly to such an adept from the other camp.

The cable across the drive to Haines's place was up, and behind the cable, trackless snow lay two feet deep over the road. Back in among the spruce and aspen, the old poet's small buildings sat cold. I hadn't tracked him over the winter; I wondered where he was.

And driving on, awakening from the deadening winter, I wondered where everybody was. I felt good. I began to see my red truck pumping along through all that white country like a fresh shot of hot blood. In the winter I had thought helplessly out across the thousands of frozen miles (from Fairbanks I could have walked on ice all the way to France). But now I was headed for its edge. I had the scent of an ice-free sea. I stuck a cassette into the dashboard player and turned it up high to feel the throb.

The two-lane Richardson Highway between Fairbanks and Valdez winds a hundred miles across the Tanana River valley, climbs up and over the Alaska Range, dips down for another hundred-mile crossing of the Copper River basin, climbs again up and over the Chugach Mountains, and finally funnels through Keystone Canyon into the country's northern-most ice-free port at Valdez.

All the way, the pavement (or in winter the lane of ice) parallels the Alaska pipeline. The two arteries wander apart for various engineering reasons and veer back together whenever at river crossings and narrow passes. In metaphor the pipeline is most obviously a silver snake, but is more accurately like a worm, segmented and having wormlike hearts in the form of a dozen or so pump stations between Prudhoe Bay and Valdez. The pump stations circulate the oil—about 88 million gallons every day—through giant heaters and send it on hot, so that it won't jell in the pipe.

On that March Saturday, the drive south was a sunny one, with the pipe gleaming, and the road looking polished and slippery, and the high snowpack in the Alaska Range shining silvery slick with melt. In Fairbanks everything was still under ice, but as I moved south patches of open water began to show in the still-glazed marshes along the Tanana River. Twice I saw early Canada geese—a pair beside an icy pool and a wedge of six winging slowly above the river. On the Tanana itself, the ice was beginning to tear and heave. In places where shelves had overridden each other, the opaque white snow ice had ripped down to streaks of translucent river ice that glowed turquoise in the sun.

Three hours later, as I drove through the Copper River valley on the other side of the Alaska Range, I shut down the tape deck and fiddled with the radio until I heard a Glennallen announcer talking with a local pilot who'd just flown over the spill. He said he'd had to be careful; helicopters were swarming the place like bees. He said the spill looked about three miles long.

I still had no inkling of devastation. I knew the sound well enough to be able to envision what a three-mile-long oil slick would look like out among its thousands of miles of shoreline. How bad could it be? The news that followed the interview with the pilot focused on concerns that the spill was smack in the middle of the sound's annual $12 million herring fishery, which was due to kick off within a week. That was one reason I figured my lanky friend Rick Steiner would be involved. As the university's marine advisory agent in Cordova, he'd worked for years with local fishermen who had long been convinced that the oil terminal in Valdez was poisoning their fisheries. In a series of lawsuits they'd filed against various Alyeska operations, they had turned often to Rick, whom they could enlist as an unbiased expert. In the last few phone conversations I'd had with him, he'd begun to sound not quite so unbiased. He was, in fact, helping the fishermen line up some legal ducks for a new suit charging Alyeska with illegal discharge of toxins from a faulty oil sludge treatment plant.

Anyway, it would be good to see him. I hadn't seen him in almost a year, and I missed his easy disregard of convention, his sincerity, and his curiosity. I liked the open side of myself that showed to him. He was the main reason I'd accepted the magazine assignment. If anybody was going to be on top of this spill, it would be him. If I could find him. I'd tried to call him at his Cordova office, but his secretary said she didn't know where he was—probably in Valdez, but maybe at the union hall, maybe down at the docks talking to some of the fishermen. She sounded rattled.

She said the harbor around her was insane, she said it was sad, she said it was a madhouse.

In the madhouse, I wouldn't find Rick for several days. When I did, and when he finally had time to recount, he told me he'd been jolted out of bed by a seven o'clock phone call on Good Friday morning and that within minutes he'd pulled on the jeans, sweater, and sneakers he would wear without a change for the next five days. Then he was out the door at a trot for his office on the creaking Cordova dock five minutes away.

"I got to my desk and started collecting as much information as I could by telephone," he said. "I remember stretching the phone cord to a window. People were just standing around the harbor sort of dazed. I remember that right down below my window there was this otter floating on its back cracking a crab, and I remember feeling kind of envious; he didn't have a clue."

The otter cracked a crab leg, chewed, rolled to wash off the discarded shell, then cracked another. News over the phone didn't get any better. Eight hours after the spill, Alyeska (which had steadily assured both state and local agencies that it could have a spill of any magnitude contained within twelve hours) was still dragging its feet, and the Coast Guard and the state Department of Environmental Conservation (DEC) were haggling over which of them should be in charge of cracking the whip.

"But is any of it getting cleaned up?" Rick told me he asked Dennis Kelso, the DEC commissioner who'd just flown in from Juneau.

"They're still getting all the equipment situated," said Kelso.

"Can you tell me what that means exactly? Are they going to be able to contain it?"

"Rick . . . All I can tell you at this point is that we're doing everything possible to ensure the maximum effort."

As he listened, getting little information and no satisfaction, Rick watched some of the dazed fishermen collect into small knots on the afterdecks of some of the larger boats. He realized they were gathering at radios, listening to reports from some of the men who'd gone out to see. After the call to Kelso he abandoned the phone and went outside to plug into the dock talk, then headed down to the union hall three blocks away.

The offices of the Cordova District Fishermen United (CDFU) were quiet. Rick found four people, all of whom appeared in a state of shock. Executive Director of CDFU Marilyn Leland was listening to someone on the phone. The other three—Jack Lamb, David Grimes, and Jeff Guard—would eventually wind up with Rick Steiner in what the media began to call the fishermen's "mosquito fleet command post" in Valdez.

Blocky, clean-shaven Jack Lamb, a father of three, was the only married man among the four. A former salmon gillnetter who now owned and operated a sixty-six-foot tender, the *Poncho,* he had lived in Cordova for twenty-six of his forty-three years and was currently the CDFU president. He had one artificial leg. Generally he was conventional, but Rick told me he had seen him panic more than one skipper by dangling his prosthesis over the gunwale to absorb the shock of collision between his tender and vessels that came alongside.

Jeff Guard, thirty, was the quartet's angry young man. This had been his winter of discontent. Until the oil spill he'd been going at it tooth and nail with the timber industry, which he said was priming the Prince William Sound shoreline for the kind of clear-cut logging that had stripped so many Native lands and the Tongass National Forest a few hundred miles south. "And now"—he glared at Rick—"they're gonna rape both sides of the waterline."

David Grimes, a man of weathered good looks with a gazer's blue eyes, whom I would get to know well in years to come, was almost always barefoot on the deck of his boat but had slipped on sandals to come onto the icy March shore. Fresh back from the jungles of Papua New Guinea, he'd swung by Rick's office yesterday afternoon and played some music he'd written inspired by bird of paradise calls, and by boys chanting to the rhythm of dugout paddles, and by tribal girls singing as they patted sago palm flour cakes on rocks. David was a salmon and herring fisherman, a wilderness guide, a river runner, a mountaineer, a musician, and a naturalist. He was an articulate gypsy; and, above all in his own view, he was a spiritualist who saw Prince William Sound as a Gaean heart, the clear, nutrient-rich Gulf of Alaska water pulsing into the southeast side of the sound, swirling up through the tidal valves, and flushing out through the Montague and Knight Island straits on the southwest. To him, the oil spill was a clot in the heart of the earth.

"Anything new?" Rick told me he asked when he walked into the union hall. Jack Lamb stood glowering at a wall chart of Prince William Sound, Grimes and Guard beside him.

"You tell us," said Lamb.

"I hear there's nobody out there. Nobody's cleaning it up."

"That's what we hear," said David.

Jack Lamb rattled a sheaf of papers—the Alyeska Pipeline Service Company's oil spill emergency contingency plan, required by the state of Alaska. "They say they can contain any spill within fifty miles in twelve hours. This one's only half that far."

Jeff Guard gave the wall chart a hard poke at Bligh Reef, then swept his hand along a path of seaward currents, past the dozens of islands, the hundreds of bays and fjords between the reef and the Gulf of Alaska. "If no one cleans it up, man, we're done for."

For an hour they talked possibilities. In terms of both commercial fisheries and salmonid biology, this was precisely the worst time of the year for an oil spill. Hundreds of millions of herring would be schooling into the sound next week to spawn in shallow water. In addition, late March and April are when additional hundreds of millions of salmon fry outmigrate from spawning streams into saltwater estuaries, where they feed for three or four months before moving on out to sea. Rick listed the ways that oil could kill them: ingestion of oiled prey, intake of petroleum compounds through the gills, disruption of homing instincts. The fishermen listened intently. The salmon fry were their seedlings, the stock for a $120 million annual harvest.

"They're killing our home," said David Grimes.

"Our money," said Jack Lamb.

Rick Steiner nodded. "I'm going to go have a look," he said, and abruptly headed out the door and down to Gary Grimes's docked Cessna 206 floatplane.

At 10:00 A.M., forty-five miles to the northwest, the Cessna banked around Bligh Island toward Valdez Narrows, and suddenly the sea, for at least three or four miles to the north, was a black and purplish blue bruise. Just below, like bubbles coming up, five sea lions bobbed and dove, bobbed and dove, sending iridescent pink swirls through the oil.

At the apex of the spill sat the *Exxon Valdez,* listing. A tug stood just off her bow, and another tanker, the *Baton Rouge,* lay a quarter of a mile off, blowing huge white plumes of water as she deballasted her holds in order to make room for the million barrels of oil still remaining in her stricken sister. There was no oil spill containment equipment there; no barges, no skimmers, no oil-absorbent booms, no suction pumps. And— Rick searched up through the narrows toward the port of Valdez—no such equipment on the way.

By the time I settled into Valdez on Saturday, some thirty-six hours after the spill, the slick had spread to fifty square miles: seven long and seven wide. Exxon divers were saying that at least eight of the ship's fourteen tanks had been punctured, and that an estimated 1 million barrels (42 million gallons) of oil remained on the ship. Exxon had tried to start pumping the oil into the empty holds of the *Baton Rouge* but gave it up when the pumping system sprang a leak. Salvage experts, marine specialists, and media teams were racing to Valdez from all over the world. Doris Lopez, a small, fiery woman usually seen with a baby on her hip, was interviewed on commercial radio saying that Valdez fishermen had had their boats standing by ready to help since dawn. "Why isn't anybody doing anything?" she asked. On the radio, too, DEC Commissioner Dennis Kelso called the spill the realization of everyone's secret nightmare. Alyeska's response, he said, was "inadequate and unacceptable."

Back in Cordova, Rick Steiner had been up all night talking to fishermen about what they might do if things got really bad. Many of them were down at the docks right now, gearing up their boats to help fight the spill. But all night, Rick later told me, he'd had this feeling of disbelief, a refusal to accept the possibility that Alyeska and Exxon Oil wouldn't have it all mopped up by the end of the day. Now that possibility was sinking in. He stared at the wall chart of the sound, then headed out the door. From his office he grabbed his files on the Alyeska operation and a copy of the National Academy of Sciences's 600-page oil spill bible, *Oil in the Sea: Inputs, Fates and Effects,* stuffed them into a maroon daypack, then walked out to the floatplane dock.

On the seventy-mile hop to Valdez, he again flew over the spill. It was bigger, much bigger now, and expanding to the southwest. It appeared to cover about half the distance to Naked Island, twenty miles out. The island and its surrounding islets were rookeries for throngs of kittiwakes, murrelets, cormorants, and puffins. And beyond those first small isles—Rick really didn't want to think beyond those isles right now— were thousands of miles of island and fjord shoreline flanking some of the richest marine habitat in the world.

In alp-ringed Valdez, the blue and gold Cessna taxied to a dock thirty yards from the plate glass windows of the Westmark Hotel coffee shop, and Rick Steiner stepped forth into chaos. His intent was simply to locate the oil spill containment headquarters and learn the plan, so he could take some word back to the fishermen and their dependents in Cordova. But he couldn't find a plan. Exxon had rented the second floor of the Westmark, which now bustled with company personnel setting up computers, consulting charts, thumbing through manuals, and keeping people out. Downstairs, federal scientists—mainly from the National Oceanic and Atmospheric Administration and its branches—were doing pretty much the same. Rick thought about throwing in with them until he realized that they'd shown up to watch, not to do. The Alyeska Pipeline Service Company, which was supposed to be overseeing the spill containment efforts from its massive Alaska pipeline terminal on the other side of the bay, was nowhere in evidence in Valdez and wouldn't answer telephoned inquiries.

Rick walked three blocks to the state building, where the DEC had quadrupled its staff in a day. "We don't have anything to clean up oil *with!*" he was told by Director of Environmental Quality Larry Dietrich. "We're a research and regulatory agency. We slap hands and crack whips. That's all we can do."

Rick had heard enough. Cordova's 500 fishermen and Valdez's hundred would be willing to attack the oil slick with Kleenex if they had to. He telephoned Cordova. "Don't ask," he said to David Grimes. "But listen; I think you guys are all we've got. I think you better get over here."

Saturday afternoon I checked in at the state building in Valdez, which according to Rick's secretary would be the most likely spot to find him. The place had been turned into a command center. It was crawling with state troopers, city police, and private cops who were making everybody stand in a line that queued out the door and halfway around the building. I didn't know what was going on, but I stood. Some people—with laminated, clip-on credentials that had their pictures on them—just walked on in. Others were turned away flat out, and some put their names on lists and then stood off to one side to wait. The woman draped with cameras two places ahead of me announced herself as Natalie Fobes, with *National Geographic,* and said she had an appointment with Admiral Nelson. A security guard looked on a list, had her sign in, and let her through the small opening at one side of the table he had blocking the doorway.

The guard glanced at the guy ahead of me, then tapped one among several stacks of paper on the table. "This one's hot," he said. "Fresh out of the oven."

The man picked it up. I glanced over his shoulder. It was a news release announcing a press conference to be held in a couple of hours over at the civic auditorium by Gov. Steve Cowper. The other stacks were all news releases too: one stack from the Coast Guard, one from the National Marine Fisheries Service . . .

"You gotta let the other guys have a turn," the cop said to the man. "Just take one of each; read 'em later." As he was saying it, I palmed my university faculty card, which had the state seal on it, and my picture over a red background, just like the credentials clipped to the lapels and shirt pockets of the wave-throughs. "I need to get a new clippy thing," I said, squeezing through the opening.

"Yeah?" He glanced at my card. "They moved, y'know."

"Oh?"

"Yeah." He pointed over his back. "All the way down, left, then first right."

So I went all the way down, left, then first right into a small room with half a dozen men and women lined up at a counter. When I got to the front, I gave a pleasant, tired-looking woman my faculty card. "Grant Sims, University of Alaska," I said.

"And what will you be doing for us, Professor Sims?"

"Consulting," said the guy behind me. I looked over my shoulder at him. He grinned. "Isn't that what university people do?"

I turned back to the woman. "Consulting," I said.

"Oil?"

"Fish."

"Ah. For how long?"

"Uh, long as I'm needed, I suppose."

"I need to put an expiration date on your credential."

A woman operating the credential camera ten feet away said, "Just put temporary."

"Temporary," said the woman as she wrote it.

"I hope so," I said.

Five minutes later I felt brazen. My laminated clip-on credential, which I wore casually askew on my shirt pocket flap, announced me as Grant Sims, State of Alaska Department of Environmental Conservation Emergency Services Official, Temporary. I stopped the first person I saw. "Can you tell me where I might find Rick Steiner?"

By Sunday, the oil slick had spread to 100 square miles, while Exxon crews had recovered only 3,000 of the 240,000 barrels spilled. Gov. Steve Cowper had declared Prince William Sound a disaster area. A National Transportation Safety Board investigation team was on its way.

I wouldn't find Rick Steiner until Tuesday. But I was busy; there was a satisfaction in getting into secured places with my new credentials, and I had bumped into some journalists I knew, and in getting caught up in the story had forgotten my own woes. Valdez seemed a carnival at first, in the way wars are carnivals these days, with as many pointed cameras as pointed rifles, and as many correspondents as soldiers. But also as in war, there was a flavor of death on the sea air, and we were in awe of it. We watched a pile of bagged-up dead birds grow into a mound and then a mountain, and watched otters die and their keepers cry, and the constant shuttling of helicopters, and all the comings of big brass and goings of big politics, and the absurd, macabre rattlings of cameras and microphones scuttling off toward every dying breath like crabs to carrion.

The population of Valdez, normally 3,000, doubled. Teams from publications and networks major and minor arrived hourly. All hotels were full, so local residents started renting out rooms at fifty dollars a bed. I paid my fifty dollars to a friendly Filipino family and had breakfast the next morning with thirteen-year-old Gina Quaddeng, who was thoroughly pleasant about losing her room. "Twelve" was the first word she smiled to me when I sat down. She looked out the dining-room window, where a big Sikorsky Skycrane was whapping out into the sound. "That's the twelfth one in less than five minutes."

Although I hadn't yet seen him, Rick Steiner was around, and busy. He and Jack Lamb, Jeff Guard, and David Grimes had rendezvoused in the closed-for-the-winter bunkhouse of Sea Hawk Seafoods, just out of town at the east end of the bay. They'd had lots of coffee far into the night, and when Exxon scheduled its next press conference at the civic center at midmorning Sunday, they headed for it in no trifling mood.

They were even more sour when they left the conference an hour later in the company of Valdez Mayor John Devens. Exxon Shipping Company President Frank Iarossi had just admitted that the spill was beyond control, at least by mechanical mop-up. His firm, he announced, now planned to use a combination of laser-ignited fires and chemical dispersants.

"What bothers me so much is the violation of trust," said Devens. "I remember them telling us over and over when they wanted to locate the terminal here that they would be ready for any contingency."

"We don't have that problem," said Jeff Guard. "We never trusted the sons of bitches in the first place."

Rick Steiner was concerned about the use of fire and dispersants. Test burns Saturday had resulted in the one hundred residents of the Native village of Tatitlek complaining of severe nausea and headaches. And the soaplike dispersants themselves are toxic, he said, maybe as damaging to the environment as the oil. "What's more, the dispersants don't get rid of the oil, they just break it down into droplets. To the environment, it's the same dose of poison in a smaller pill, which means that smaller critters die first. For some people it's out of sight, out of mind. But the reality is that if the oil gets into shrimp, it gets into whales."

Jack Lamb stopped on the sidewalk. "I'm not going to go back and tell our people that they just have to sit back and watch the show again. It's time we do something."

The foursome, along with Sea Hawk Seafoods boss Ray Cesarini, returned to the seafood plant. They strategized among themselves and by telephone with their fellows in Cordova. Some wanted to blockade the Valdez Narrows with their boats to stop all tanker traffic to the pipeline terminal. Others, eyeing the charts and currents, were more concerned with trying to save three Prince William Sound Aquaculture Association hatcheries that were in the path of the spill. If oil coated the spawning estuaries and destroyed the natural salmon run, the hatchery stock would be all the fishermen would have left with which to reseed.

Out in the sound there was no moon. Roy Corral stood on the deck of the *Pagan*. A Fairbanks photographer, he had been sent out by the Cordova fishermen's union to document the Valdez spill. While the union members were stranded ashore politicking, he was to be their eyes. He kept a meticulous journal of his time on the dead black water, and on the slick black beaches; and when one of our breakfast conversations one morning turned into a sort of interview about what he had seen, he carefully thumbed through the journal to reference his answers. I was curious, and when I asked he let me read it. I was struck by the depth and transparency of the man's emotions behind the numbed simplicity with which he recorded a world that lay dying as he watched.

On that first night out, he wrote, he hadn't yet seen the oil, but he could smell it, feel it slide by the throbbing hull.

Skipper John Herschleb and his three-man seiner crew felt it too. When they left Valdez, the water hissed and lapped, and the wake swirled with the biophosphorescence of blooming plankton. But now they had sailed into what looked like a black hole. It neither gave nor reflected light. Corral and the crew and the boat's only other passenger, *National Geographic*'s Natalie Fobes, stood silent, as if listening for life, but the oil slid by dead against the hull. After a while, though, the sky began to lighten with a display of auroral light. It was a slow dance of green and blue-green swirls fringed with a violet that rippled in reflection over the snows of 5,000-foot peaks. To Corral, who had lived in Alaska for twenty-five years, it was the first time the auroral swirls had looked like whorled oil.

Herschleb had anchored the *Pagan* in a small cove off Disc Island.

Corral slept on deck. When he awakened, he saw the oil. It was thick and sludgy. Two red snappers rode the surface of it belly up. Corral saw no other dead wildlife. But as the *Pagan* left the cove he watched a small flock of murrelets trying to lift off ahead of the hull. They flapped and floundered; beyond them, five sea otters appeared frantic. Oil-soaked, they were having trouble staying on top. They popped up through the inches-thick mousse and swam fast and violently, rolling, trying to scrape their thick coats clean, until they sank.

On Sunday I bummed a ride on a tug out to the *Exxon Valdez*. It was big: three football fields long, a chalky, oil blue hull, brick red deck, some big yellow booms amidships, and at the stern the squat T-shape of a white wheelhouse that seemed to be a hundred feet over my head as I looked up at it from the tug. We circled, bringing into view another tower behind the wheelhouse, dark blue, with *Exxon* in ten-foot-high red letters within a white stripe. We swung seaward to skirt a small sailboat that a photographer was maneuvering so he could shoot the tanker through a water-sculpted hole in the ice. Another tug was stringing a semicircle of floating absorbent boom around a small oil slick that was drifting over toward Bligh Island. The pump system that had sprung a leak on the smaller tanker *Baton Rouge* had been fixed, and she now lay snugged up against the deepwater side of the *Exxon Valdez,* held in place by yet two more tugs as she sucked out the million barrels of oil still within the wreck's unruptured holds.

The slick itself wasn't as visible from the tug deck as from the air. Too, the oil was camouflaged today by choppy water, and by overcast skies that lent a nacreous look to even the unoiled sea. I'd planned to hitch a ride farther out among the islands to get a closer look at the shoreline damage (helicopters and boats were everywhere now; with my little badge, my walk-on passengering hadn't even raised an eyebrow), but the tug skipper said there was about to be a hell of a blow. He headed in; the wind waxed; and before we'd chugged half the twenty-five miles back to Valdez, we were pounding through troughs that turned me green.

That night I could hear the whole sound howling, and the Monday morning news was that overnight winds had whipped to seventy-three miles an hour, smearing oil thirty miles out into the sound. Planes couldn't fly to see just how far it had gone, but word crackled in via fishing vessel radios that the eastern ends of several islands had been hit hard, with oil even coating the shoreline spruce to a height of thirty or forty feet. In addition, the gale had whipped the oil and water into a froth the oilmen call mousse, which can double the volume of a slick. Exxon announced that the stranded tanker had shifted twelve degrees in the wind. Of the barrels left aboard after the spill, 120,000 had been pumped into the *Baton Rouge,* with 880,000 left.

Rick Steiner and the three fishermen, up all night, had decided to hold a press conference of their own.

"It wasn't exactly a press conference as much as it was an educational forum," David Grimes would tell me the next day. "We were tired of hearing Exxon tell these nightly bedtime stories to the nation about the harmlessness of biodegradable oil." The press had realized that the people here were angry and the fishermen out of work. From Exxon, they weren't going to hear about that—or about how oil kills plants, fish, mammals, and aesthetics.

The fishermen held their conference early, right after the press had eaten breakfast, and it worked. Immediately the Sea Hawk Seafoods phone started ringing with interview requests, and that night millions worldwide began to see news features on how oil kills.

Monday afternoon, a coincidental meeting occurred which finally catapulted the sound's fishermen from frustrated inactivity into frontline frenzy. It happened when Jack Lamb and David Grimes, upset about a report that Exxon had sprayed dispersant illegally in a herring catchment area, dropped by the state building "to raise Cain" at the Department of Environmental Conservation.

They were standing around jabbing charts and saying how they thought things should be, when the DEC's Larry Dietrich wandered in and listened for a while. Dietrich, one of the department's two top officials on the spill, had just been told by an angry Gov. Steve Cowper to sidestep Exxon, get creative and *do* something. In Lamb and Grimes, he creatively saw several hundred fishermen, with boats that could corral oil with strings of floating booms, deliver crews and absorbent cloth to shoreline cleanup sites, haul hardware, and shuttle cages of oil-tainted wildlife.

"You fellows have a minute?" he said. "We'd like to get you involved in this thing."

Five minutes later he had the two fishermen behind closed doors in a private DEC office. "Listen," he said, "we're going to try to do something. What do you think it should be?"

Jack Lamb went to the Prince William Sound chart—there was one on most walls in town these days—and pointed out the aquaculture association's three hatcheries at Port San Juan, Esther Island, and Main Bay. "We have to protect where the most salmon are," explained David. "If we save these, in a worst case scenario we could reseed the natural environment from the hatchery stock."

Dietrich listened. His boss, Dennis Kelso, listened. Rick Steiner, who was off trying to arrange for a helicopter to deliver some floating booms to the Port San Juan hatchery, happened to telephone Dietrich during the meeting and was told to "get your butt over here right now."

At midnight the trio, along with marine biologist and union board member Riki Ott, were ushered into the presence of the oil spill brass: Exxon's Iarossi, DEC's Kelso, Coast Guard Admiral Edward Nelson, Jr., and their respective lieutenants.

Kelso, of course, knew that the fishermen were coming, but the oil executive and the admiral at first "looked at us like, 'Who are these nobodies?' " David Grimes told me the next day. "Then pretty soon Jack is telling them how the water flushes in here and flushes out there, and I'm telling them how the sound is a Gaean heart, and Rick and Riki are giving them some impressive biology, and they're leaning forward in their seats to see the chart better, and they start asking us questions . . ."

In the odd late-night lucidity, the fishermen and the bureaucratic muscle realized together that there was no way possible to stop the spreading slick. "That shouldn't stop us from acting, though," said Rick. "What we have to do is focus on something else, something that is based on a probability of success. I think Jack is right. We can *defend* with success if we put all our effort into a few key defenses: here at the hatcheries, here at Herring Bay and Snug Harbor, here along the northwest shore of Montague Island, and at the mouths of a few escapement streams."

"When there's nothing you can do," said David Grimes, "you are freed from limitations. You can go for it."

When it was over, at 3:00 A.M., Dietrich pulled the Cordovans aside. "Okay, folks, you're in. The Operations Committee meets every night at eight, and between meetings you tell us what you need and somebody'll get it."

Steiner, Lamb, and Grimes were too exhausted to drive back to Sea Hawk Seafoods. Lamb found an office chair, propped his feet on a desk, and was soon snoring. Steiner and Grimes stretched out on the DEC kitchen floor.

"For half an hour it was quiet," Rick told me later. Then he heard David chuckle. Rick thought it was maybe the same sort of mild hysteria he was feeling himself, and then David said, "Rick?"

"Yeah."

"We come in like bums off the street, and they put us in charge."

"Yeah. We got to get the admiral to get us booms. Many booms."

"Yes, sir," said David. "Yessir."

"And, Frank," said Rick to the apparition of Iarossi, "helicopters. Lots of helicopters."

At breakfast the next day, I read the latest entry in Roy Corral's neat hand.

At first light the day before, he had beached the *Pagan*'s skiff on Ingot Island. The oil ashore was deep, more than a foot deep in depressions, and had been splattered by high winds up among the rocks and spruce. Ashore he'd seen no life, no death. There was only the sticky silence, broken by the chugging of a small skiff out in the bay, where *Pagan* crew members Ian Payne and Torie Baker struggled to contain a patch of sludge within the loop of an absorbent boom. Then Corral had realized that one of the oil-covered rocks he was looking at was not a rock at all. With a stick, he lifted the body of a cormorant that looked as if it had been dipped in molasses. He scanned the beach. It was covered with lumps, some obviously rocks, some now obviously not.

After a while he'd climbed up to a high, grassy point from which he watched and photographed: flock after flock of floundering seabirds, families of otters, small herds of blackened sea lions on rocks, the futile efforts of Ian and Torie against a drop of oil in a wasteland of oil. When he finally lowered the camera and walked away, it was with absolute certainty that he would be a rabid environmentalist for the rest of his life.

For four days after North America's worst-ever oil catastrophe, the fishermen had stood ready to help but were frustratingly excluded as official efforts steadily lost ground. The slick from the *Exxon Valdez* had spread to 500 square miles. Exxon, the Coast Guard, and the state of Alaska were still sniping at one another over whose fault it was that the oil hadn't been contained within hours after it leaked. Only about 5,000 barrels of the 240,000-barrel spill had been recovered; but the Department of Environmental Conservation's Larry Dietrich told the press that, "frankly, no one is really trying to recover oil now. We're beyond that. All effort is now in the defense of very sensitive areas."

On Tuesday, March 28, the fishermen got their chance; their lost war was to begin. Those "very sensitive areas" Dietrich was talking about were theirs: the three hatcheries and the few most important bays in the herring and salmon fisheries.

At 6:00 A.M., after two hours of sleep, Rick Steiner, David Grimes, Jack Lamb, and Jeff Guard carried paper cups of hot coffee into the DEC offices in the state building.

"We walk in, and they say, Here's phones," David Grimes told me when I wandered into their command post at midmorning. "Here's tables and stuff. They give us a courtroom, and we convert it into an office. Someone comes in and tosses us the keys to a van. Stan Stevens opens up his home so we can use his charter business computer."

The fishermen went to work. Jack Lamb parked his briefcase on the judge's rostrum and immediately telephoned Cordova. Until today, only fifteen fishing boats had been officially employed in the cleanup effort. Before the day was out, another eighty vessels would have headed from Cordova into the sound, without their skippers knowing whether there would be anything for them to do when they got where they were going. Their main tools would be floating containment booms, which could be linked together and stretched across bay mouths or towed in a loop between boats to drag oil. Only about a mile of the booms had been dispatched by Exxon into the sound so far, and it was all in constant use by the fifteen boats already at work. Within the next few days, however, Exxon and the Cordovans would locate more than 260,000 feet of booms—about fifty miles' worth—throughout North America, Europe, Scandinavia, and the Middle East, and, when Exxon hesitated to pay the transportation bill, the Cordovans would recruit the Coast Guard to fly the booms in.

They also located enough additional boats to swell the defense fleet to about 200 vessels, plus skimmers, tugs, and barges, "supersuckers" that vacuum 8,000 gallons per minute, generators, portable living quarters, floodlights for night work, food and clothing, and skiffs for shoreline cleanup. On their behalf, DEC officials commandeered two state-owned passenger ferries to anchor near the hatcheries as floating bases for research and cleanup efforts.

At the Cordovans' request, big Sikorsky Skycranes went whapping off across the sound with the heavy stuff, and smaller Bell helicopters made dozens of daily trips ferrying light supplies, researchers, photographers, writers, video crews, politicians, and delegates from probably every major conservation organization in the world. Semis loaded with North Slope oil gear came barreling 800 miles down the still-frozen highway from Prudhoe Bay.

In the windowless courtroom, the Cordovans lived what Rick Steiner told me he came to think of as "the absolute nightmare of trying to jury-rig a war.

"It's a war driven by equipment rather than planning," he said. "It's not like you can say, Let's draw what we need from some vast inventory; you have to say, Look what we've found, let's ship it out there and see if somebody can use it."

Exxon said it would pay the bill, and the Cordovans ran it up into the millions. The whites of their eyes were vein-laced from sleeplessness, but they stayed wired; it was a heady atmosphere.

But underneath, said David Grimes, was an "enormous grief and anger" that occasionally dragged them all into a pit. One night, for instance, Rick Steiner's girlfriend, Claudia Bain, showed up with fresh clothes. She was a therapeutic masseuse, a toucher who coaxed people into corners for back rubs when she sensed tempers close to the edge. This night, when all the hatchery reports were bad, and islands and animals were dying, she herded the group back to Sea Hawk Seafoods, insisting that they get some sleep.

Instead, they picked up a big bottle of Old Bushmills and sat on the bunkhouse floor, drinking until they cried. A hundred years ago, Alaska was all over the world, and then it was just here, and now they could feel it out there dying in the dark. They sang. They grieved, and talked of the very deep love that had caused the grief, and of whatever hope there was on the far side of it. David Grimes read poetry: a long one first, a ballad by Irishman Michael Coady that David had copied from the wall of O'Connor's Pub in Doolin, County Clare. "The tiding old sea is still taking and giving and shaping," he intoned.

The gentians and violets break in the spring from the stone.
The world and his mother go reeling and jigging forever,
In answer to something that troubles the blood and the bone.

In the wheelhouse of the *Pagan,* said Roy Corral's notebook, skipper John Herschleb sat slumped. He had heard that the fifteen or so fishing vessels trying to protect the sound's hundreds of miles of threatened shoreline had been dubbed the mosquito fleet, and that was what he felt like. He felt desperate and strong, like he should be able to do something. "But there's such a futility to it all," he told Corral.

Corral went ashore. Six waterfowl had beached themselves and were trying to preen. But when he tried to work close enough for photographs, they flushed back into the sea, into the oil. He grimaced. He wouldn't do that again.

Along the beach he found two dead loons, a scoter, a merganser. He walked over a small rise and saw ahead a frozen waterfall, an icicle-walled cliff that was irresistible to his photographer's eye. He shot it until, shifting to another vantage, he came across a deer carcass and bear tracks and bear scat. Uneasy, he retreated back over the rise and saw that he had missed by seconds the shot of a lifetime: a bald eagle, its golden talons oiled black, had just lifted off the beach, leaving behind the half-eaten body of an oil-smothered bird.

Corral went down and looked at the wet red against the wet black. He knew that no one could really feel what had happened here unless he came out into the sound, into the sensuousness of it.

He needed a break. Three helicopters had landed down the beach, and he bummed a ride with one of them back into Valdez. On the way, riding high, he saw the oil for the first time from the air. Ahead and below was a single boat, towing a length of floating containment boom. For perspective, he held his right hand at arm's length and measured between thumb and forefinger. The boat was a quarter of an inch high. Then he spread his arms as wide as they would go, but he couldn't measure the oil.

The oil slick grew to 750 square miles, then to 1,000, then to 2,500 and beyond. The clot now plugged a full third of David Grimes's heart of the earth. The fishermen's defense had saved the hatcheries they'd so worried about, and helped protect some of the bays and spawning stream estuaries. But they had no way of knowing whether the shoreline, the wildlife, or the fisheries would recover. Answers would be years and hundreds of millions of dollars in the future.

"I guess the satisfaction is in knowing that we've done what we could," Jack Lamb told me the last night spent with him and the others in the Valdez command post. "This is our home. I don't know how we could have stood it if we couldn't have fought."

David Grimes, who to that point in life had modeled his escapades, larks, and adventures after his Ozarkan hero Br'er Rabbit, found himself looking at life much differently. He had sensed the shiftings within himself from serenity to outrage to resistance to concession to hope. He looked to the future and wondered whether the ripple from Prince William Sound would jolt us, help us realize just how much killing power we have in our complacency. "For those of us here," he said, "life has taken on an utter clarity, because in the face of something like this you have to drop all the white lies of your life and know who you are."

It was two o'clock of a morning a week or so into the spill, and David was exhausted, almost unconscious. "The world may lose a last best place," he said.

Rick Steiner scratched his beard. "Frank Iarossi says he's going to polish every single rock."

"It won't be the same rock. Even if he scrapes off every drop, it won't ever be the same rock."

"Well, we'll hold him to it anyway."

"Yeah." As if sleepwalking, David walked to a cassette player that lay on the floor. He stooped, put in the tape of his New Guinea composition, and stood listening to the song of the girls patting flour cakes onto rocks, and the chant of the boys to the rhythm of their dugout paddles, and the fluting call of a bird of paradise.

"Life is music," he said. "We have to sing the song we are."

Then he crawled under the magistrate's table, stretched out full length, and fell asleep.

7

Grave Waters

War's a game, which, were their subjects wise, kings would not play at.
— William Cowper, "The Winter Morning Walk"

"Maybe it was his way of doing you a favor, of trying to polish every rock," I said.

Rick Steiner's laugh was short. "If I had two favors like that, they'd kill me."

We were talking about Exxon President Frank Iarossi, fifteen months after the spill. Rick had offered me an early-morning cup of instant coffee in his hut of an office on a dock overlooking the Cordova harbor. The June weather was clear, the water calm, and every two or three minutes another of the bow pickers—so called because they are built to winch their nets up over their bows—would clear the breakwater, turn left, and gun out toward the fishing grounds on the Copper River Flats, forty miles southwest.

Rick had aged. He might be right about Iarossi's favor, I thought. His ruddy skin looked as if it had been used hard and rehung carelessly. And I realized, as I watched him tell me of the long fight, just how addictive, and how ravaging, this grappling for power must be.

Six months before, while in Washington, D.C., to lobby for a quick settlement of civil action against the Exxon Corporation stemming from the oil spill ("So we could start putting some money into habitat restoration"), he'd met with Iarossi across from the White House in the Hay Hotel coffee shop. The meeting had been at Iarossi's request, and the executive had gotten right to the point.

"There's something I must tell you," he'd said. "We are very close to a settlement with the Justice Department regarding the criminal plea."

141

He was talking, Rick knew, about the criminal charges stemming from the spill. But a settlement? A plea bargain? No one Rick knew had gotten wind of anything like that.

"Even after all those months of walking up Surprise Valley, I was more than mildly surprised," Rick told me. "This guy was letting one hell of a big cat out of the bag. Why would he do that? The plea bargain had to be about the fine, something maybe in the neighborhood of a billion dollars; and if they were having secret negotiations, it must be to save money. Tens of millions, maybe? Hundreds? Why would Frank Iarossi tell me something that would cost his company that much?

"So I asked, 'Why are you telling me? Is there something I can do? Some way I can help?' And the guy nodded his head! Just a little nod, one nod. And I thought, 'Holy Moses! What would he need help with?' And you're right: It was for polishing those rocks. He owed us one, but something in his corporate circumstance wouldn't let him pay. Not directly, anyway."

"How close are you to a settlement?" Rick asked.

Iarossi said nothing.

"Within a week?"

The Exxon president nodded.

A week. "How much is it for?"

"I can't tell you."

"A billion? I heard maybe eight hundred million on the criminal charges. Is that close?"

Iarossi shifted uncomfortably. "No, less than that," he said.

"So I figured it was probably half a billion anyway," Rick told me. "A lot less than everyone other than the feds thought it should be. And the plea bargain, I was sure, meant that the feds would back out of the several billion dollars' worth of civil suits that had been filed.

"I got in touch with the Alaska attorney general, Doug Baily, and he didn't know anything about the secret meetings, and he got in touch with the governor, who didn't know anything about it, and the governor got in touch with the general counsel for the National Oceanic and Atmospheric Administration, which had been appointed damage assessment trustee, and he didn't know anything about it.

"Nobody knew anything. So I called the Justice Department and talked to a bunch of incredibly nervous people. Finally they got their chief criminal people around a table and put me on a conference phone and told me they couldn't confirm or deny what I'd been told. But one of them said, 'How did you get this information?'

"I said, 'Frank told me.' And he said, 'He can't have; that's privileged information.'

"And I said, 'Well, I consider myself privileged to have received it.'

"And that was pretty much the end of the conversation; they weren't going to shed any light. So I went to see Chuck Hamel, who's a lobbyist sort of person I'd been working with on Alyeska pollution issues before the spill, and is big oil's worst enemy in Washington.

"And he said, 'Well, there's a pretty easy way to put a bee in its bonnet,' and he called someone he knew at *The Wall Street Journal,* and the whole thing between Exxon and the Justice people fell apart within a week."

Rick stood with his back to me, watching boats leave the harbor. "It cost Iarossi his job, I think," he said. "Within a month he was gone, and the couple of pipelines I have into the Exxon hierarchy say he was fired."

"So do they have a bread line for people like that?"

"Oh, he's okay—out of this mess and doing just what he wants. He's head of the American Bureau of Shipping—the global shipping standards institute."

I thought of the boat Rick had bought just before the spill, *The Buddy.* I hadn't even seen it yet, hadn't seen Rick, in fact, since that week we'd spent in a Valdez courtroom over a year ago. "So how about you? You been able to fish your boat yet?"

"No, this thing has a good solid hold on me. Still and for a while."

Cordova had been my favorite coastal town in Alaska since Rick introduced me to it in 1983. "It's a Shangri-la," he said; "you have to come." We'd taken a canoe down the Eyak River just a couple of miles out of town and caught half a dozen silver salmon fresh up the river on a high tide. It was one of those days filled with lazy water and warmth, and the metronomic clunking of paddle against canoe. You knew there was no one else on the river, and you could stand and cast and look across the delta to a long horizon of serrated, snowcapped, unpeopled peaks in the Chugach Mountains. There were no other human footprints in the Eyak sand, but whenever we beached the canoe to fish from shore, we walked beside fresh grizzly tracks twice as wide as our own.

I went back whenever I could, and Rick helped my brother Russ get a summer job at a fish cannery there when Russ was in college, and some friends of mine and my wife's opened a rustic lodge at Whitshed Point ten miles out of town by boat, so we started going there, occasionally, too, and gradually our portfolio of Cordova memories grew rich and among our favorite. Few of our subsequent days there were as sunny as that first one I spent with Rick on the Eyak—the place gets more than a hundred inches of rain a year—but Joan and I came from the dry interior and welcomed the coastal drizzle as refreshing. Cordova was quiet, quaint, and removed. No roads led in. The only ways to get to Cordova were by boat—for us it was a six-hour ferry ride from Valdez—or by plane into the Merle K. (Mudhole) Smith Airport. Downtown Cordova was all fish port; it didn't cater to tourists and attracted few.

This time, Rick had asked me to come write a proposal for a marine science center the community planned as a research base for the several thousand miles of Alaska roadless coastline that stretched southward along the Gulf of Alaska, and northerly around Prince William Sound.

I was finding Cordova changed. The hysterics of the summer before were gone, but cleanup crews had been deployed by the thousands again into Prince William Sound after a six-month winter hiatus, and the big fights nowadays were over who was going to pay, and who was going to get paid. Actual cleanup costs had run into the hundreds of millions, and predicted habitat restoration costs into the billions. By the tens of thousands, fishermen, Native tribespeople, private salmon hatchery owners, tourism concessioners, public agencies, and research scientists were all clamoring for what they hoped would be a windfall of atonement money from Exxon. (Regardless of what the penalty to Exxon would be, the American public had already paid for it—and, because of the illusion of shortfall, Exxon's profits were on track for an all-time high.)

In the meantime, Exxon *was* shelling out money for the cleanup effort—half of Cordova's 2,600 people were getting a lot of oil money by contracting their boats and bodies to the cleanup effort (at $100 per foot per day, a thirty-foot fishing boat could net its skipper $90,000 a month), and the other half wouldn't touch the money. The town and its harbor were choleric with tension and to me appeared proud and sad in a circumstance that was pitting the locals against the corporate slicks.

Cordova was factionalized by other new controversies as well. Business had been brisk with all the comings and goings of media crews and bureaucrats during the spill. Some Cordova business owners liked the new economics very much and were now pressuring to open a tourism access road into town along eighty-two miles of abandoned railroad between Cordova and the nearest accessible road's end at Chitina.

And finally, the untouched old-growth forests of Sitka spruce lining the shorelines and slopes of Prince William Sound were beginning to fall to the saw. Clear-cutting was planned for several hundred thousand acres, mostly on land granted to Native corporations during the Alaska Native Claims Settlement Act of 1971.

"What we have here is the metamorphosis of a tragedy," Rick said. "It's not even an actual event anymore. It's a political event, a business event. And I'm beginning to believe, I really am, Grant, that the main purpose of the exercise is simply to create the illusion of accomplishment."

He turned from the window to look at me. His eyes were smiling the old way again, although through red veins, and over small pouches. "You can't break down," he said, "you have to break through."

Before the spill he thought he *had* broken through.

"I remember sitting in this same chair just hanging out," he said. Again, as with almost everyone I talked with about their lives these days, the day before the wreck of the *Exxon Valdez* was an important point of reference, a point of interruption, that was definitive of life before the spill.

"I was waiting for a call," he said. "I remember it was too nice a day to've let myself get stuck inside. I felt like a cat." He looked at me again. "Restless, but content. It was a good spring day."

About midmorning, he said, he'd felt a small thump, a gentle sway. It was either a very small boat or a pilot with a very light touch. Most of the boats came in with a jolt that sent a tremor through the dock and set the floor beneath his feet to creaking. He rose from his desk, walked to a window.

Out in the small boat harbor the water still lay slack on the high tide, and at the waterline just below Rick's office was the aluminum skiff that had just bumped in. Aboard were Pete and Belle Mickelson, just in from their lodge out at Whitshed Point, ten miles west. It was a sunny day, but the Mickelsons had come in on a stiff breeze and were wearing slickers against the spray. Rick watched Belle step from the skiff and whip its bowline around a cleat. She lifted out her stout little five-year-old, Mikey, and peeled off his slicker. Pete cut the motor. He looked up toward Rick's office, spotted him in the window, and waved. Rick waved back, then stepped away from the window to give the family back their privacy. He'd be meeting with Pete later on to talk about the new marine science center.

Rick had moved to another window, one that looked inward on the harbor, which was jammed with work craft and bustling with fishermen gearing up for the herring, the halibut, and the salmon seasons. In the lee of the dock just below his office an otter floated on its back, cracking the legs of a Dungeness crab. It was a big male, a campground-bear sort of animal that had staked its territory here in the harbor. Almost every time Rick stepped to the window it was loafing down there somewhere with a crab or a clam, those bright black eyes glancing up at him unconcerned out of a face comic with stubble.

The otter rolled lazily to wash the debris off its chest. Rick looked beyond the animal into the hurry of one of the prettiest ports on earth. Out among the boats some ducks had come in, the first of the season. They were old-squaws, the handsomest of sea ducks, which had probably been overwintering just a few hundred miles down the coast. Rick watched long enough to see whether they were diving for the herring that had begun to flash about the harbor, harbingers of the $150 million fishery that would kick off within a few weeks. But the ducks just paddled about, gabbling their constant *owly, owly, owly . . . ah, ah, ah,* the mating chant that had inspired their name.

He watched the boats. There was a lot of white paint and rust out there. White paint, rust, and black wool watch caps. Most of the 350 or so vessels had gaping holes on deck amidships where hatch covers had been pulled off and fishermen were climbing in and out, making repairs, stowing gear. Greasy men came blinking like moles out of engine rooms. Other men and some women were scraping paint off, brushing paint on. Some of them had herring nets strung out along the docks so they could knot in some last-minute mends. Other nets were being wrapped onto big drums aboard the vessels, and the decks that weren't rigged for nets were being outfitted with skeins of longlines and hooks for halibut.

Most of the galley stoves had been cranked up. A thin pall of smoke hung over the harbor from the smokestacks, and Rick imagined that he could smell the coffee from three hundred–something pots.

But over in slip 62, he noticed, the forty-eight-foot seiner *Prince William* still had two feet of snow on her decks. David Grimes was back in town, though; he and Steve Smith should be showing up soon to shovel her off.

It had been no day to be inside. The Cordova winter had been month after month of cloud cover, wind, and snow, people getting tight as strung fiddles. And now two days after equinox you had this sudden clarity, the seascape crisp all the way out to Hinchinbrook Island, the sun baking all the sailors' black watch caps hot, and at night the stars out and the aurora rippling up above the snow on the Chugach peaks.

It was a palpable awakening of the harbor, and it had his heart beating faster. He would like to be out there. He had been in Prince William Sound long enough to know that you didn't desk-bind yourself on a sailor's perfect day; you canceled meetings and didn't take calls. Today he was making a willing, if anxious, exception. He had spent much of the past winter trying to put together a partnership of his own—a third of a million-dollar investment in a forty-eight-foot seiner called *The Buddy*— and was standing by for the promised banker's call that was to seal the deal.

He'd wandered back to his old gray metal desk and sprawled his long frame into the old chair. That's okay, he told himself; there'll be plenty of these days. It was just hard to wait when everyone else was out there in the starting blocks. This partnership would be the first of anything like it he'd ever done. He was anxious about its prospects, and anxious, too, to get on about the business of being part of this community rather than simply an adviser to it. He'd been here what, now—six years? Six years on the outside, so subtly osmosing through the membrane of community that he hadn't realized he was on the inside until a couple of months ago, when it suddenly seemed that the logical thing to do was buy a home. So he bought one, out on the road to the lake and facing the big green Henry Range, with snowpeaked Mt. Eccles right outside the door. He settled in; and last week when Ed Abbey died he tacked one of the grand old steward's quotes to the wall: "Like all desert tortoises, he knows his house, loves it, stays there, guards it."

Now, telling me about it, Rick sighed. He did like it here. He loved it here. He loved a woman here. When he first came, it had seemed to him that he had stumbled upon a Shangri-la—perpetually green, hauntingly misted, isolated from the rest of the world by brilliant white peaks and an enormously rich and sheltered sea. The past half dozen years had done nothing to change his perception. It was still a breathtaking small shelf, and there was sublimity here, and a satisfying mingling of friends.

So Rick Steiner had become a Cordovan. He made his rounds of coffee stops in shops and galleys along the waterfront, and he palavered with all the boatmen about salmon prices. He got together with neighbors to pluck music and sing. He put on puppet shows for the little kids down at the school. Just a week before the spill, the program had been a St. Patrick's Day thing he cowrote, featuring a leprechaun and some Bryan Bowers music.

> Money can't buy back your youth when you're old,
> or a friend when you're lonesome, or a heart that's grown cold.
> And one thing's for certain: It's so hard to find
> one man in a million with a satisfied mind.

Youth, friends, warm hearts, a satisfied mind. Know it, love it, stay here, guard it. Guard it. Even before the spill he'd had this growing sense of threats hanging poised over paradise. There'd been talk of a new road slicing in along the Copper River. Talk, out at Two Moon Bay, of cutting Prince William Sound's first commercial timber ever. Talk of pollution spreading from just around the corner at the Alyeska oil pipeline terminal. Talk of fishermen shooting whales and sea lions, and of Taiwanese and

Japanese fleets illegally intercepting Prince William Sound salmon out at sea. Talk about the ocean becoming so junky with debris that out at Hinchinbrook Entrance, where the current funneled into the sound from the Gulf of Alaska, beachcombing locals were calling Hinchinbrook Island's trash-stacked shoreline the Hinchinbrook Mall. It was out there, all right, the rest of the world.

But those hadn't been worries for that day. "That day I felt anchored," he told me. "I liked feeling settled, liked the great buoyancy of riding high with the rest of the town on the crest of a big salmon price boom. I could feel it out there, everybody pumped up, investing their psyches into the prospect of another good year."

"You need to get out of here," I said. "Take the cure."

"I thought my boat would be the cure," he said. "But the boat has turned into a $330,000 hole, and no pay dirt for fill."

He was at the window again. We'd had our day of meetings, hammering out a draft of a proposal to various agencies and endowments in hopes of funding the proposed science center. David Grimes had come up from his boat to use the phone before we all walked uptown for dinner, and Rick had turned off the office lights so others wouldn't stop by. "Actually, I have gotten out of here," he said. "Twice."

Just a few months after the spill he and David Grimes had gone to Sullum Voe in the Shetland Islands to see how the Brits did their disaster contingency planning at what was supposed to be the world's most state-of-the-art oil terminal. And in the fall of 1989—while national interest in the Alaska disaster was still hot—they'd done a whirlwind speaking tour of all the coastal states in the United States except Texas, warning audiences of the dangers of oil transport and drilling activities.

In Scotland, they'd been met by Jonathan Wills, editor of the *Shetland Times* in Bressay and author of *A Place in the Sun,* a then in-progress book which would label Sullum Voe's £1.3 billion Shetland Oil Terminal a disaster waiting to happen.

"Jonathan had been struck by how much coastal Alaska was like the Shetlands when he visited Cordova during the spill," Rick said. "And in Scotland we were reciprocally struck by the openness of the country, the wild tundra, the scattered villages, and the way the people are all in partnership with the sea, and the frontier nature of the place, and the intense coastal weather, and the high-risk fisheries with the potential for high reward. . . .

"There were big differences, of course: the buildings all of old gray stone, and the old Scottish seiners in the harbors, and the thick brogues and Scottish beers, and everybody with their peat bogs and stacks of peat blocks, and that odor of peat that gives such a great smell to the houses. And nasty, nasty wind, two-hundred-knot gusts. 'Our bloody hurricanes,' Jonathan called them. . . .

"But there was a kindredness of spirit. We met with the Shetland Fishermen's Association, and they were all intensely interested in the spill, and anxious to compare notes on how accommodating or unaccommodating our respective governments and tycoons had been. We were struck by their great love for the place, and how they'd long feared, as we had, the Big One.

"And even the Brits out at the terminal itself were very gracious and interested. And awfully formal chaps; they kept giving us ties. They'd flown us by helicopter out over some scenic cape lighthouse country with names like Muckle Flugga and Sooth Moothers, and then over the terminal with all its tanks and pipes and stacks, and flames burning off the excess gas; and they explained how they handled their oil better than we did, how they cooled off the crude so it wouldn't be volatile, and they told us all about their preparedness, and pointed out their spill containment equipment, and their high-tech tractor tugs, and their sophisticated tracking techniques, and told how all the mariners who operate the port have to be trained and licensed, and how helicopters fly over vigilantly to make sure the tankers don't deballast oily water. . . .

"We were, after we saw it, resentful. Yes, they did handle their oil more consciably than it was handled at the terminal in Valdez. And why? Because British Petroleum, the company that was the majority player in both their terminal and ours, had applied a double standard. Our colonial terminal was out of sight, out of mind, and had gotten second-rate treatment while the home water was coddled.

"But we couldn't tell the oil people, or more important the fisher-

men, what they wanted to hear. We couldn't tell them that they had
prepared well and were safe. We had to tell them that from what we had
seen, in spite of all their toys, they were victims of fallacious thinking on
two critical fronts—One: 'Don't worry, it can't happen here'; and Two:
'If it does, we can take care of it.' "

Rick chuckled. "On the seat right next to us on the plane out of
Aberdeen—just coincidentally, mind you—was the very persuasive head
of public relations at Sullum Voe, who tried very hard to convince us
otherwise."

He sighed. "The idea of pollution control is so sifted by the corporate mind that it evolves into the idea of image control. The illusion of
trustworthiness that placates us while we die."

David Grimes was finished with the phone and now stood in the
doorway between Rick's and the front office, listening. "I particularly
enjoyed the swimming," he said.

Rick grinned. In August, he said, the two of them were in the midst
of their media blitz tour of coastal states when they were invited to speak
aboard a yacht regarding pending offshore oil leases in North Carolina
waters.

"But we lost our invitation. The yacht was in a secured area of the
port in Morehead City, and the guard at the gate turned us away. You
know how we always look, me with a beard, him with long hair, both of
us in sandals; we couldn't convince him that we were the keynote
speakers.

"So we drove around, parked, and swam in. The cops saw us in the
water and were on a vector course for us when we climbed out, but we
made it to the gangplank and went aboard.

"Soaking wet, and all the socialites agog. And David says, 'Sorry
we're late, folks; it's a long swim from Alaska.' "

Rick was soon back in the thick of it. After he broke the news of the
secret plea bargaining between Exxon and the Justice Department, the

governor of Alaska, Steve Cowper, had come to Cordova to meet with him. *"You* live here," he told Rick; *"you* figure out how much it's going to take, and that's what we'll go after from Exxon."

"Do I have a ceiling?" Rick had asked.

"No, but I want you to have a consensus. If it's three billion, then it's three billion. But I want everybody who lives around the shores of the sound to be agreed on how it's to be spent. That's everybody: fishermen, Native communities, tourism concessioners, everybody."

Rick had come up with a plan quickly enough—already had it spelled out in detail that day I spent with him in his office, just a few weeks after the governor had passed him the buck. It was the habitat that had been damaged, he told me; the logical action would be to spend the money on habitat restoration. "After the spill, we realized that there wasn't much that all us king's men could do to put the sound back together again," he said. "You can't *fix* a dead murrelet colony. But you can help *compensate* by acquiring and protecting some undamaged but clearly threatened shoreline."

The Prince William Sound Oil Spill Restoration Fund was formally established in federal court late in 1991, some months after my last, brief stay in Cordova—months during which Rick had reared his brainchild through a successful grassroots campaign. I worried about him the way you worry about people who are doing too much good work for their own good and tracked his progress by phone, by friend, and occasionally in person.

One day in Anchorage—another year had passed—we met and settled into a window booth at Simon and Seaforts restaurant; it was the first beer booth we'd shared in years.

"I hear you've got a whale by the tail," I said.

"It feels like one."

After Exxon's half-billion-dollar secret negotiations collapsed, his fledgling coalition had pressed for a $2 billion fine of the oil company but agreed to $1 billion as a faster way to settle litigation that otherwise almost certainly would have tangled on for years.

But to get the consensus the governor had asked for—from Native groups, timber companies, fishermen, tourism concessioners, public agencies, and all the other factions milling around Prince William Sound in the wake of the spill—was to take him another year. It was a year in which I tracked him by phone.

The lengthiest and trickiest of his maneuverings targeted the lands his coalition most wanted to see saved: some half a million acres of shoreline threatened by clear-cut logging operations that had already been launched by several Alaska Native corporations. The new logging—along the northernmost range of old-growth Sitka spruce—was the first large-scale coastal timber harvest north of the notoriously administered Tongass rain forest. By the end of the decade, the clear-cuts could wipe out a quarter of a million acres of old-growth timber along the Prince William Sound waterfront alone, not including tens of thousands of additional acres southwest of the sound: out along the Kenai Peninsula, Kachemak Bay, the Kodiak Archipelago, and the Alaska Peninsula.

"It's *where* the logging is planned that particularly bothers us," I'd been told by Pam Brodie, an Alaska representative of the Sierra Club, which had been the only national environmental organization to remain seriously involved in watchdogging Prince William Sound once the oil spill media hype was turned off. "Most of it will be on Native inholdings *inside* national and state parks and refuges—and not only inside them, but in the most choice areas inside them."

The inholdings were among the 44 million acres granted to Alaska Natives as part of the Alaska Native Claims Settlement Act of 1971. Native groups were allowed to pick the lands they wanted, and although the idea the Natives put forward in justifying their settlement claims was to select "cultural" territories used in traditional hunting and gathering activities, most of the lands in timber country were selected on the basis of their lumber value. Because the selections were made before the 1980 Alaska National Interest Lands Conservation Act that set aside 106 million acres in new conservation units, many of the state's parks and refuges had to wrap around the choice lands the Natives had already claimed. "In places like Kenai Fjords National Park, all the park really includes is the rock and ice," said Brodie. "The 77,000 acres the Natives selected there include almost the entire coastline."

The citizens' alliance insisting that the restitution money be used for land acquisitions had already bargained with Native corporations whose

ownerships accounted for about 904,000 acres of shoreline. Those included 262,000 acres of national forest inholdings within Prince William
Sound itself, plus 77,000 acres in Kenai Fjords, 312,000 in the Kodiak
National Wildlife Refuge, 200,000 acres on Afognak Island, 23,000 acres
in Kachemak Bay State Park, and 30,000 acres in a Gulf of Alaska area
called Suckling Hills, which would be added to the Yakutat State Game
Refuge. The negotiated price averaged about $1,000 an acre, putting the
entire 904,000 acres of inholdings within the capabilities of the $1 billion
fund.

Native corporations initially were so incensed by Rick Steiner's idea
of buying their inholdings—which they saw as meddling with their plans
to have the land logged—that they tried through the Alaska Federation of
Natives to get Steiner fired from his post as a consulting biologist for the
University of Alaska. But since the spill the logging contracts they'd once
seen as so potentially lucrative had actually driven some of them to the
brink of bankruptcy, and none were doing very well. Faced with the
prospect of owning clear-cut land with nothing to show for it, the Natives
now strongly supported the sale of their inholdings, which would result
in their still having a million acres of old-growth timber in the neighborhood and a billion dollars in the bank.

The money that would buy their land was in two kitties. One was
a $100 million criminal penalty, with $50 million each going to the Alaska
and federal governments. State legislation had been passed, and federal
legislation introduced, requiring that that money be spent on wildland
acquisition. The second, $900 million civil settlement, was to be paid into
the restoration fund over ten years. It was the latter, larger fund that was
overseen by court-appointed trustees including Secretary of the Interior
Manny Lujan, Secretary of Agriculture Edward Madigan, National Oceanic and Atmospheric Administration chief John Knauss, Alaska Attorney
General Charlie Cole, Alaska Fish and Game Commissioner Carl Rosier,
and Commissioner of the Alaska Department of Environmental Conservation John Sandor.

"Now that the bureaucrats have got hold of it," Rick told me in his
office, "they're being even less cooperative about oil spill restitution than
was the culprit."

Rick's plan to buy endangered wildlands with the money had the clear support of communities affected by the spill. But the six federal and state trustees quickly found themselves bogged in what they themselves labeled "a quagmire" of 460 proposals on other ways to spend the money. In addition, the Bush administration lobbied adamantly against using it to buy the wildlands. And in the year it had taken Rick to solidify a consensus plan, Alaskan voters had replaced Steve Cowper with a new governor, conservative independent Walter Hickel, who proposed that the fund be transformed into an endowment.

"It was a simple bait and switch," said Rick. "We were asking for $2 billion, not $1 billion, but Wally Hickel talked everyone into settling for the lesser amount to save time. He told us, 'We need the money now so we can get on with the restoration.' So as soon as he gets it, he puts the first $55 million in the state's pocket, and then has the nerve to propose that the rest of it go into an endowment fund rather than the habitat acquisitions that everyone had approved."

Once the money was placed into an endowment, the "restitution" would be financed by the fund's interest. "But they're not going to go out and buy habitat with interest money," said Rick. "If you're going to buy habitat, you buy it now when the price is lowest. No, what they want to do with the interest money is finance research"—research that would be conducted, of course, by the six agencies represented by the fund's six trustees.

And the squandering, said Rick, had already begun. Of the first $90 million payment made in 1992, the state of Alaska immediately paid itself $55 million for expenses incurred during the spill and locked up another $19 million to finance its own postspill research.

"They sure got that $74 million out of the quagmire fast enough, didn't they?" said Rick.

"If there's a quagmire, it's of their own making. That money was to be used to buy wilderness lands, purely and simply. The whole idea was to preserve resources, not bureaucracies. But now we're facing a scheme that would see almost $300 million going to reimburse the state, the feds, and Exxon itself—*Exxon itself!*—for oil spill cleanup expenses; another $300 million winding up in the six agencies' coffers as 'administrative overhead,' and most of the rest financing yet another couple of decades of research proving that oil and water don't mix."

★ ★ ★

In the booth at Simon and Seaforts, Rick interrupted his rambling to take a sip. "You been following this stuff?"

I had. Just days before, Dave Gibbons, who worked for the trustees as administrative director of the Oil Spill Restoration Team in Anchorage, had told me that the team was just proceeding carefully to develop a restoration plan and to make certain that the money went to restore habitat and other "resource services" such as fisheries and recreational facilities lost or damaged as a result of the spill.

Gibbons also said the team opposed pending legislation that would mandate that the money be used to buy wilderness. "We oppose it because under the settlement agreement the trustees were given the authority to decide how the money would be spent, and because a legislated mandate would take public involvement out of the restoration planning process."

"Yeah?" Rick said. "Did he happen to mention the $74 million they've already paid themselves? Was the public involved in that process?

"Besides," he said, "the purchase of wilderness lands with the money has been supported by the public ad nauseam. It was a plan that was *born* of public involvement, and of public concern that the money would be bureaucratically wasted if it wasn't spent quickly and on something substantial."

I told Rick about a conversation I'd had shortly after talking with Gibbons. "A friend of yours, I think. Jeff Petrich."

Petrich, a lawyer attached as counsel to the congressional House Interior Committee, had updated me on goings-on at the federal level, where Interior Committee Chairman George Miller, a California Democrat, had authored two amendments to the National Energy Bill that would force the fund's trustees to make acquisition of wilderness lands the fund's "primary purpose."

The three federal agencies involved as fund trustees plus the Department of Justice had all filed official protests to Miller's amendments, saying as did the state's Dave Gibbons that legislative mandating of how the money was to be spent would not follow the protocol giving the spending power to trustees as established by the court, would preclude public participation in the restoration process, and would prevent completion of a full damage assessment.

"It's ironic and hypocritical," Petrich had said. "Here you have Bush on his way to the Earth Summit in Rio saying that he wants to spend $150 million of taxpayers' money to help save the Amazonian rain forest. And at precisely the same time he's adamantly opposed to spending a billion dollars of private money—at absolutely no expense to taxpayers—to save a million acres of American rain forest.

"What those guys are doing," said Petrich of the fund trustees, "is trying to cache the money in a Bureaucratic Perpetual Employment Fund—their own pockets.

"Of course they oppose land acquisition. In demanding that the money be used the way it was intended, we're taking away their spending discretion. We're playing with their toys."

"Another?" said Rick.

"Maybe several anothers," I said.

"Like old times."

He still looked tired. More tired. I thought of the years and easy wildness of our early friendship. "Not much like old times," I said. "We've changed."

He nodded, sighed, and gazed through the window, out across the fast tide sweeping seaward down Knik Arm. "Well, we didn't used to fish for whales," he said.

8

Polarized in the Arctic

This concept that the Arctic needs to be preserved as a wilderness for visitors is a crock. This is a flat, crummy place. Only for oil would anybody want to go up there.
    —Harold Heinze, former president of ARCO, Inc., presently, Commissioner of the Alaska State Department of Natural Resources; *Anchorage Daily News*, October 12, 1986

On July 2, 1989, two days before Stu Pechek and I took the walk along the Beaufort Sea that began this story, he and photographer Mark Kelley and I caught a 400-mile flight north in a twin-engine twelve-seater from Fairbanks to Alaska's northernmost shore. We had crossed the spine of the Brooks Range and begun a long descent when I first saw what I'd been sent to write about: the thin strip of the arctic coastal plain where oil developers wanted to drill, and where preservationists were figuratively digging in for what they predicted would—in the wake of the wreck of the *Exxon Valdez* at the other end of the Alaska pipeline a few months before—be the biggest environmental battle of the century. It was springtime down there: a hazy, flat land struggling toward green between shriveling patches of snow.

Dead ahead twenty miles north, two giant radar grids stuck up like tombstones from one end of a small island in the Beaufort Sea. The pilot sighted on these and dropped his flaps a notch. The grids were leftovers from the old DEW Line, a chain of Distant Early Warning system outposts in Alaska and Canada. Most of the dead receptors had been ripped out, said the pilot, but the younger whalers and caribou hunters among the locals had asked that these be left. Reared on the easy visual fix, they never learned to navigate by star.

"I get scared when I can't see 'em," said a boy in the seat behind me of the grids. "My snow machine don't have a nose for home."

The boy's name was Dahrone. He was unusually outspoken for a rural villager, and at eleven or twelve was impressively spontaneous with one-liners. In Fairbanks, as we waited with four other passengers for the plane, I'd asked him what his name meant.

"It means they broke the mold," he'd said. "There ain't another Dahrone in the whole world."

And now, as we slipped from a Brooks Range rainstorm into a blue sky above the arctic plain, he tapped me on the shoulder, leaned to my ear, and told me that of course there ain't another Kaktovik, either. I'd done my research, though, and knew better. Dozens of kaktoviks, or seining places, were spread along the northern seaboard. Like most Native arctic nomenclature, Dahrone's village name was simply descriptive of place. Until the turn of this century, his ancestors were nomads, not villagers. Kaktovik was a char-netting autumn stopover for Dahrone's great-grandfather, who at other times of any given year might be encamped on Tigvariak (portage) Island waiting for bowhead whales, or along the Okerokovik (blubber cache) River netting grayling, or up at Anuktuvuk (caribou dung) Pass ambushing the mighty antlered mass as it funneled through.

I turned in my seat. Dahrone was bright-eyed and ready to talk. "So tell me what it's like," I said. "Kaktovik."

"Right now? A war zone."

His village of 200 was "swarming with gussuks and helicopters," he said. *Gussuk* is a legacy of Russian colonization, a particularly vehement bastardization of *cossack*. In this case, the cossacks were corporate flacks, environmentalists, biologists, geologists, anthropologists, paleontologists, media production teams, politicians, and writers such as myself. A lot of us, I suspected, would be the same bodies and voices whapping around in the same helicopters that had whapped among the pandemonium in the wake of the wreck of the *Exxon Valdez*.

Dahrone was right; his Inupiat Eskimo village—which consisted of a dirt airstrip, a few dozen modest clapboard homes and shacks, some old Quonset huts left over from its occupation by the American military, and a new multimillion-dollar school paid for with oil money—was the staging arena for a war. I was struck by the irony of his perspective. We had come swooping in, all of us wearing white hats, but carefully segregated, philosophically factionalized, formidably armed with money and rhetoric, the designated warriors for a nation facing the Battle of the Last Wilderness Alternative, and to Dahrone we were gussuks one and all.

With the exception of the Alaska pipeline and the gravel road that parallels it, the Brooks Range runs wild for some 625 east-west miles across Alaska, from Canada to the Chukchi Sea. Rivers flowing down the spruce-timbered south slopes of the range tend to meander among miles of gentle hills before they empty into the westerly valleys of the Yukon and Kobuk rivers. The north slope of the Brooks, however, is treeless and precipitous, and its rivers are fast. They spill a lot of pebbles and grit onto an alluvial shelf that has, over the ages, risen above the Beaufort Sea to create a coastal plain.

For nine months a year, the plain is simply a low platform of ice. For a few weeks of summer, in twenty-four-hour daylight, it erupts, and the caribou—180,000 of them—come to drop their calves in the new grass of the long lowland sweep of vulnerability that keeps the wolves and grizzlies away.

About 95 percent of this plain has long been open to oil development. But at its easternmost and narrowest end, a band of tundra 125 miles long and averaging about 15 miles wide has been closed as part of the Arctic National Wildlife Refuge (ANWR). Of the refuge's 19 million acres, 8 million were designated wilderness in 1980 with passage of the Alaska National Interest Lands Conservation Act. That same act, however, left the fate of that 1.5-million-acre coastal strip undecided pending a study of its wildlife and petroleum potential.

That study, by the time I was sent north as a journalist to look into the row nine years later, was in. State biologists and the feds' own Fish and Wildlife Service predicted that oil development would either displace the 180,000 caribou from much of the plain or substantially reduce the herd size—possibly both. Oil company geologists estimated only a 19 percent chance of finding recoverable oil within the refuge, and if the anticipated

3.2 billion barrels were recovered, they would be equal to only 200 days of American oil consumption.

Nonetheless, the Department of the Interior was recommending that Congress authorize full-scale development—which would include a 150-mile-long elevated pipeline, as many feeder pipelines as necessary to connect wells to the main stem, plus a 150-mile paralleling haul road and 160 miles of fanning spurs.

The jury, however, was still out. Although a go-ahead to drill in the refuge was part of the National Energy Bill then in the hands of Congress, voters were in no mood for it in the summer of 1989. To open another oil spigot in the face of the biggest human-caused environmental disaster in the nation's history would be akin to political wrist slashing. Prudently, Washington would bide its time.

A few months after the spill, public attention shifted to the arctic refuge—750 miles farther north, near the other end of the Alaska pipeline—because preservationists saw the congressional lull as another chance. The pendulous national mood had swung into their corner. Before, few knew where the refuge was; fewer cared. Now, in a time of collective guilt about the damage done, the country was plump with earnest folk looking for ways to make amends. The arctic refuge was amendable. More than a hundred environmental organizations funneled support for its preservation into a Last Great Wilderness project coordinated nationally in Fairbanks by the Northern Alaska Environmental Center.

Suddenly, a distant, stately barrenland, which heretofore had drawn only a few hundred pilgrims a year, was swarming. By August, the several hundred researchers hired to load the biological data guns for both sides would be outnumbered by helicoptering politicos and news teams. The tiny village of Kaktovik and its fifty families sat squarely in the cannon's mouth. They would be journalistically prodded and politically milked by teams from journals and networks major, minor, and international: by, for example, CBS, NBC, ABC, and BBC; by *Time, Newsweek,* and by the Associated Press, United Press International, and Reuters; by the *Los Angeles Times, The New York Times,* and *The Wall Street Journal;* by the National Geographic Society, the Wilderness Society, and the Sierra Club.

★ ★ ★

Stuart, Mark, and I got in a little ahead of the crowd.

We were met at the hangar end of Kaktovik's gravel airstrip by Roger Kaye, who at the time was the U.S. Fish and Wildlife Service's assistant refuge manager and also the official pilot who flew biologists in a grid over the refuge each July for the annual Porcupine herd count. I'd talked with him a couple of months before in the federal office complex in Fairbanks, where I was struck by his earnest infatuation with northeast Alaska and by the fact that his guard was so ingenuously down. He'd been unabashedly rapt, when he'd shown me that ANWR pamphlet, about the humility and respect and awe he still felt in the face of nameless valleys and horizons unexplored.

Also at the airstrip was an old man named Charlie Sims, who was picking up supplies from the plane we came in on and who said the Kaktovik Hilton—which was pieced together from old army Quonset huts—was filled with National Geographic staffers and helicopter pilots. But inasmuch as he and I might be distant kin, he said with a wink, we could stay at his bunkhouse for two bucks a bed.

We tossed our gear and ourselves into the back of a one-ton flatbed with sidegates, and Charlie bounced us over the gravel and through the dust to the front door of a dilapidated two-story place with chipping green paint. It was mostly bare inside, and hollow sounding, but it looked weathertight and clean.

"Twenty-five beds," said Charlie, showing us two long rows of bunks upstairs. "Two bucks a bed, that's fifty a night. Apiece. Including the kitchen."

And so, with beds from Charlie and an escort from the U.S. Fish and Wildlife Service, we settled in.

Roger Kaye, I soon realized, seemed disaffected by that bureaucratic guardedness you see so often in the faces that agency spokespersons turn to the public, particularly when they're on as hot a seat as ANWR was just after the trouble in Prince William Sound. His blue eyes, and the smile under his blond beard, were so open they looked almost naive. In the years to come, you could see the mask creep onto his face more often, although he was always clearly uncomfortable with it, and it kept slipping off. Not long after our meeting with him in Kaktovik, rumor would have it that as the ANWR controversy built, his candor was censored, and he was demoted a notch from assistant manager to refuge pilot and subsistence liaison.

In those early meetings, though, at a time when I was enduring or maybe indulging that undefined disillusionment with Alaska that had set in during the previous winter, I found myself uplifted by his enthusiasm. When Stuart, Mark, and I stepped off the plane into what at first looked to me like one of the bleakest landscapes I'd ever seen, it was Roger Kaye who immediately began to freshen the experience. He walked and drove us through the grit-winded landscape like a dazzled patron, painstakingly introducing us to a ramshackle whaling waterfront and its elders and young turks, talking always of a richness of human and natural history, and of the importance of the *idea* of a last wild land to humankind.

In the years to come I would learn just how inseparable Roger was from that idea. I would begin to see the Arctic itself mirrored in him, and to see the story of the land merge with the story of the man and his passion for the place and for the two little half-Native daughters it was soon to thrust into his care.

From Charlie's bunkhouse we walked to the village, a square mile of gray wood and peeling paint, and a stark harbor knocking with drab, functional-looking boats. A few of the boats, Roger said—including a couple that had been mothballed above the waterline among sprouting weeds—were old longboats from Yankee whalers that had anchored in the harbor around the turn of the century.

On the other side of the airstrip from the harbor was a beachfront that smelled of sour fat and was littered with marine mammal bones. The boat-sized remains of a bowhead whale sat among small ice floes in several feet of water just offshore. About town, yellow-white polar bear hides lay drying on rooftops or on porch railings. Adolescents buzzed perpetually

around the village on three-wheeled all-terrain vehicles, churning a constant fog of dust into the constant wind. And everywhere we were shadowed by small children with big-cheeked smiles.

We tried talking with adult villagers about how they felt about their
village council's endorsement of oil development—a stance that pitted a
few hundred Inupiat Eskimos against the few thousand Gwich'in Athabascans on the other side of the Brooks Range who were worried about their
caribou supply. But the Inupiat aren't open about their private affairs, and
we all knew enough not to push too hard for answers.

I settled for a secondhand analysis from Roger, who said the Inupiat
had sided with money ambivalently. "They would like to have their cash
and eat caribou too." But during the winter night that lasts up here for
almost three months without a sunrise, Kaktovik villagers could see the
Prudhoe Bay gas flares glowing like an unavoidable fate beyond the
western horizon, 110 miles away.

"These people are great believers in fate. They're at a cultural intersection and have little choice other than to take the road most traveled
by." In Kaktovik, that road led beyond the old village with its weathered
and ramshackle cottages to a modern subdivision in which each of the
community's newlywed couples was given, courtesy of oil-based revenue,
a sparkling new home.

In the evening, after that midday Stuart and I spent taking stock of
our world from its far northern shore, Roger Kaye dropped by our
bunkhouse for dinner and stayed to talk. As a pilot, he naturally talked
about flying; but rather than the usual hangar bravado, it was talk in which
the conversational flying was simply the medium, the narrative vehicle
through which he told his life.

In spite of my own uncomfortableness in the air, Roger spoke of it
with such affection that I quickly found myself comfortably up there with
him, skimming along at 200 feet as he rolled the wheel of his Cessna to
follow some sweep of shoreline below.

My own trip to Kaktovik and to the throngs of caribou on the coastal
plain was important to me in a sensory way. To understand them I needed
to see them, to hear the brisk, percussive music of their hooves, to watch

their flanks shudder under the relentless blackflies, to smell the dung and hide.

But to be whole, a place needs to have a story. We humans give voice to locality. And when we apply ourselves to a place, we have a way of incarnating it—of absorbing its bits of fur and ice and predicament into ourselves until it has passed through us wholly, from chaos to coherence.

As I listened to Roger Kaye, I began to see the Arctic itself mirrored in the man. And from that beginning, as their stories intensified and merged, I would come to realize that the north and the man were of one nature, one and the same.

Now, of course, it's easy to look back and see how he was so taken by the whole of the place and its people that he was bound to possess them. Even as he walked the dirt streets of Kaktovik establishing for me the human geography with which we must always overlay a land in order for it to mean anything to us, he was reciprocally overlaying the land with himself. The arctic north was growing his skin.

Not that that sort of thing is particularly unusual. I suspect that most of us identify our friends with their places. The differences in these northerly reaches are of wildness and size. It has seemed to me that most friendships up here are like they must have been among fur trappers or feudal lords, when adding a new acquaintance also added a significant chunk of real estate to your repertory. Alaska is too big to know wholly; after you've been up here awhile you realize that if you're going to have some home water or home turf, you're going to have to pull in your horns a bit, decide your druthers.

Roger Kaye, as I got to know him, had bigger druthers than anyone I'd met. His official shire included the eastern arctic coastal plain, the eastern third of the Brooks Range, and several Yukon River tributary drainages, including that of the 460-mile-long Porcupine River. It was an area that was not only his responsibility but also his passion. He was in love with every inch of it.

And his story became the latest chapter of its story, the ironies of his life the latest manifestation of that chain of ironies so common to men who have great affection for a place: in knowing it so well, they become the logical choice for its frontline defense, and as its champions they are robbed of the peace that inspired them to love.

Not the night in Charlie's bunkhouse, but later, Roger told me that he, as did so many Alaskans, remembered precisely where he was on that March day when the *Exxon Valdez* hit Bligh Reef.

"It was midmorning, up along the Coleen River two hours out of Fort Yukon on a blue day. You could see the end of winter. The way March had burst open, it was turning into flier's paradise."

Up ahead of the plane, among the high peaks in the north, the sun had begun to glaze some of the southerly snowfields. They glistened and flashed. The last time he'd flown here those same slopes were wind-polished to a cold blue sheen. That was in January, when he'd veered off up the Sheenjek to the Richard Hayden place, at a time of year when there was only an hour of good daylight and you had to race the sun, timing the flights from cabin to cabin so that you could set your skis on ice before nightfall. But the sun was shining fourteen hours a day now, and gaining an hour a week. The light was bathing, clean. The cockpit windshield felt radiant. "So much glow after so much darkness was like standing under a hot shower after you'd gotten a chill," he said; "it took a long time for the heat to work its way to the bone."

Roger's mindflight was more substantial than the one I had taken while standing with Stuart and thinking southward from the edge of the Beaufort Sea. Mine had been a way of connecting my life with other lives. His was a connection of life with sky and land. He was more comfortable with his flight; it had more confidence, more dimension; it drew you further in. And before you knew it you had spent an hour seeing and feeling how spring germinates within another man, over a white ribbon of river, flanked by thick stands of spruce.

The river wended toward him out of Alaska's northeast corner. It was an ancient trade route, he said, between the Athabascans and Eskimos. Few traveled it now, though some of those few were illegitimate. Wolf poachers were one reason he flew low, looking for signs of the region's dozen or so wolf packs, and for human campsites and the skid tracks of ski planes. Roger considered law enforcement a minor part of his job as assistant manager of the Arctic National Wildlife Refuge. For the past several winters, the Coleen River Valley had been occasionally targeted by men in planes who left carcasses in their wakes. But this year, except for the trapline pathwork of the valley's resident trappers, the Coleen had appeared undisturbed, a quietude that Roger suspected had a lot to do with Earl Remsing being out of circulation. Remsing's case was one of the biggest ever cracked up here, after Fish and Wildlife investigators discovered a set of journals in which the North Pole dentist wrote of killing Brooks Range wolves, grizzlies, and flightless, nest-tending geese.

Roger Kaye flew for another half hour, watching his quick, black shadow flatten and jump with the contours of the snowdrifts and the river's buckled floes of ice. He spotted a cow moose, belly-deep in snow, munching some freshening shoots of willow from a clump of the plants lining a slough beside the river. He saw some urine-stained and trampled snow, and circled to investigate. It was only a cluster of caribou, no more than half a dozen, bedded in a coppice of spruce. Still flying low, he swung back over the river. The ice of it was dusted with recent snow, and the snow was laced with the stitchery-looking tracks of voles and snowshoe hares, the straight-line punctuations of fox paws, the carefully splayed two-toes of a moose, and then a clutter where some caribou had crossed. The Cessna 185 throbbed warmly, clean and trim, red and white.

The river bent sharply, and, rather than steer through the zig, he climbed into an easy turn. He was 107 miles above the Arctic Circle now, and seventy above the Coleen's confluence with the Porcupine. In order to fly on up into the headwaters he'd have to overnight at Bob Hart's place, where he had cached some five-gallon cans of aviation fuel. Hart was a short, strong, tough character, suspicious of bureaucracy but a good man—and his wife, Nancy, was an artist with a woodstove.

Roger sighed. When visiting folk of the bush, he sometimes felt his professional tightrope begin to shimmy. His was the agency charged with managing the wildlife refuge, and on top of that, he, personally, was the liaison between the agency and the refuge's natives and settlers. With the exceptions of five isolated families, some 400 people lived within two communities that bordered the refuge—the Athabascan settlement of Arctic Village in the foothills of the Brooks Range at the refuge's southern border; and the village where he spent so much of his summer time: Kaktovik, on Barter Island in the Beaufort Sea. For them all, Roger explained policy and enforced it, held meetings and conducted conservation programs for school kids, delivered mail and sometimes Christmas presents, counted caribou, looked for poachers.

It used to be that the refuge attracted a few hundred visitors a year, and got little attention from the press except from the Wilderness Society magazine, and that only because its founders and a couple of subsequent presidents had played key roles in establishing the refuge. But since the first proposal to drill for oil on the refuge, things had been getting hotter. Several thousand people visited the refuge each summer now, many of them on media- or research-related business. Millions of dollars had been poured into wildlife surveys and research projects stemming from congressionally ordered development of conservation plans, an environmental impact statement, a wilderness review, and plans for the refuge's wild rivers. To complicate matters, a rift had begun to develop between the refuge's Eskimos, who supported oil exploration, and its Athabascans, who opposed it. And of course the oil company people and the environmentalists were here, in a mad race, churning out political fodder. When Roger was alone with the refuge, walking it or flying over it, he felt the paradoxes of coating these humanless distances with hype, and of turning solitude into a media event.

Professionally he was trying to strike a balance. When it couldn't be both wilderness and people, which should the U.S. Fish and Wildlife Service go with? It was a hard fence to walk, and with the superimposition of oil development, national energy policy, and oil spill wrath over the whole of it, it was getting harder.

Still, Roger Kaye had come to love this country and its people. He had studied it, scoured it, scrutinized its history, knew all its white pioneers, and knew Native history better than did most Natives. He was a biographer of naturalist-explorer Bob Marshall, whose proposals in the 1930s eventually led to the creation of the arctic refuge. His own adoptive grandmother, a Koyukuk Eskimo, had been a friend and dancing partner of Marshall's. Roger was a link, a buffer, a filter between these people and the mounting attentions from an increasingly interested outside world. To many of them, the America beyond was a mysterious southerly haze, full of alien complexities. Roger translated it to them when he had to. But his heart was more engaged by their lives beyond his duty.

And behind his passion for the place played the background melody of his own small daughters. They were four years old now, half-Yupik Eskimo twins, whose mother's family had them sequestered into village life. They were the progeny of only a brief affair, and their mother had gone on to a troubled life. Where were his daughters today? How were they? What were they doing? To Roger Kaye, the children were becoming ever more pendent symbols of his intense feeling for this arctic north and its northerners. How long, how strongly, did you have to love before you could truly be a part of a people or a place?

Below, Roger saw the homeward-bound sled-runner tracks from Bob Hart's trapline, and moments later he spotted the smudge of cabin smoke. He braced himself. Bob would have some strong concerns to talk about; it would be a lively discussion. But, all in all, Bob was a good man. Besides, there was Edna, his Eskimo wife, to soften the conversation. And of course the three dark-eyed daughters. Children who must be so much like his own. He had brought them some small gifts, and he could already see the lights in their eyes.

He lined up the Cessna, lowered the flaps, and glided down to meet his shadow. The plane flared and dropped, and he felt the reassuring rattle and cut of skis on ice.

The long daily flights over the Porcupine herd, Roger had told us that night in Charlie Sims's bunkhouse, was a fascinating chore of which he never tired. And the next day, as I flew with Stuart, Mark Kelley, and another pilot, Don Ross, along the Beaufort shoreline, it was easy to see why.

Down on the swells and swales of the brown and green tundra, the beasts teemed like mosquitoes on flesh. It was midnight, or around midnight, during that vivid, rare flooding of light from a sun almost touching the northern horizon. The caribou cast shadows a tenth of a mile long, each animal a bright, golden brown speck at the north end of a long black line. With the lowering sun, the shadows of the animals had sprouted quickly, as if the treeless tundra was growing its own forest of darkness during a season when night never came.

To the north, out my window, the Beaufort Sea ice lay flaked so intricately that the floes seemed to pose a labyrinthian question: *Which way?*

The sea was flat calm, the reflection perfect. As we flowed west, the mirrored sky appeared to glide east, and the ice to float alongside us through a firmament that was variously salmon-colored, pearlescent gray, and unfathomably black. The traceries of open water that coursed between the floes to beyond the horizontal east and west and north, I remembered, were called *leads*. *Which way?* The question had been posed before.

In the years that have followed my own trip to Kaktovik, whenever I talk with Roger after the annual census to ask whether the count is up or down, invariably I recall that first sweep like a tern over the skylit sea, and over the plain with its thousands of hexagonal lakes and tens of thousands of converging trails, the black lakes flaked with snow geese and swans, and to the south the massif of the Brooks Range breathing with mists, and flexing with shadow and light.

When he was up there in the far north, he had told me, he was absorbed by the wildness and the human history of the place. And from the intensifying crowds and controversy, flying was always a relief.

"And sometimes," he said, "it's about the only time I can really think."

"About controversy?"

"About the struggles: the one for this place, and the one for my girls." They seemed to be struggles oddly aligned, he said, as if they had more in common than being just *his* concerns. Because of his job, he couldn't speak for the one or reach to the other, at least not the way he would like to.

To history, wildness, and solitude, his vast north had added a dimension most personal, and at once more marvelous and more rotten.

A few weeks before, he had learned that his twin daughters had been turned over to a foster home in the small Yupik village of Lower Kalskag after their mother, allegedly drunk, apparently left them outdoors at night. He flew straight there.

He hadn't seen them since they were eighteen months old. Now they were toddlers, lovely, light brown little ladies with olive eyes and long, dark hair, but already tough and undisciplined. In his mind they had been small, vague figures, indistinguishable in their twinness, but in Lower Kalskag he surprised himself by almost immediately recognizing their individuality: Polly, the impulsive free spirit; Lolly, a meticulous child intrigued by detail. He found himself suddenly, deeply thankful that they were unstricken by the fetal alcohol syndrome that had mentally limited an older half brother. Roger had visited with them for three days at the foster home, made a model airplane for them, played with them beside a river, read them books. And when it was time to go, Polly the Bold gripped his hands. "We want you to be our daddy," she said.

Naturally, her declaration made him feel misty, but for some days he didn't consider it seriously. The foster parents were nice folk rearing a good family, and they were willing to keep the girls. It made sense.

But now? Good lord, if he took them they'd come with all that emotional baggage. So rowdy, so unruly, so needful.

And what about Masako? They'd been considering marriage; he had even flown to Japan to meet her family. She was a woman he didn't want to lose, at once conscientiously traditional yet untypically independent, a mountain climber who had traveled to the wilds of Alaska twice alone.

And beautiful.

Would she marry into motherhood?

"And then I'll look off the my-side wing and think, 'And then there is this!' " he told me. The lovely, haunting Arctic had been his home for almost two decades. "Twenty years, and it still has magic."

But whereas then it had seemed an impregnable wildland, now it seemed sometimes helplessly mute and suffering from a malingering frontier image. He felt its vulnerability, knew too much of the bad news, and he was convinced that the arctic north couldn't much longer survive laissez-faire public policy and individual waste fostered by the myth of frontier abundance and freedom. Alaska's special character and options for the future, he felt, were losing ground to frontierist misperceptions that the state had unlimited natural wealth.

"We've done a lot of irrevocable plundering," he said. "A lot more than our generation's share." The loss of Alaska's character was evident here, in the scars of the scramble for North Slope oil, and elsewhere, in the overcutting of irreplaceable old-growth timber, and in the conversion of public wildlands to private, developed inholdings. It was evident in the strident calls of politicians and industry cheerleaders for almost any kind of growth that was immediately profitable. And it was evident even among the tens of thousands of mostly good-hearted folk—the recreationists, tourists, and sportsmen—who were lured into the wildlands by promoters who ignored the cumulative effects of the swarm.

He was convinced, though, that there were real possibilities for passing the north on as we had found it, for preserving vestiges of the old cultures that hung on; but it could be done only if Americans stopped trying to prolong their intemperance by robbing their children. All it would take would be some good planning and restraint, but to accomplish that modest, logical end was going to take some loud, persistent persuasion and surely, regrettably, some fierce fights.

Commitment. Roger just had to figure out the trick of how to be the common denominator to a wildland and two small girls. They were confusing, inspiring trusts. Even as they fragmented his energies, he could feel himself pulling them all back toward himself, into a wholeness that he couldn't yet define.

Over the months, Roger would tell me later, his life got steadily knottier. But he could still occasionally retreat to places and companionships in which the new complexities faded behind the symmetry of the country.

Occasionally at noon, he said, he would roll up a topographic map of Northwestern Alaska's Koyukuk River, and walk north through Fairbanks to visit a friend, an old woman who was his favorite among Alaska's Native elders. She was in her eighties now, and he had been recording her reminiscences for fifteen years. Early on, the sessions were just pleasant, history-collecting visits. But there was more between him and Tishu Ulen now. Now he was her adoptive grandson, and she a grandmother who sewed him mukluks, patched his parka, and made him lunch. The visits were personal.

He particularly remembered one day, darker than it should have been under an August sun, because lightning fires to the east and south of town had been smoking the sky for the past few days, and the sun through the smoke cast a red pall.

It would have been a beautiful day to fly out of the mess, but he had been stuck in the office, forced to watch from his window the slow grazing of clouds across a loosely flocked sky. His flying was tapering off. It was paperwork season now, and he could only wish back to those daily census flights over the big herd up on the coastal plain.

It was only a few blocks from Roger's office to South Hall, a state-owned apartment complex for the limited-income elderly. At apartment 214, the old Inupiat Eskimo greeted him with a soft laugh that crinkled her eyes down to jovial black slits. "You been lost, Grandson?"

"Just real busy, Tishu. How are you?"

Beckoning him in, shuffling toward the kitchen, she said what she always said. "Oh, still pining for the old ways. But I'm okay. You hungry?"

"This poor *Tannik* is always hungry."

"You know what I have; you brought it. He's a good young bull this time."

"I told you he was."

"Did you? Well, a caribou hunter will tell you lots of things, but you have to wait to taste the truth of it."

As Tishu rattled around in the kitchen, Roger unfurled the topographic map on the dining-room table and weighted its corners with salt and pepper shakers, an ivory owl, and a small vase.

"You been up to Wiseman?" Tishu asked him.

"You know I wouldn't, not without you."

Tishu eyed the map. "I would rather go up there than talk about it," she said. But Roger knew that she would enjoy the talk enough.

Tishu Ulen was born a nomad in 1905 on the shore of Chandalar Lake, more than 200 miles north of Fairbanks, and east of what is now the 8.5-million-acre Gates of the Arctic National Park.

Roger had met the crinkly-eyed old woman years ago among the southerly foothills of the Brooks Range in the Koyukuk River village of Wiseman, while trying to identify peripheral people in some old photos of wilderness advocate Robert Marshall. In 1930s Wiseman—more than 200 miles from road or electricity—Marshall believed he had found "the happiest folk under the sun."

"He was a pretty happy man himself," Tishu had told Roger Kaye at their first meeting. "I was one of his dance partners. Oomik Polluk: Big Whiskers. He could dance all night."

Tishu, it developed, could repeat those stories about as tirelessly as Oomik Polluk could dance. But Roger didn't mind; he was fascinated by Marshall, whose wildland passions were so similar to his own. He had become a Marshall biographer, collecting the man's letters, recording reminiscences of his old acquaintances, and corresponding regularly with Marshall's expatriate brother George in England. In Tishu Ulen, Roger had found ears that had listened to Marshall's, hands that had touched Oomik's own. In a voice as breathy as if fresh from a Circle City two-step with Marshall himself, she relived for Roger Kaye the all-night dance fests once a month at Pioneers Hall between the Wiseman Eskimos and white gold miners. And then her voice would tone down to the near whisper of remembered gossip among the *nivershaks* (meaning "chickens," in reference to young, unwed women), and she would tell of Marshall's fathering of an illegitimate child by one of the Wiseman Eskimo girls, or of Marshall swearing to secrecy his companions on a climb up Mt. Doone-rak, where he suffered a seizure that was probably related to the undiagnosed illness that killed him in his sleep at age thirty-eight.

So grandchild Roger had become. And over the years—he a blond and bearded young man with an affinity for things wild and past, she an octogenarian with thick white hair, strong traditions, and a strong smile—they left the here and now together, to share the then and there.

That memorable noontime, with the kitchen going steamy and him sitting with her at the table, she had leaned over the paper topography unfurled there, as if seeing the hills and rivers from the sky. Her hand wandered to a spot; her forefinger tapped it absently. Roger leaned to see. It was at a wide bend in the Kobuk River, some 200 miles west of her home country. She told about camping there as her family floated down the Kobuk in plank poling boats for the trading rendezvous in Kotzebue. Families, whole villages, were funneling down for the rendezvous, and the closer they got the more people would be collected at the campsites; and the fiddles would come out, and the young men and the *nivershaks* would dance. . . . You could tell her heart was there, sixty years ago; and he noticed, now, that she even wore the beaded moccasins, cotton stockings, and loose cotton print dress—this one blue and white—in the style she would have favored then.

For a few moments she stopped talking. It was after midnight. Her eyes had gone distant. He furled the map and walked back to work in the red glow from the smoky sky.

A year later, in the autumn of 1990, the Arctic National Wildlife Refuge issue had settled to a dull roar, at least temporarily. Roger had his children. Friends told me he would have a certain parental air about him as he gave the place a parent's unconscious security check. In his wake the girls would bounce in like fawns, mischievous and shy.

He seemed to have positioned himself a step back from his idealistic absorptions with the wildland and its history. And though I knew that those topics as well as ANWR politics still concerned him deeply, he had with his children evolved a separate peace into which he didn't allow the other to intrude. I don't know what compromises, if any, it had required, although he seemed to me not compromised but redefined. I had recently gotten into a habit of looking for the *place* in people I met, sort of the way one might try guessing what sorts of dogs they'd own. Roger's place was changing. He reminded me, oddly, of a man who has just shot a moose: the hunt is out of him; his passion quietens from animistic to domestic, his cunning from predation to purveyance.

Whenever I telephoned, it was family more than ANWR that he wanted to talk about, and I realized that it didn't matter which; they were inseparable—the floe of his life among the leads of the land, the pattern certain but undefined, and always the question: *Which way?*

One day, he told me, he'd sat on a split-log bench with Lill Fickus outside her home in the John River valley. Lill was giving advice.

"The main thing is, you have to give them habits," she said. "And not habits from a TV."

Roger had glanced toward his five-year-old twins, who were romping out toward a barn in the wake of Lill's husband, Bill. Habits. He'd had the girls just three weeks, and the most notable habit they'd manifested was a fractiousness that so far had resulted in him being firmly asked to leave Lamont's department store and the Fairbanks city library.

He had flown the girls here—the Fickus homestead was in roadless wilderness 180 miles northwest of Fairbanks—to get his new family away from the city for a while, to camp at a favorite spot upstream from the Fickus spread, to study the children without distractions, to find the right ways to set limits.

"Be firm," said Lill. "They want boundaries; in their hearts they really do."

Involuntarily, he'd glanced at Lill's hands. Firm indeed. They were stronger than most men's, prominently veined, calloused, weathered, and heavily creased. She was not a woman a stranger would seek out for advice on parenting, with her chiseled brown face under a red Marlboro cap, her black hair chopped at the shoulders, and her lean figure dressed in faded jeans, a frayed blue-and-red-plaid flannel shirt. Dark glasses hung from a red lanyard around her neck, and, behind her, a scoped, high-powered rifle leaned against the cabin logs, handy. But you didn't have to be around her long to become an admirer—and her big-game hunting clients from around the world included a good many admirers. One, Roger knew, was Johannas von Trapp, one of the *Sound of Music* children who had escaped from Austria with his parents during World War II.

And as far as Roger Kaye was concerned, Lill Fickus was a model mother. She had reared four children, none of whom had succumbed to drug or alcohol problems (one daughter was a Miss Alaska), and in whom she had instilled her own "habits" of a lifetime, including homemaking, gardening, hunting, guiding, horse wrangling, ranching, mining, trapping, skin sewing, and beadwork. And all that on a wilderness homestead in the John River valley, way up here in the Brooks Range, in Bob Marshall country, where subsistence living was still the rule. The village of Wiseman, fifty miles east of them, had become the model for *Arctic Village*, Marshall's classic 1933 study and celebration of wilderness and subsistence living. Lill, a Gwich'in Indian, was born in the real Arctic Village, even more remote than Wiseman at another 130 miles northeast, and still today probably the continent's most traditional Indian society. Roger had come to her because his girls had never had what Lill's four grown-now children had without TV, without booze, and without abuse. As young as they were, his twins seemed already to be hiding behind shallow eyes that darted with quick savvy and for quick gratification. He wanted them to grow up with the love of hills in their eyes. He wanted them to learn the music of water, the spirituality of the long arctic night. And because, as the old Gwich'in so firmly believe, you are what you eat, he wanted their fast food to be caribou.

That's an overidealization, of course. He knew he'd never be able to decontaminate them entirely, from either the past or the future. He wouldn't really want to; he just wanted them to have choices. But he wanted, too, to give them the exposures that would equip them to make those choices.

He said he was beginning to love them. Not that he hadn't cared all along, but, until these past few weeks together, there'd been no basis for a bond. Still, they were his and he was obliged. He had read the social service's report on the girls and their mother and her boyfriend, a documentation of repeated drunkenness and violence. And then he talked with the girls themselves again and learned of other things, things that left his conscience no option. He just couldn't leave them there. They were his. They were strangers, but they were his.

"In Bethel, at the end of all the court stuff, one of the social workers drove me and the girls to the airport," he told Lill. "She handed me a white plastic bag. She just handed it to me and said, 'Good luck.' And when I got onboard and looked inside, I saw this pathetic wad of clothes and a couple of other things. It was everything they owned."

And now here he was, and here they were. "I figure I'll write to Masako soon," he said. "Maybe tonight."

"Pretty good chance she'll come?"

"I think so. I think me and the girls are having a good run of luck."

On the bench beside him, Lill Fickus pointed with her chin toward the barn where Bill Fickus was lading the girls with small armloads of wood. The John River lay beside them, the green and reddening hills beyond. Together with the children and the old man, with the pole corral and the log barn, it was an idyll, and in response to it Lill said, "If a TV ever started to control my kids' lives, I'd take it out and shoot it."

9

The Hardest Hour

I can't sing. As a singist I am not a success. I am saddest when I sing.
So are those who hear me. They are sadder even than I am.
    —Charles Farrar Browne, *Artemus Ward, His Travels*

On that spring night in Valdez when David Grimes sprawled beneath the magistrate's table to sleep, he had crawled out shortly before dawn, poured coffee, and crossed the courtroom to where I sat going over notes. Some of the others in the impromptu command post still slept, some were conducting business in murmurs.

"I woke up realizing I'd been drawing from my memory bank," David told me quietly. "And I thought, 'Why *that* memory?' And of course it's because it was a recollection of a life we might never have again."

Nine months before the spill, he said, he'd been in one of three kayaks that slipped seaward past the Cordova harbor jetty half an hour after dawn on a blue last day of June. The water sat flat calm, the boats rode slim and low, brightly enameled in reds and yellows, looking like shards of glass on glass. They cut small arrows of wakes toward Mummy Island, six miles out, where David planned to release an orphaned crow. He knew there were other crows out there. The story went that there was a crow on the island for every one of the kelp-wrapped Chugach Eskimo mummies discovered in caves by fox farmers late in the last century. Two hundred mummies, two hundred crows—a fluttering of phantasmata from the mists of sea and time.

The kayaks, he said, had turned left, southwest, into Orca Inlet. The bird was apprehensive—"It didn't yet have its sea legs"—and spent the first of the journey gurgling small complaints, wobbling on the spruce

179

bough that Grimes had rigged just aft of his own seat, and ruddering its balance with a reactionary tail.

Its name was Caurin Po Crow, a name that sounded southern, like corn pone or Edgar Allan Poe or maybe an Uncle Remus character, but actually was a commingling of the creature's specific Latin name, *Corvus caurinus,* and the name of a T'ang dynasty poet, Li Po. In the wild and natural China of twelve hundred years ago, Li Po incongruously was a seeker of wilderness solitude, a champion of nature. In naming the black crow, Grimes passed over the fact that Po means the white one and looked instead to the poet's boyhood reputation for taming wild birds, and to the wings of his verse.

Even in ponytail and sandals, David looked too much the rugged fisherman to be possibly the only thirty-four-year-old ever to spend two months of his life doing almost nothing other than rearing an orphaned crow. In a working harbor from which men and women seafared out to long, death-tempting days on slimy decks, the idea of spending the salmon season at home nursing a baby bird smacked of piddling indulgence.

Indulgent David might be, but never piddling. Tall and well-muscled, sincere to the point of intensity, he had a reputation for putting his back into work and his heart into play, and for sinking the teeth of his soul into the great mystery. He had a degree in natural sciences from the University of Missouri, and the same Gaean riddles that drew him initially to the study of nature stirred him still, although he had not yet translated his diploma into a conventional profession. He had spent the past sixteen years working seasonally, mostly as a commercial fisherman, but some summers as a temporary biologist and, occasionally, as a smoke jumper. During the rest of the year he explored. He explored himself and human-kind and the earth and the universe. He traveled, wrote poetry, composed music, studied history, and contemplated natural and metaphysical law. He was probably as close a specimen as we'd yet produced to the perfect holist, living conscious of himself as only part of an organic whole, and regarding that *tout ensemble* of what we are—our history, our biology, our spirituality—as having a reality independent from and always, infinitely, greater than the sum of our parts.

Two months before, David had returned to Cordova from a winter in Japan, where he'd explored the ancient, animist Shinto religion, to which he found in himself an ancient, animist response. Shinto gods are the deities of wild waters, savage lands, and feral creatures. As he told me of it, I was skeptical; his story was beginning to smack of new agism. But when I wondered aloud if that's where he was heading, he didn't smile. "Since I was a boy," he said, "I have felt the wildness dying in myself and in the world."

He said he had felt it ever more wistfully, as if being abandoned; and when he pilgrimaged to some of the old Shinto shrines still tucked into river valleys across the isles of Japan, he found in them a concentration of that same pathos. In the days when the emperor was himself one of these gods (before he denied his own divinity), the spritely Shinto deities were virile, vivifying powers. David found during his visits that their influences still hung heavy. The old gods clung to the shrines like mists, their expiring wildness still tainted by vitality, the way swirls of smoke in the wake of a vanished magician both hide and define the mystery.

So he came home influenced. He did not come home a Shintoist, but Shintoism did rekindle his awareness of humankind's more primal attachments, he said, and sent him back to Prince William Sound with a patron saint, a clay statuette, a reverent habit, and some serious questions. The patron saint was Ebisu, a god of round belly and wonderfully smiling face, who is said to be the deity of good food, honest dealing, and fishermen. The clay effigy was of Tanuki, the little raccoon dog, god of fertility, mischief, and illusion. The habit was of David clapping his hands twice in reaction to moments that struck him as holy—a modification of the Shintoist practice of clapping hands between prayers, perhaps to keep the gods awake. David mimicked it—in reaction to a breaching whale, a certain aspect of light on water—just to get the attention of the cosmos in order to say thanks.

David's commitment to Caurin Po Crow came about as a result of the questions. He had come away from the Shinto shrines with a sense of loss, a loss that he felt was sequel to our possession of, and divorce from, the earth. Should we have loosed our grip so permanently from the soil, and our spirits so finally from the traditions of our ancestors? Was it right to always be escaping from what we were? In our drive to possess, had we

181

lost the profound excitement of being possessed by the whopping and secret forces of the earth? The earth "is never 'taken possession of,' " wrote Thomas Wolfe; "it possesses." Had we gone the wrong way?

When he got back to Cordova the small black bird was there, raucous, demanding, and dependent. A friend of David's had found it fallen and wandered irreplaceably from some high nest. The friend couldn't care for it; he had to go fish. Until that moment, David had planned to go fish, too. But suddenly here was an opportunity to explore humankind's lost naturalness by plugging his own life, at least for a while, into this bright black, bright-eyed jolt of primal vim.

Ah, ahh! the crow said when it saw David. The two of them imprinted on each other quickly, David setting about the process of becoming a parent crow, and the flightless young bird applying itself seriously to the center of the universe. *Ah, ahh!* it would repeat hoarsely a hundred times a day. Sometimes the cry was demand or complaint, but just as often it was a marveling comment on yet another new wonder of life.

David learned almost immediately that the crow, like many other perching birds, was a projectile excreter—a lesson that dictated the positioning of their quarters and their relationship. He also learned early on that crows can be taught only when willing to learn, which is often at four o'clock in the morning and never after the sun has dropped below the yardarm. When the sun sets, birds sleep. David's active cheerfulness on the warm early evenings of spring were met by a heavy-lidded glare, and by mutterings as petulant as those of a sleepy child.

And Caurin Po (a name that displaced an earlier choice, Raven Charles) just as quickly learned that a parent is actually a sort of giant yolk sac; if you tug on its ear persistently, it will rouse itself to feed you worms, cream cheese, or salmonberries. For the first few days, that knowledge was the alpha and omega of existence.

But Caurin Po soon blossomed beyond appetite. David found the bird engaging, gregarious, bright, and inquisitive. It not only learned quickly but performed with verve, hollering and flapping, strutting like a wind-up toy, commenting on most of what it encountered, tasting much of it, snatching the best and brightest household baubles for its own collection, or sorting solemnly with its beak through David's more subtly attractive collection of seashells, unable to decide.

One afternoon a week or so into the relationship, when David and the crow were on their daily outdoor constitutional, Caurin Po hopped into an inch-deep rain puddle. He froze, almost panicked, and then— David will remember it always—the small black countenance was washed by an expression of comprehension. Spontaneously, the genetic machinery kicked in; Caurin Po spread his wings, dunked his breast, dunked his head, and launched into the joyous splashing abandon of a bird at its bath.

That evening, David watched the archetypal, almost ritualistic, way the crow courted sleep, flexing first a leg, then another, then stretching one of its growing young wings, then the other, spreading them out, fan-folding them back, ruffling everything into place with a single settling flounce, then slowly dropping beak to breast and nocking its head beneath a wing.

And he wondered: Exactly how far have we come from such primal memory? And in that distance, what have we lost?

On Mummy Island, David said, the streambed next to his campsite had been absolutely chockablock with blue forget-me-nots. "I remember walking through them, with the sun toasting my back and my neck and radiating this faint, steamy sweetness up from the flowers."

They had camped for three days, most of it too windy and rainy to risk a run for home. Caurin Po had perched on some large rocks near the tents, swooping down for food at mealtime and hopping up among the thick branches of a big Sitka spruce when it showered. Evenings, he cocked an eye to the sky as the island's resident colony of sea crows came cawing back to their rookery from the mainland. Caurin Po didn't return the cries; he just watched and paced.

But the day the sun touched David's shoulders brought a break in the weather with which they would have to leave. From the blue-on-green sweep of forget-me-nots, David walked barefoot back to the grassy shelf above tide line where the others had already broken camp. He stuffed his sleeping bag and spartan gear into the kayak's small stowage and carried the craft down to the incoming tide. He settled the boat in the water, then walked back to the cluster of mossy, copper-brown boulders where Caurin Po perched facing the sun.

183

The bird's eyes were closed; the sun on his feathers had baked him into a drowse. David reached toward him, hesitated, withdrew his hand. He stood looking at the bird for a full minute, hardly believing the fatherly catch in his chest. He backed away—and lightly, without sound, clapped his hands twice, then turned and walked back down to the kayaks. He shoved off, slipped into the seat, unclipped the paddles from their brackets, and stroked into the rhythm of a six-mile run with the tide.

you were
like a flower
broken from a cloud
above you
the blue depths
of high heaven
below
swelling waves
of green water

The crow and he had been as one; or, perhaps more accurately, the crow had been a metaphor. "For us all. We're all born wild but pulled away from the wildness and brought up in a culture that represses our animal selves. Then we come of age and are set adrift. We try to make sense of our choices. We hear the call of the wild. We know that there is a siren song in the water, in the sky. There is great meaning. We don't know what it is. We don't know how to find the melody of it. We are afraid out here, so we fly back to town.

"I would submit," he said, "that all of us are natives in a dying culture. We are going to have to recognize, with humility, our place, or we will lose it. We will die."

In the months that followed the spill, while Rick Steiner was going after the money and law he figured it would take to save the waters and shoreline of Prince William Sound, David Grimes appointed himself a champion of its spirit.

He bought a boat, the thirty-eight-foot converted troller *Orca II,* as a matter of conscience and conviction and contribution, after a friend's chance remark that there really ought to be a fair witness vessel out in Prince William Sound during the cleanup effort. The spill had been a powerful magnet to people from all over the world wanting to come see, but access to the sound was limited. Exxon had employed virtually every available boat on the West Coast at contracts ranging from $1,000 to $5,000 a day, and if people wanted to see the spill, they almost had to go out on one of Exxon's guided tours.

David was taken by his friend's idea of a fair witness vessel, and for a while he tried to get such a boat funded with grant money; but the slough of grantsmanship, he found, is alternately becalmed or blown with such fickle winds that after a month he decided it wasn't going to get done, at least not in time, if he didn't just go out and buy a boat himself.

The notion was to have a way to get concerned people out into the sound without telling them lies. Just take them out there and let them see for themselves what had happened, what was happening, and let them make up their own minds about it and take their unlobbied judgments back to whatever constituency they came from.

When I chartered the *Orca II* in July of 1990 for a trip around the sound with my wife and son to revisit the path of the spill, David told me that for the past year bereaved people from throughout the world had telephoned him day and night to talk about Prince William Sound—or had come to charter his boat and see the damage for themselves. He would sit in the *Orca*'s wheelhouse and talk with them for hours, strangers and friends, sharing what he called commiserables and comparing philosophies, bolstering hopes, plotting strategies.

Again and again, on his small boat in its small harbor in its tiny town, the phone that he had plugged into a receptacle on the dock would ring and he would marvel at how much human passion had funneled into Cordova, and how many alliances had been formed, and how, even considering the magnitude of all that had transpired, in the end there really weren't that many phone numbers in this holy wildland for the sunk of heart to call, and not that many willing ears to listen. He felt that if he unplugged the phone, he wouldn't be surprised to see the line squirt blood.

And finally on a June day not long before I showed up with my family for some fair witnessing of our own, he'd found himself sitting topside on the warm, whale-black planking of the bow, fingering a penny-whistle and contemplating the boat's anchor, a Norwegian fifty-pounder with thick flukes that swiveled on the shank. The anchor was attached to fifteen fathoms of chain and another forty fathoms of line, the whole of it wound onto a capstan inside an oiled cedar housing.

He'd gotten into a habit of sitting there when he needed to feel anchored, he told me; not so much by the reassuring symbol itself, but by the solid wisdom of the friend for whom that particular anchor was a memorial. *Lars,* said the bead weld on the iron, for Lars Holtan, two years dead.

On that day, the reassurance wouldn't come. Something was very wrong. For no reason he could articulate, he could feel himself slipping into a depression he was unable to check.

But *why?* He still felt strong; he still felt a sense of destiny, and a certainty that he had been doing the right thing. He hadn't been after money for the past two years, or any kind of profit other than a heightening of awareness, both for himself and for the dozens of parties he had taken aboard the *Orca II.* People didn't sail with him into Prince William Sound to mop up oil. They came to set their spirits straight; they came to mourn a loss, to love the company of their misery; they came looking for balms, and for good omens and silver linings; they came to be buoyed up, to take heart. And he had been a conduit for all of that, and it had felt precisely right. At the helm of the *Orca II,* he had felt humbled and privileged and absolutely certain of the direction to steer, and of the direction that humankind must go.

"So why the woe, Lars?" he'd asked the anchor.

Lars Holtan, he knew, would have answered something practical, something obvious. You're run down, he'd say; just take a break.

The last time they'd seen each other, David was feeling very mortal, having just bought the *Orca II* near Juneau and risked the 500-mile run home across the Gulf of Alaska with no insurance, no sideband radio, and a forty-year-old engine. He'd felt it an act of faith, a tossing aside of the cloak of doubt, a spiritual quest. Lars, he knew, would have reminded him that adventure is the result of poor planning.

He'd known Lars was dying of cancer but hadn't visited him in five weeks and was unprepared to see what emaciation had done to the handsome, angular face. "I like my life," Lars had reassured him. A few days before, he'd insisted on taking his boat out to the commercial grounds on the Copper River flats to fish for reds. He'd fished such a full day that his wife, Landa, finally collapsed and made him take her home. "That's what you want to do, live the way you want to die."

Lars, like David, had been a wildlife biologist (they'd met out on the Copper River delta, where Lars was developing a master's thesis on Aleutian terns and David was studying dusky Canada geese); and Lars, like David, had given it up so he could stay in Cordova and live the Cordovan life as a commercial fisherman. Both of them loved to travel, loved languages, and spoke several (although the Norwegian, Swedish, and Danish on Lars's list were not on David's). And they both loved music. It was Lars who introduced his friend to the Irish ballads that had struck such an immediate and powerful chord within the Irish American that they had become one of the great loves of his life.

The great love of Lars's life was Landa. She was lovely, dark, bright, outspoken, calm. As a Native (was she Haida or Tlingit? David must have heard, but couldn't remember), she had a seasonal response to things, and David remembered that in that first summer, in a berry-picking mode, she'd dragged the two men out among tall green vines where each ripe salmonberry was as plump as a thumb. Her black eyes flashed, and Lars Holtan the Norwegian sang her an Irish tune.

So on that last day, David had taken one of his own loves, an old air from the Isle, along with his guitar, to Lars Holtan's deathbed.

"There is a ship and it sails the sea," went the last verse,

Its keel is deep as deep can be;
But not as deep as this love I'm in;
I know not if I sink or swim.

The water is wide. I cannot cross o'er;
And never have I wings to fly.
Build me a boat that will carry two,
And both shall row, my love and I.

When he got through, Landa was crying. Lars took her hand. She said, "It's true, Lars. I don't know if I'll sink or swim."

And, dying, Lars was so very alive, his pale gray eyes watching his wife, then shifting over to David with a smile.

"Just float," he said.

She laughed through tears, and shook her head. Then Lars said to David, "Speaking of floating . . ."

David told him the new boat was fine; it and he had bonded fine. "I'm still not sure why I have it," he said. Then he said, "For fellowship. All these people coming into the sound, they need fair witness, and like-mindedness, and someplace to heal."

"Sounds like a church," said Lars.

"I think maybe it is; a spiritual entity, anyway."

"Like me, pretty soon."

David smiled. "Kindred spiritual entities, I'm sure. I'll name a part of her after you."

The gray eyes brightened. "Which part?"

And that stumped him. He didn't know. He'd have to get back to Lars on that.

But a week later Lars was dead. Landa had asked David to deliver a eulogy, and David was tinkering about the *Orca II,* thinking about what he might say, when he casually noticed that the anchor was a Norwegian brand, a Forfjord, and that made him think of Lars; and thinking of Lars, he suddenly remembered that Lars's nickname was Hooker, a sobriquet he'd earned in the Norwegian merchant marines by falling off a ship and cracking his chin on an anchor fluke.

So the anchor became Lars, and vice versa, and after the eulogy David went down to The Reluctant Fisherman and sang songs and got beery with his friends and with some Soviet sailors from the big oil skimmer, the *Vayda Gubsky,* who had come ashore offering fresh baked bread and plum preserves and looking just like neighbors needing friends.

On the day he told me about Lars and the anchor, David and I were sitting at that same spot on the bow. As he talked, the sun began to set, the deck began to cool. My wife, Joan, came up from the galley with hot tea, and she and our small son, Cody, sat to hear. All the while he talked, David's fingers trifled over the note holes of the small, shiny flute he held, as if rehearsing. Cody occasionally eyed the instrument curiously; and when the story was finished, David smiled at Cody and lifted the whistle to his lips. For such a five-and-dime piece of tin, its notes floated out startlingly pure; and after he played, he sang:

> Don't mind the wind or rollin' sea;
> The weary night never worries me.
> But the hardest hour in a sailor's day
> Is to watch the sun as it dies away.

And unabashedly, with the three of us beside him, he spoke aloud to the dead: "Two years, old friend. The boat has begun to feel like a shrine, and I have begun to feel perpetually reverent. Maybe I do need a break. Maybe to heal, maybe to Ireland. Or maybe, as the balladeer says (or is it you, Lars?), all I need is a large, cold bottle and a small, hot bird."

Even though it was more than a year before we left Alaska, I knew when we chartered David's boat in 1990 that we would be leaving, and there were times aboard the *Orca II* that I felt as though we'd just dropped by on our way out. I realized how tired of it all David was getting to be, too, and I felt as guilty as if visiting a hospitalized friend before bolting off on vacation.

I'd come to look at some of the island beaches I'd visited a year before—beaches oiled and some that had escaped the oil—and to try to get a feel for whether the place was dying or surviving. I'd asked David to take us out to one anchorage in particular, West Twin Bay on Perry Island, where I had spent ten days the previous June helping take a wildlife census with biologist Pete Mickelson. I had mapped seaweed beds and the nest sites of eagles and mergansers and Canada geese and other birds and had counted rock crabs and limpets and anemones, and had tracked otters—four pairs of them—to their dens. It was the one place in the sound in which I would be able to tell whether there was as much life now, or less.

David's boat was a beauty, all cedar and oak, a thirty-eight footer built as a troller in 1946 and converted into a small yacht. She was comfortable, with the main cabin and galley expanded and glass all around, and the wooden feel and sound of her taking you back, as if into a grandparents' cabin.

David flew strange, multicolored flags on the *Orca II,* and as we motored out of Whittier harbor, the flags whapping against a backdrop of snowcapped peaks, I asked him what they meant. He said they were borrowed from his heroes. One—black, red, and yellow—was the Australian Aborigine flag, meaning "Land Is Life." Another was the flag of Ethan Allen's Green Mountain Boys, who, legend had it, got tipsy on applejack before winning the first battle of the Revolution. And a third was the coat of arms of Thomas Paine, who had helped inspire the Declaration of Independence and had, at least as important to David, coined the term Age of Reason.

Inside, the wheelhouse was neatly crammed with navigational charts, books, photographs of friends and lovers, and bits of memorabilia. On the port bulkhead, David had taped an excerpt from John Muir's 1915 *Travels in Alaska.* Joan copied it into my notebook. I thought of Rick Steiner when I read it, and of his struggle to save the old-growth Sitka spruce forests lining Prince William Sound. "No doubt," it said, "these trees would make good lumber after passing through a sawmill as George Washington after passing through the hands of a French cook would have made good food."

West Twin Bay was tranquil. There were no other boats. We cruised back the mile-long arm of water almost to its end, where a sandspit—our old campsite—poked out a hundred yards from the island's main bulk. We anchored up and took a skiff to shore. Cody had brought his new springer spaniel pup, Freckles, and both of them greeted the firm footing of the pebbled beach like rediscovered security.

My wife came to stand beside me. "This is where you worked?"

I knew what she meant. There was no work to be done here. This was paradise; work would be a transgression. The rich green of the island rose high above all three sides of the bay. At the head of the bay a small waterfall tumbled into shallow, clear water. A bald eagle sat on a white snag beside the fall. A skittish family of mergansers cut wakes over to the other side of the narrow bay, away from the dog and the boy. A profusion of blossoms—sundew, bog orchids, daisies, and even a few clusters of chocolate lilies—grew among the tall grass that carpeted the spine of the spit.

"Well, not to work, really," I said. "Just to observe."

"Did the oil come in here?"

"It hadn't when I left." I had pointed some oil lines out to her on the shoreline rocks as we turned into the bay, but apparently the tide had swept the stuff on by.

"It's changed, though," I said.

"How?"

"I don't know. Maybe it's just that there's no atmosphere of urgency anymore." I looked up. "No helicopters. And there was a big ship, the *Defender,* the one I hitched a ride back to Valdez on, anchored out at the mouth; and Pete Mickelson buzzing around in the *Zodiac.* Seems different, though. My perception of it? The context? I don't know."

And it kept seeming different all the time we were there. Was there less wildlife? I'd thought I would be able to tell, but I couldn't Whenever I sectioned and quarter-sectioned the sky the way the ornithologists tell you to, I counted fewer eagles, fewer other birds, than I had a year ago. And the merganser and sea crow nests weren't in the snag out at the end of the spit the way they'd been before, and the gull and tern and oyster-catcher nests weren't on the rock in the middle of the bay, and the one pair of river otters I had time to look for were either gone or had moved their den.

But it was July this year, not June. If there had been nestlings this year, they would have fledged by now. I wasn't a biologist; I didn't know enough to interpret the evidence, or the lack of evidence, that would tell me whether the lives that had been here before were gone for good or had just moved on.

We hiked up the ridge behind the spit, up through a spruce wood to where smooth mounds of stone poked above the tree line, and where dozens of small, moss-lined tarns lay in pockets in the stone, reflecting the sky. Where I had come up to bathe alone, and had thought that I could sense the dying as I sat in a great muteness broken only by the distant warlike sound of helicopters, and between the helicopters the soft warbling of eagles overhead, my six-year-old and his pup now splashed in with the future, and with the yips of oblivious youth.

The next day we tried to race a gale to port, and lost.

We'd left Perry Island to cruise among other islands of the sound, but at the urging of a gale warning on the radio, we'd turned in choppy seas to run. I had watched uncomfortably as the waves built, and finally David had kicked away the stool he usually perched on at the helm and stood spraddled, wrestling with the wheel. Outside, wind howled, but the seas weren't running and cresting the way they do before or against a wind, but shuddering and frothing straight upward into wild, tossing peaks.

I lurched forward to stand beside David. "What *is* this?"

"Crosswind," he yelled. "You got a gale force wind slamming into a fast-running tide. The tide runs real fast through here, and when you got a wind like that off the glacier, it's real hard to get through."

"It looks real impossible to me."

It wasn't the realization that I could die that terrified me; it was the helplessness. If the boat went, we went. Those heaving, glacial seas would suck the life from us all within minutes, and there would be nothing I could do. I couldn't even bargain for the life of my family: Take me, save them. I think I could have found some measure of composure in that. But there was no entity around with whom to effect the trade. There was only Alaska coming down on us full force, and the desperate hope that this time of terror and exhilaration would not be our last.

At least that's the way I felt about it. David, his legs braced and tense as he struggled with the wheel, kept singing:

Got a full crew onboard,
and faith in the Lord.
Comin' in on a wing and a prayer.

And Cody slept. I had staggered belowdecks, bracing myself against the bulkheads, and had wedged and padded his small body with pillows and sleeping bags while books and paraphernalia fell and flew. I marveled. I thought maybe he'd been knocked out. I poked him. He opened an eye and said, "Hi, Dad," and closed it again, at peace, his trust suddenly more appalling to me than unconsciousness.

I went back up. Joan was gripped to a wooden pew at the rear of the wheelhouse looking acutely suspicious but a lot better than I felt.

We wallowed deeply to port then, and as I staggered for balance, I could hear dishes smashing to the floor in the galley; and then something closer, right behind us, cracked against a bulkhead and fell to the floor.

"Is that my umbrella?" asked David.

Joan looked. It was.

"I always wondered what it would take to knock that thing loose," David said.

Then he decided. "We're not making headway. We can't turn and run with the tide, it'll swamp us sure. We'll have to run with the wind, crosswise to the sea.

"Make sure the doors are shut tight. Hold on. I'm going to turn, and when I do, all hell's gonna break loose for a minute, just for a minute, so don't worry, it might feel bad, but we're just gonna have to take a little pounding while we swing around."

I latched the doors; he spun the wheel. I braced myself in the bench seat beside Joan. A huge peak grew under us, lifting one side of the *Orca* high and then dumping her into a deep trough where the boat bucked and wallowed until another sea slammed into her hull and sent her reeling, stern high, toward a sickly silvery wall that thundered up over the bow into the glass windshield of the wheelhouse. The *Orca* moaned. Dishes crashed.

Half an hour later, running southwest, we passed a point of land that cut the wind, and we slipped from chaos into a merely poppling sea.

The *Orca II* thumped through the bumps of the chop into the mouth of Cochrane Bay. Ahead, and to port and starboard, the Kenai Mountains rose sheer, and between the peaks, the blue-green edges of ice fields lipped over saddlebacks onto the seaside slopes.

I left the wheelhouse and went aft through the galley to open the stern hatch. Back the way we had come I could see for maybe twenty or thirty miles, across Wells Pass, where the gale had trapped us in the tide and was still whipping the sea into a spray, and on northeastward up the long finger of Port Wells to the white cliff face and funneling slope of the Harvard Glacier, and above the glacier to where a tatter of cloud clung to a shoulder of Mt. Valhalla.

I went back in. Joan was uncluttering the floor of the galley. David was on the radio, talking to the skipper of a fifty-foot cruiser off our port bow.

". . . not the first to duck and run," said the radio. "I talked to a couple of boats already anchored up ahead."

"Whereabouts?" said David.

Another voice came over. "Three Fingers Bay," it said.

"How is it back there?" asked David.

"Flat calm."

"Anybody on up beyond the buoy?"

"Guy in a seiner went up the south finger. Nobody else, but we just pulled in a while back."

David was back on his stool. I stood beside him as we listened to the chatter. By the sound of it, we figured, at least three other skippers were somewhere behind us trying to beat it out of the gale. David pointed out Cochrane Bay on the chart and slid a finger up the ten or fifteen miles to where the head of the bay branched into three narrow channels. "There's an anchorage buoy at the mouth of the fingers," he said. "A couple of boats can tie up at the buoy, but there's no other anchorage unless you go on, and there's only one good anchorage up each finger." He pointed along the tiny north channel and said, "Pretty place. Hard to get in sometimes, but we should hit it at slack low, which is good: no current and you can see the rocks."

The bay narrowed and pinched away the last of the wind. We slipped over glass and through an almost unearthly quietness. "We're in stove weather, Joan," said David, and she answered, "Water's on." I answered a whine at the forward cabin hatch and let out Cody's springer pup, and I was carrying him out to the afterdeck to pee when Cody stuck his head out of the hatch and said, "Where are we?"

194

"You're alive," I said; and he said, "Barely." Then he said, "My hungry wants beans."

We anchored up at the head of the bay's middle finger, at a place from which we could see eleven waterfalls, and where the grassy shore was purple with wild iris. Cody caught a fifteen-pound halibut off the afterdeck and then, while it was cooking, sat at the rear of the boat with a horn David had made him from an eight-foot length of kelp stipe, blowing deep notes that echoed like Viking war calls off the high stone cliffs all around.

David and I went ashore and followed the tracks of a big grizzly up a gully that steepened until we were on all fours, pulling ourselves up by holding on to brush. We emerged on a ridge high above the boat, the spindly waterfalls all around on the cliffs, the notes from the kelp horn floating up among the white sound of the falls, and below the ridge on the side opposite the bay, an alp-ringed lake toward which the grizzly tracks led on an even more precipitous looking route than we'd taken up.

It was getting dark. We took a breather and stayed too long, saying nothing at all for maybe half an hour, until at the end of a loon call from the lake below, David got to his feet.

"This is it," he said. "The highest value for Prince William Sound is what it already was."

He stood and in the vague light looked down the tangled green way we had come. "The thing to do now," he said, "is see if we can find an elegant way back."

Later that night I found him in the wheelhouse, fingering through a volume of Tennyson's collected works. He was sitting on the stool he had kicked aside during the storm, and I pictured him then as I have pictured him so often since, braced at the wheel, saving lives.

"So," I said. "You've had a year of people like us, and you're getting a bit tired."

He grinned up from the Tennyson in his lap. "That's a non sequitur. The last year has been the richest year of my life, and I've enjoyed everyone very much. In fact,"—he held up the Tennyson—"I was just thinking about the first ones, the beginnings, and wondering as usual where it's all going to lead."

A year ago this full moon, he'd been thumbing through the same volume of Tennyson, he said, looking for a passage he could almost remember but couldn't quite, something that he knew would be appropriate for the passengers he'd chartered for a week in the sound.

Two were already aboard—a small, keen woman named Kate Bowens and a thoroughly Bohemian and robust man who had given his name only as Pavel—both of them from the Perseverance Theater in Juneau. They had flown into Cordova to board the *Orca II* and had gone below to sleep in the forward bunks during the last half of the quiet, twenty-hour run across Prince William Sound to Whittier to pick up the third member of the charter.

He had run the boat through the night. There wasn't much darkness in Alaska in June, but he had kept the boat moving through what there was of it, the sea swells easy, the sky clear, many of the stars paled to invisibility by a milky wash of light from the first-quarter moon. In the brightness he could only occasionally see the Big Dipper with its two pointer stars, Dubhe and Merak, at the front of the cup aiming up toward the North Star, Polaris. But Polaris itself was luminous enough to stay with him, hanging there ahead in the northwest like a bulb in mist. They'd remained asleep as he eased into a slip in Whittier's small boat harbor and shut down the engine, and they still slept now, in the morning quiet not long after dawn. He kept looking for the passage in the *Collected Works*. What was it in? The Arabian Night poem? Maybe the one about Lancelot?

In a few minutes, when the train rolled into Whittier from Anchorage, he would walk up the ramp from the small boat harbor, and two blocks over asphalt to the terminal to pick up the theater's director, Molly Smith. It was an unusual first charter. When the woman had telephoned her reservation she told him that when the *Exxon Valdez* ran aground, her theater troupe was beginning production on the *Odyssey*. "But the spill has been so much on our minds, so much a part of our lives, that we can't keep it out of the production," Molly Smith said. "It's going to be there no matter what we do, so we decided it would be better to put it there consciously, to come see, so that we can convey some images of the tragedy to our audience."

The three dramatists—Bowens, Pavel, and the Perseverance Theater's imposing, sardonic director, Molly Smith—David felt, were the ilk of passenger he wanted for his new boat. And there seemed to be so many. He hadn't advertised; the word had just gotten around, and the calls had come flooding in, all from people who talked as though the wound had been to themselves, and they had to be able to see it, to fix it in their minds, in order to find in themselves the strength to heal. David had no clear idea why this particular type of searching was attracted to the *Orca II*. The lovely old boat, whose wooden hull had thrummed so firmly over forty-three years of seas, seemed to invite it somehow. She seemed to have taken on a will of her own; to have abandoned fair witness as too dispassionate, perhaps, and relegated herself to the spiritual cleanup.

The sun was over the yardarm, the train was almost due; it was time for David's passengers to hit the decks. With the ball of a bare foot he thumped on the bulkhead between the wheelhouse and the forward bunks. In Tennyson, he'd found the lines—he should have known; they were in *Ulysses*—and now he hollered them down:

"Come, my friends!" He gave it the force that he imagined the poet was calling for, hearty enough to ring above full flapping canvas and a crashing sea:

'Tis not too late to seek a newer world.
Push off, and sitting well in order smite
The sounding furrows; for my purpose holds
To sail beyond the sunset; and the baths
Of all the western stars, until I die.

The second day out from Whittier had dawned a color that David decided, upon reflection, was golden blue. None of his three passengers had been on Prince William Sound before and could not know how fortunate was the weather in which they'd sailed the past hundred miles. The clouds were few if any, the breeze light when any, and the swells were broad, shallow troughs of sunlit water through which the *Orca II* sliced with the sound of a small brook trickling over stones.

In this oddly stormless, golden light of June he had steered these people into the narrow necks of fjords past silent blue ice floes that had calved from glaciers and now lay crowded and bobbing, waiting for an offshore wind to herd them, screeching, out into the shipping lanes. He watched these people watch the dark eyes of harbor seals on the floes, and then he took them to kelp beds to watch otters, and to a kittiwake rookery; and he took them out into the open channels, where they could watch the great mountains slip by with that latticework of white Ys etched into the dark basalt up where snow is still packed into the veins of erosion that drain from two to one, shallower to deeper, down into their golden green skirts of spruce. At Harvard Glacier, up beyond Port Wells at the head of College Fjord, when he killed the motor you could hear the fluty warbling of the eagles and could look thirty feet down into clear water where lion jellyfish with pulsing golden manes palpitated by like slow heartbeats.

But he had skirted the oil. He had not shown them the black beaches or the scum. The mousse from the spill slid through Prince William Sound from northeast to southwest, out through the sound's archipelago of islands and on along the coastline of the Kenai Peninsula. Because of the direction of flow, the oil hit hardest on the northeastern shorelines of both the islands and the mainland peninsulas. Tomorrow, when he would take his passengers around Knight Island to Snug Harbor, they would be struck by the sudden appearance of thousands of workers in bright orange rain suits laboring against a backdrop of black oil, and around and among the workers a fleet of machinery hovering and clunking, the whole of it clouded by steam pluming up from the jets of hot water with which they were all trying to wash the rocks. It looks like hell, Molly would say, her eyes following the heavy black line of oil along the rocky beach all the way from Point Helens to the surrealistic bustle of Snug Harbor's city in the wilds. "Like the somber shade of death," she would quote from Homer, and that would be the most striking of the images they would take back to the Juneau production of the *Odyssey*: a thick oily line painted on the stage backdrop, substituting for the rope Odysseus followed to hell.

But, so far, David had meandered along southwesterly shores away from the spill because he didn't want them to see the oil just yet. He wanted them to see parts of the sound that remained the way all of it was before, so that when they finally saw the damage it would register, in contrast, fully as ugly as it was.

So far, the only signs in their path of the cleanup activity were the persistent, urgent whappings of helicopters shuttling gear and personnel between the islands and Valdez, Whittier, and Seward, back and forth, all day, all night. Today there hadn't even been much of that, for he had steered the *Orca II* into the thirty-mile-long Knight Island Passage, along the westerly shore of the island itself, opposite the path of the spill.

He had decided to show these people one last special place before he took them to see the oil. "One last best place." It was too true. It used to be (only a few short months ago!) that the sheltered inlet toward which he now steered was the perfect pure nugget of wilderness at the remote heart of wilderness, a place David considered the soul of Prince William Sound, and now it was just over the hill from devastation. Ten thousand workers were scouring the beaches of the sound right now, several thousand of them on the easterly beaches of Knight Island. David suspected that with the exception of casual passers-through on pleasure cruises, the sound had not seen a total of 10,000 whites in all the 212 years since George Vancouver first sailed around these isles naming things after Prince William, Sir John Knight, and his other favorite British royalty.

At the southwest tip of Knight Island, David had spun the big wooden helm hard to port and motored toward the island shore.

Ahead, a narrowing neck of water constricted, constricted more, and seemed to disappear against the sheer walls of a fjord. David knew that if he followed it, the channel would open onto the serene bay that was his favorite anchorage in the sound. It was a mythical place, at the head of a fjord with more than a dozen waterfalls cascading down the high basalt walls, the fjord channel meandering below eagles and hurtling kingfishers for a mile and a half, then opening onto the small bay from which the mountains spread away more gently, the bay studded with small islands, the rocky islands covered with wild iris and plush, golden green moss, and stunted Sitka spruce. And if (as most boatmen didn't) you maneuvered the tricky channel beyond the last of the islands, it opened yet again onto another small cove, a placid cove, a soul, a sanctuary, where he was sure that tonight, because of all the dying hereabouts, the hush at the soul of the sound would be elegiac.

George Vancouver had missed what David considered the loveliest sanctum in the sound, and nameless it remained until, about the turn of the century, some anonymous sailor inked it ignominiously onto the local charts as Lucky Bay. The name had sounded cheap to David, too, until he thought about how, if he were inbound from open water and being chased by a big blow, it could be luck indeed to be able to duck in here. If you tucked your vessel a mile and a half back at the head of the bay, you could rock to sleep on unruffled water while a sixty-knot gale whipped the open passage to a froth.

He had made sure that his passengers were topside and alert for this. Molly Smith had come to stand beside him, looking out through the windows that wrapped the front and sides of the wheelhouse. Kate Bowens was in the galley brewing tea, and the Czech set designer Pavel stood out at the rail, humming deeply to himself.

David had thought it appropriate, their being here, discovering a part of their home they'd never explored. The dramatic piece they were working to adapt, the *Odyssey,* was of course about that search far and wide that leads to home; and to represent that homewardness, the Juneau group had five writers trying to Alaskanize the script. So far, some of the gimmicks seemed more whimsical than artistic—the Cyclops had become a one-eyed grizzly, and the dances had become Eskimo rituals performed in togas—but this oil spill was a serious haunting of the art, and the thespians were saying they needed to deal with it, somehow, as artists. David sympathized. After all, "The deep moans round with many voices," as Tennyson said, and he hoped that what he was doing—showing them the song of this deep drama before he showed them its moanings—would provide the contrasting images they needed to convey the tragedy from sea to stage.

Kate Bowens came forward with two cups of tea, and just after she handed one of them to Molly the two women leaned abruptly forward with widening eyes, and Pavel's humming terminated in a sort of grunt. David heard himself sigh. Dead ahead of the *Orca II,* four killer whales had lifted quietly to the surface between the boat and the picturesque channel leading to Lucky Bay. They were very close to the boat, so close that David could hear the soft pops as their blowholes opened to expel six-foot clouds of mist. Whenever he'd seen this happen, David had always felt as if it was a conscious gracing of humanity by these creatures; and it made him feel, oddly, each time, as though he was on the right track, and along the way had just kept an appointment. Instinctively he reached to the ignition switch and killed the engine.

For moments, the orcas rested at the surface, their eyes above water-line fixed on their namesake, the *Orca II*. The big male was longer than the boat; behind him, the shape of his high dorsal was echoed by a peak of dark basalt, the highest point on the island, miles away above the head of the fjord. The four whales, in the symmetric cleanness of their black and whiteness, appeared to be etched against the softer free forms of sea and stone.

The five orcas drifted. In the belly of one, David Grimes felt like Jonah with a window. No one said a word.

In September of 1991, fourteen months after we'd shared his boat, David called to say that he had finally reached a weariness in which he felt that no cause in the world could be as important as a long, restful walk.

"I have to leave here for a while. To rest. I have to."

"Where will you go?"

"After some small, hot bird," he said.

And a week later he found himself half the world away, marveling, as he would tell me later, at how easy it had been to escape.

He spent three months in Ireland, in a beachside cottage with a woman named Beth whose long brown hair and fawn eyes went a long way toward ensuring that they would be months he could draw on for the rest of his life.

He loved, too, the long, tranquil amble along the country lane that wound among the stone walls and brambleberries of County Mayo, on Clew Bay, three and a half miles from the nearest phone.

He recited it to me like a story with a moral, the walk up and away from the beach, where it meandered along a high shelf above the sea. The first day he walked it alone, he said, he followed it through a small oak wood, then stopped beside a brambleberry hedge, remembering that this was supposed to be the last day of the year that the berries could be eaten. The day was *Samhein,* or Halloween. That night, the *Puka*—the Pucklike

Irish spirit of mischief that wandered the isle in the form of a goat or a red-haired boy—would spit on all the wild fruits and vegetables, rendering them into faerie food. David tasted the black berries, which were plump and October sweet, and suspected that a little Puka spit wouldn't stop him from snacking again tomorrow.

He looked back at the oak wood, so very small that—of a land known among the locals as the Alaska of Ireland—it was an almost pathetic vestige. Although it was mostly oak, the woodland was, like Alaska's coastal spruce, a remnant northern rain forest. This one, along with a few others like it, was what was left of Eire's vast canopy, stripped away by the British viceroy Charles Cornwallis in his brutal zeal to drive the rebellious Irish to hell or to Connemara.

David shifted the sling of his guitar from his right shoulder to his left and walked on, headed for Newport to buy victuals and strike up a few notes in the pub where he'd waited for Beth over a pint of ale when he first got to town, and to which they'd invited him back. As he walked he was conscious of the peace he felt and realized that when a man is at peace a part of the world rests, untroubled, gathering strength. At first he wondered, then on reflection was convinced, that rest like this is a periodic obligation, a contribution toward restoring Gaea itself.

The rural Irish countryside, of course, looked as though it had been at rest for some time, with its wanderings of stone fencing over a soft repose of hills, its lazy curls of peat smoke, and the meander of its brooks and lanes. West Mayo was more rugged than most of it, though, and had a more dynamic look and feel—not so much where the tide breathed up to the gate down on the shore where Beth caretook the cottage, but up here where the wind buffeted him as he walked, and where he could hear and smell the sea pounding in and watch the late autumn squalls and their own stark shadows boring into the dark canyons of the glaciated hills.

The gravel of the lane crunched almost like light snow. He stretched into a full stride, appreciating scenery. Big Clew Bay, with its treeless islands that looked like floating potatoes, stretched off toward Nova Scotia to his right, its surface shifting to green, to gray, to the color of a pearlescent bruise. Above the south shore of the bay rose the green pyramid of Croagh Patrick, where the saint himself was said to have spent forty days and forty nights in A.D. 470, wrestling with demons before he finally whipped them and tossed them all into Clew Bay. Nearer, tall autumn grass, still green, rippled in the lazy fields. Up in the hills he could see the stonework of dwellings in which no one had lived for a thousand years, maybe two. Faerie forts, the locals called them. And across the slopes lower down, the welterings of old raised potato beds created a corduroy pattern that swept across the hills like staffs of music.

The country tugged at his genes. He felt again, as he had whenever he had come here since Lars Holtan first introduced him to Irish music, that this was his ancestral, musical home. There was a plaintive lilt to the very country, so wildly sensual at one moment, and at the next so very dissonant with pain. And so bittersweetly rich in its bereftments. All the losses—of heroes and lasses, and of broad oak forests, and of saints and snakes and wolves and dragons—remained keenly here. In America we supplanted the peoples who were interwoven into the fabric of the land, and even after some centuries we remained largely strangers; but here the ancient rhythms prevailed. The place was resonant with wildness that was. He felt the ghosts.

Ah, Beth. Even when she was not with him, she lingered on the country. He inhaled her, and she lingered on his lips. He felt her coming on as a song, so he unstrapped his guitar and sat at a low place in a rock wall beside the lane and sang her for a while. He had to grope for the words, but the keening came out purely and naturally Irish, so that he knew he was born to it, and was pretty sure, whenever it all happened like this, with the music indistinguishable from the land and the love and the ghosts, that he was intended to be a bard.

He returned to Prince William Sound reinvigorated, ready for another round of fair witness aboard the *Orca II*. And yet it was different now, he would tell me. The sound was subtly beginning to heal. In the tempering distance of time passed and perspective changed, his sense of urgent concern had shifted. His solicitude now was less for the waters, more for himself.

He sailed restlessly. He wrote songs. He jumped at chances to travel with Rick Steiner to Scotland on an oil-spill cleanup technology reconnaissance, and again on an Eastern Seaboard speaking tour. Eventually, he realized that the one particular emergency that had consumed him was over. His role in crisis hadn't carried over fittingly to life in the wake of crisis. "I think it must be part of the disorientation a soldier feels returning to civilian life," he would tell me. "You have to redefine yourself, find a new usefulness. You have a great yearning to slip into some old, comfortable uniform—and you try to; you fish, you sing, you love—but under the facade of sameness everything is new, and you begin to wonder whether you'll ever wear life comfortably again."

10

Prisoners of Hope

Angry as one may be at what heedless men have done and still do to a noble habitat, one cannot be pessimistic about the West. This is the native home of hope. When it fully learns that cooperation, not rugged individualism, is the quality that most characterizes and preserves it, then it will have achieved itself and outlived its origins. Then it has a chance to create a society to match its scenery.
    —Wallace Stegner, *The Sound of Mountain Water*

To Stu Pechek, bush planes are a great consolation, are, in fact, time machines. When one of them takes him back to his Brooks Range trapping cabin in November, it will be to precisely the life and time he wants: just him, a couple of hundred years ago.

Stu occasionally invites me to fly to Grayling Lake with him in the Super Cub he bought so he'll no longer have to depend on other pilots. I have traveled with him in the arctic north but never yet to his winter home. Intruding is a precarious business. That cabin—its isolation and the unconfined life it represents—defines Stuart in a way that I would like my favorite fly-fishing stream to define me: as a manifestation of spirit. But laundering your soul in a river or hanging it over a mountain can, like draping underwear, be a personal ritual that loses something in company.

On the other hand, sanctums can get to feeling thin-shelled and lonesome. I do like to share my home water once in a while, and the result is often a pleasant enough reaction by one to things important to another, a mutuality of glimpses, and a stretch of good water—or in Stu's case a stretch of trapline—covered companionably.

So maybe someday I will go. Stuart has, after all, been a boon companion. In our few long travels he has kept the bush life simple, tackled the rough stuff matter-of-factly, and has been a good listener and quick to smile. I've not seen him angry; to the contrary, he seems to have infinite patience—with the village kids who hang on his arms and pester him for treats, with belligerent boors in bars, with interminable delays in weather-plagued flights. Within a few weeks one summer, I heard three women—family women who'd been recipients of some favor, or of a package set on a doorstep in the nick of time—describe him as a saint.

In the bush, Stuart always seems to be granted deference at a glance. Reactions to whites vary among Natives from person to person, from village to village, and even in some basic cultural ways from Eskimo to Athabascan. The attitudes of a village's young turks, however, are often barometric. Some whites regularly get sullen glares. Some, like Roger Kaye, earn village respect through perseverance, dependability, and a genuine interest in Native affairs. I generally get cautious looks, which seem to me to be looks of judgment reserved, and I feel a degree of respectability in those, and am content with them. But with Stuart, the same quick appraisal is followed by immediate acceptance. The eyes flick cautiously past me and go to Stu, and you can see them say, "Well, okay."

And that is Stu Pechek's value to his place: that straightforward honesty that seems to be universally recognizable in those few people we all know who have it. He is the man who first made me wonder whether we really mourn for wildness or for simplicity—for qualities disappearing from the earth or from ourselves. We tend to campaign more vigorously for an uncontaminated backyard than for uncomplicated lives. But if one reflects the other—if simplicity mirrors pristinity, if we dream of the life as well as the land—then preserving the rare artless existence is the same as safeguarding the wildlands themselves.

Stuart likes to write; I wish he'd put his memoirs to hand. If, as I believe, clarity and story are the essences of good writing, his winters at Grayling Lake hold a latent literary power. I hope he gets them down. I don't know who else could do it. He is the last Dan Boone I know.

I've said that the wreck of the *Exxon Valdez* changed us all. In Stuart's case, it sent him into a couple of serious rounds of antioil politics, although the change was not permanent in any dramatic way, and in retrospect seems to have been just a temporary shift away from his pattern of seasonal trapping, fishing, surveying, and solitude. He reacted to the

LEAVING
ALASKA

spill, and even contributed time and conviction to antioil politics, but did not head off into permanent new directions as did Rick Steiner, say, or David Grimes. While Alaska began the business of turning a good many of us into someone else, Stu Pechek kept hold.

The day before the wreck, I was helping him ax and haul big chunks of aspen and spruce for his annual spring bonfire—a symbolic melting of winter on the night of the vernal equinox. I was sweating, but Stuart couldn't shake a chill. He blamed the week he'd just spent in Hawaii for thickening his blood. "My body cranks out the thermal units, but the sap won't push 'em."

"Push 'em?"

"Out to the ends of my fingers and toes and nose."

He took off his mittens, blew in his hands, then stuck them inside his parka, under his armpits. It was twenty below—not cataclysmically nippy if you're dressed for it, but about a hundred and ten degrees colder than it had been two days before in Honolulu. "Infernal equinox down there," he told me, "has definitely got less of a bite."

He was tempted to light the fire right then, and just keep it going until everybody arrived. Man wasn't designed to go from the Equator to the Arctic in six hours, he said, although going the other way wasn't so bad "if you can get down to the water before the humidity danks you to death." Hawaii had saved his sanity more than one winter, and March was always a good time to go. "Around here, people tend toward odd temperament in March. Wet ice, rotten snow; champing at the bit to do all the chasing around they won't be able to do for another two months."

We hauled the logs and sections of small dead trees up to a wide place in the dirt road where it forked down to his cabin. The packed snow on the steep drive had gotten wet and refrozen into slick ice. Rather than fight the glaze, we found it easier to break trail off the road, up through the crusty snow. After a couple of hours and a dozen or so trips, Stuart paused partway up to blow on his fingers again. He looked back toward the cabin. "One more load, we'll go in and bake by the stove. Boil some water, coupla mugs, coupla jiggers Jack Daniel's . . ."

As if she'd heard him, Marta came out on the cabin porch. She didn't have on a coat, so we knew she wasn't out to stay.

"That's a pretty ambitious heap," she called up.

He eyed the eight-foot pile. "Yeah, well, I find myself craving the thermic."

"There's lunch whenever," she said.

He sat with his feet toward the stove, letting his wool socks steam. It'd been a busier, more peopled winter than were the Brooks Range trapline seasons to which he was accustomed. For the first winter in many, he had stayed in town to do some course work at the university but thought of the fallow trapline often, with its humanless snow and the almost absolute silence of the high Arctic on a windless day.

"But I'd be done with trapping by now anyway; I'd be right here, hung over from Hawaii, and ready to burn away winter with a real big fire."

Stuart's cabin—one big room and a loft—was ten or fifteen miles out of Fairbanks, and down several steep off-turnings of dirt road along the north bank of the frozen Tanana River. Stuart was a private man, and although we had begun to be friends, I couldn't yet reconcile what I took to be his shyness with all the work it was taking to attract a whole bunch of people to a pagan bash.

"I like people very much," he said, "just not very often." He motioned toward a wall calendar featuring a beauty in an ermine bikini. "It's the only time you can corral all your friends in one place. Soon as the ice is gone they'll fan out, fish or carpenter, do some field research or survey for BLM. Come fall they'll hunt, and after the first snow they'll run around trying to pack in enough wood and do all the other winterizing they put off again until it's almost too late."

But right now everyone was at the mercy of the weather. The sky was a bluebird sky, and we felt the energy accumulating for the seasons to come, but we couldn't really do much with it because all of interior Alaska was still locked up. When fresh snow fell in March, it was the most beautiful part of winter, and it made us all want to get out and do things, but we were nervous about it because we knew it was going to give way to April, which is the ugliest month, with all of the interior a churning mass of mud and ice, and about all we could do for long weeks on end was buy tickets to the lottery that gives a hundred thousand bucks to whoever guesses the exact time the tripod will tip over on the fracturing ice down at Nenana. Stuart's annual fire gave some of us a chance to crackle at each other with all that energy, and to find out how everybody else's summer was shaping up.

Himself, he was looking forward to the first halibut opener, which was a pleasant way to start each work season because it was a gamble and you never knew whether you were going to walk away from it with $50,000 or nothing. "It isn't very often nothing, and not very often fifty thousand, either; but the gamble of it gives you a healthy reckless feeling going into summer."

And after the halibut, because he'd stuck around the university instead of trapping over the winter, he was going to have to do something more for money than fish—at least he would if it wasn't a blockbuster of a halibut opener. He could stay down in Kachemak Bay and get a crew share on a salmon seiner, he supposed; it was shaping up as a fair year for reds. Or he could get on the Bureau of Land Management survey crew again, although beating through the bushes and the devil's club wasn't as much of an adventure as it used to be, and he was just getting to know Marta, and the survey work would keep him away from her for some months with no breaks. But she might be away anyway, if she got on with Fish and Game up on the Noatak.

He sighed. "Sometimes I wonder if I should've stayed a government biologist myself."

"You never wonder it for very long," Marta said.

"Nope. Likely all the stability I need is the occasional fleeting glimpse."

He would be tempted briefly to anchor up, he said, then he would think about Grayling Lake and his months of solitude on the trapline, and about his migration to the sea every spring, and about wrestling the halibut gear and the salmon seine nets, and about all the drudgery and beauty of life on a calm ocean, and about the drama and robust fear of standing up to an ocean beset.

He had no idea of it yet, of course, but the next day his plans would begin to change as would mine, and within a couple of weeks he'd be running a skiff for Exxon down in Kachemak Bay, making good money shuttling goods from the service boats to the shore crews. "But there was always an acuteness about it," he would tell me later. "You always had the feeling that a good place was on its knees." In June he'd be aboard the *Peggy J,* her anchor ropes moaning in an eighty-knot gale, the sea pounding like a sledgehammer on the hull, and the scream outside like rage and mortal pain, the wind driving the oil thirty feet up into the branches of the spruce, and then the company people out at Gore Point bringing in a big crew after the storm and telling the workers to scrape the beach but only down an inch or two, and then bringing in the network TV crews to see the big mob at work, and then laying off almost all the workers as soon as the cameras were gone.

His big woodstove glowed red. Beside it, we finished our Daniel's and hot water. "In northern Minnesota," he began, but didn't finish. He was dozing. I was pretty sure I'd heard what he was about to say before: In northern Minnesota when he was a boy, he spent all the time he could in the Boundary Waters Canoe Area, and that's what he loved best, and that's what he was still doing, staying away from the uppities in the city, and away from the false slick face of bureaucracy, and staying close to the least contaminated wild, and close to himself.

Marta brought a bowl of salmon dip and chips to a table beside the stove, then stood looking down at Stuart. "You asleep?"

"No," he said, but it was a lie. And when she lifted his baked feet from the stool down to the cooler floor, he rumbled a purr, as if conscious of being grateful but unable to make his sleeping lips say thanks.

Two years later, Stuart called me back to the same chores and the same stove. He and Marta were fresh back from the arctic trapline, both of them with frost-nipped cheeks and noses. Marta, tendering a sprain she'd suffered on snowshoes, limped out the door to do some shopping, and after she was gone, Stuart told me that the trip to Grayling Lake had been her first.

"She liked it?"

He grinned. "Have to ask her."

"How about you?"

He dodged: "Just waiting for her to come in got me through a lonely Christmas and a lot of weeks."

He reached to a shelf to pull down a thin black book, thumbed through it, and handed it to me open. It was the latest volume of his journal: small, maybe five by seven, and thin-lined. The writing had a workmanlike personality with a left-handed slant. The entry to which he had opened was Jan. 14, 1991, 4:20 P.M., $-10°$ F, calm and foggy.

The afternoon before, it said, long shadows had spurted from the stunted arctic spruce, and the teal snow around Grayling Lake was flooded by brilliant white. Out at the woodpile, Stuart blinked and squinted. It was the first sunlight he'd seen in two months. It spread; the south sides of all the black trees turned suddenly green. Stuart grinned, wiped his watering eyes on the back of a mitten, and kept watching. The sun was back, the weather was fine, Marta would be here in two days, and all was bright under the arctic blue.

That night he stood in brittle air outside the cabin and watched green tendrils of aurora feel and swirl among the constellations. He glanced at a thermometer hanging on a nail outside the cabin door. It was twenty below. He was wearing insulated boots and insulated overalls and his old down parka with the wolverine ruff that held a pocket of warm air in front of his face. His hands perspired inside his heavy wool sledding gloves with the nylon overmitts. He should have gone in, but he was restless.

He walked across the spruce pole bridge over the gully and the frozen creek, and made his way 200 yards down a well-packed trail to the lake. Under the starred sky and the aurora, it was bright enough out for easy walking, but the snow had gone blue again, and the trees black; after today's brief sun, it was a reversion to winter's dark sameness, and it had him in a funk. It happened often enough that he had come to respond to it habitually with this walk, down out of the eclipsing trees to the flat white plain of Grayling Lake, with its unobstructed view of a broad sky and an upward sweep of hills to the pinnacles of the range. It was not so much that he needed the view (although watching the horizon dilate as he walked down the slope did tend to ease his midwinter claustrophobia); it was that he needed to see life. He came down here in the slim hope of finding an iota of vitality—an owl, a raven, a vole, a hare, a fox, a wolf, a caribou, a moose. Anything. Back around the first of December he'd gratefully watched a silver fox trot nervously across the lake, and a week or so later a small band of caribou. Usually he saw nothing. He would stare for an hour or more, occasionally mistaking a windblown wisp of snow or a tremoring tree for warm life. He would welcome a fly; he would happily let it crawl around on his nose. He had no idea what a fear of lifelessness and silence might be called; it probably didn't happen enough anymore for humankind to pay it much attention. But it happened here, and when it did you had to do something about it, or else content yourself with lying all night with a fast heart, staring at the colorless, moss-chinked logs of the ceiling.

So in darkness under the dim aurora he stood down by the lake on watch. He remembered his eyes watering earlier in the day in the sudden brightness, and in that recollection he saw the color of his sunlit eyes. What color, he wondered in his journal, did the pigment reflect in darkness? What color were eyes when there was no one to see their blue?

I was still interested in how they'd gotten along for six weeks of togetherness in a place that had hitherto been exclusively his. To me, anyway, it wasn't just idle curiosity. The role of solitude in human affairs had been important to me over the years and seemed particularly a key to defining Alaska's best value to humankind. Stuart knew that; we'd talked about it before, and had puzzled together over the mystery of why some people so crave to be alone. So I risked offense and pried:

"How did it work out, having company?"

"Oh, it got to be a test. It was a disruption of the reason I go, if that's what you're curious about, but mostly not a bad disruption. It always gets to be a test up there, and if you go through it alone, I think you come out a bit stronger individual. And if you go through it together, you come out a stronger couple. I don't think of it as solitude; to me, solitude is still strictly going it alone. With Marta it was a step away from solitude into a special kind of communion.

"There were times that, when they were over, you realized there had been a real tempering process at work. Particularly when there was danger."

★　★　★

On the day they saw the worst of it, he said, they sat inside a wall tent at Stuart's Rabbit Lake camp, about thirty miles out along the trapline from the home base cabin that Marta had come to call the Grayling Hilton. It was February 4, three weeks into a cold snap in which the temperatures had ranged from forty to sixty below. Usually Marta stayed at the cabin when he went out to check the marten traps in this kind of weather, but she was bored stiff with the Zen of floor sweeping, she said, and Stuart knew what she meant; he was sick enough himself of the Zen of a large woodpile.

"I figure," said Marta, "that there's a hundred and thirty degrees difference between inside and out."

He smiled over at her. She was a lump in a sleeping bag. "I figure that our caloric intake is about ten thousand a day," he said, "and we're getting skinny. We could start a fat farm."

"Or write a diet book," she said. "But I'd rather have a cracker and a stick of butter."

He sat on a stump in long underwear next to a hot stove, his feet propped on a coat to keep them up off the cold tent floor. Even the animals weren't moving much; usually he'd have ten or a dozen marten by this far along on the line, but this round he'd picked up only two marten and a red fox. On the trail yesterday he saw none of the little > > > > > trails of voles that crisscrossed the snow each morning before the wind smoothed them over, and none of the usually prolific ptarmigan tracks down in the willow bottoms. And no moose, no yard-apart marten hops; nothing fresh at all except the tracks of a small band of caribou and a trail cut by the Monument Creek wolf pack. The pack had plowed a single-file path in deep snow parallel to his own trail for several miles without ever taking advantage of the well-packed trapline route. They were probably as frustrated as he was by the cold, but not yet hungry enough to trust a human path or to start robbing traps. They'd left the trailside to follow the caribou spoor.

"In all these years," he told Marta, "I never realized what those dimples are that you see in the snow around caribou tracks. Little twin dimples here and there like a baby's butt, and every once in a while some scrapes where they paw down through to the moss. Yesterday it just came to me: they're nose prints. They must be able to smell good forage through the snow. I bet they can tell how deep down it is, and the vintage and everything. They don't have to waste energy pawing down until they know it's going to be worth it."

He looked at Marta. She was asleep. He was mildly surprised. Usually it was the other way around.

But good. She could use all the sleep she could get. She had sprained her leg snowshoeing, and pain like that got to be a hole that sucked out the warmth faster than you could generate it. She hadn't ventured away from base camp for days and didn't want to go anywhere until the weather warmed. He didn't blame her. Yesterday, out checking the line, he got chilled even while shoeing as hard as he could to stay warm. He frost-nipped his cheeks; the balaclava froze to his beard, his outer mitts got so stiff he couldn't bend his hands, and clouds condensed from his body heat, throwing up a vapor trail as he walked.

But they were going to have to get out of here. This snap might go on for weeks, and they had food for only two or three more days. He could make the thirty miles back to the cabin in a day and a half alone, but he didn't know how long it would take together.

They were going to have to get out of here tomorrow.

He looked at the couple of wisps of Marta's blond hair that curled out to shine on the gray cloth of the bag in the red glow of the stove. He listened to the boom and crack of ice out on the lake and knew that tomorrow wouldn't give them any breaks. He thought back to almost three weeks ago, when the plane had come in with Marta. He and she were still pretty new to each other; she'd never been here before. He'd been sleepless for two nights and was popping muscle relaxants. When the clear weather gave way to steady snow, he worried himself sick that the marginal weather might delay the flight; on the other hand, he was almost paralyzed by a dread that when she did step out of the plane he might not be able to think of a single thing to say.

He needn't have worried. He'd brought her big malamute, Melozi, in with him back in November, and when the 206 buzzed the cabin and landed down on Grayling Lake on skis, she stepped out and went for the dog. That big blue-eyed dog was all over her, and she looked up at Stuart, laughing, and her eyes were green, and she came over and gave him a hug.

That summer Marta did get the job with the Alaska Department of Fish and Game 440 miles northwest of Fairbanks on the banks of the Noatak River, counting spawning salmon. And Stuart went east from Fairbanks 150 miles, surveying for the federal Bureau of Land Management in the Yukon–Charley Rivers National Preserve, a remote wildland known mostly as a center of peregrine falcon nesting activity.

And that fall, when they returned to Fairbanks, Marta was offered a full-time directorship of the Last Great Wilderness Project, a coalition effort by more than a hundred environmental groups to block oil drilling in the Arctic National Wildlife Refuge. It was administered locally through the Northern Alaska Environmental Center, but Marta realized that, with congressional debate heating up again on the issue, she was going to have to do some stumping in the home districts of fence walkers and key swing voters in the Lower 48.

Stuart decided that he couldn't, in good conscience, enjoy a winter of solitude at his cabin within the refuge while Marta was out on the front lines fighting the good fight for its preservation, so he offered to help. Together, they planned a five-state eastern seaboard sweep that would continue a road show campaign they'd helped put together as volunteers shortly after the latest spring bonfire at Stuart's place. In September they loaded Marta's 120-pound malamute husky and an Athabascan Native from Canada named William Greenland into an oxidized blue Datsun pickup with a camper shell and headed southeast.

They knew they would face audiences heckling as well as sympathetic, but the prospect of antagonism didn't worry them nearly so much as did the news. All reports indicated that the oil industry had enlisted enough support to see George Bush's National Energy Security Act passed complete with a rider authorizing oil drilling in the refuge. The bandwagon was already on the roll, pulled by senior Republicans, the White House, Big Oil, Big Gas, and Big Business.

The prospect of such an uphill battle, Stuart told me, almost defeated them from the outset, particularly one day in October, in Philadelphia, where, all things considered, they would rather not have been. They had walked out of the *Inquirer* building, editorial page editor David Boldt's barked questions still jarring around their insides as coppery as Boldt's red hair. Stu's stomach was feeling sour. Marta trembled. William Greenland had withdrawn into a black depression. "So what's so special about caribou?" Boldt had barked at Greenland. "Why can't your people eat canned food?"

"We define ourselves by our relationship to the caribou," William Greenland had said. "Seventy percent of our diet is caribou. They are the one constant of our history."

"Oh?" said Boldt. "So what gives you the right to define yourselves by caribou, and us not the right to define ourselves by oil?"

Donald Kimelman, the page's deputy editor, had rolled his eyes sympathetically behind thick lenses. Stu had had the feeling, then, that the two editors were just good cop–bad copping them—a suspicion that the editorial page later would confirm. But that consolation was some days away. Now, walking out of the drab hulk of a building into the drab October afternoon, Stuart felt like he was walking away from a whipping.

"You got a ticket," Marta said when they got to the truck.

"It says 'Parking Allowed.' "

"Except four to six."

He looked at her over the Datsun's fading blue hood. Six months ago they'd driven the truck through the Northwest and Midwest and parked it in Boston after giving forty slide-show talks to friendlies and hostiles, wrangling with a bunch of editors and talk-show hosts, and forever angling off to hit the home district of some congressional fence sitter. They'd been optimistic then, when the issue seemed undecided. But now, at the beginning of a long and probably futile haul from here through Pennsylvania, New Jersey, Delaware, and New Hampshire, the sharp chops from the *Inquirer* editor had already drained their sap.

"I need a ticket home," Stuart said.

Marta grinned. "Chin up. Think about the Grayling Hilton."

Stuart opened the truck door. "Get in back, dog."

Melozi looked through him with that inscrutable blue-eyed stare that had so impressed audiences across the country on the last trip. Parked on his butt next to Marta while she stood at a microphone, Melozi would stare through and beyond everyone with those chips-of-ice eyes, never wagging his tail, just sitting with his big chest out and those eyes not focused on anything fathomable but still pinning everybody's conscience, his massive head waist-high to Marta as she stood, her hand often dropping unconsciously to stroke the dog between the ears. Stuart had stopped wondering what Melozi might be thinking. He doubted that the dog was a thinker. The dog was a doer; he pulled a good sled.

"Back, I said!" They should have taken him inside, let him fix those fangs and icy blues on Red the Rude.

He white-knuckled the truck through the city and out to Valley Forge, where they dropped William Greenland off at the Valley Budget Motel.

"You okay?" Stuart said.

William, a short Gwich'in Native who wore round glasses on a round, friendly face, was normally quick to smile. But when he got out of the truck his jaw still had the hard set it had taken on in the *Inquirer* offices. "Okay?" he said. He gave Stuart an Indian-to-White-Man look. "Sure."

As Stuart pulled away, Marta watched William disappear into his motel room. "Think he's all right really?"

Stuart shrugged. "We'll see, I guess." He knew it was booze she was worried about. Just a few months ago in northern Canada, William had been in a coma for so long that they'd almost pulled the plug on him. The Gwich'in elders came in from William's village, Inuvik, and prayed over him until he snapped out of it. Stuart had had his doubts when William had volunteered for the Arctic National Wildlife Refuge road show. Not only had he been looking forward to the months alone with Marta but here was a man with a real problem wanting to go out to campaign for a cause in an alien culture. On the other hand, he lent good credentials to the effort. His people depended upon the caribou. He was articulate, congenial, and a pretty good speaker—had, in fact, trained to be a disc

217

jockey, and even won an award from the National Aboriginal Communications Society for some documentary he produced up around Great Slave Lake. He certainly wasn't going to hurt the cause if he held up.

And so far he'd been a pleasure to travel with, and when he talked he exuded authenticity. You could tell he was determined to climb back up from the bottom he'd hit. He was truly terrified of booze, wouldn't sit at a table with it. But a couple of times already, after some antagonism or sniping from a Philadelphia audience, or just because of some creeping inner debasement, you could tell he wanted a drink. He exuded that, too.

"We'll check on him," Stuart said.

He drove back to Sarah Nichols's place in Westchester. Sarah was a lawyer for the Clean Air Council. Her home, which she'd opened to them for a week while they politicked, was on the fancy side and artsy, with framed things on the walls and gold faucets and a baby grand. Stuart hated to think of William out at the Valley Budget Motel, but William had a violent allergic reaction in his one night at Sarah's, probably to the cats, but maybe to the poodle, the parrots, or the snake.

Sarah wasn't yet home. Marta opened two beers, and she and Stuart sat in the dining room, leaned on the table with both elbows, and drank from the bottles.

"We'll win," she said.

He shook his head. He had loved her for some time, but until this trip he hadn't really appreciated the strength (he still wasn't sure whether it was a strength of depth or blindness) of her faith. The Republicans had the votes to pass the energy bill right now. How was it going to shake her when they did?

"I'm not sure the nice red-headed man got the point about West Sak," he said. They'd tried to convince the two *Inquirer* editors that oilmen were going after ANWR not because they needed it but because they wanted to grab it before it was legally locked up as wilderness. The real key to maintaining North Slope development lay in another, bigger oil field that the industry was trying to keep under wraps. The West Sak field, on 260 square miles of state-owned land just west of Prudhoe Bay, held an estimated 15.0 to 25.0 billion barrels of untapped oil, compared with an estimated 3.2 billion barrels beneath the arctic refuge. And because of the locational and geological differences between the two fields, West Sak oil could be produced profitably at prices of $18 to $25 per barrel, whereas profitable ANWR oil production was predicated on a barrel price of $33.

Marta thought it through. "I don't know what else we could have said."

"Just seemed like it wasn't what they wanted to hear."

She looked at him out of the tops of her eyes. "Licked, are we?"

He smiled at his beer bottle. "It just wasn't a real good way to start the trip."

"Remember Montana?"

He looked up from the beer, surprised at the shift. Last spring in conservative Butte, within sight of one of the biggest open-pit mines in the country, they'd thought they might be tossed out of town. But after the talk, an old redneck came up and clapped their shoulders and said, "You folks keep it up," and a couple of other miners with him nodded, and one of them said, "Amen." And the old man said, "You want to see how they keep their promises, you go look at our hole."

And in Great Falls they'd given their talk in an outdoor amphitheater on a brisk, clear, darkening evening, standing with their backs to the brink of a sheer cliff and listening to the warm applause sweep past them like leaves crackling on a breeze, out and down into the wide Missouri Breaks.

"You do win some," he said.

Early Sunday morning, he drove a few blocks to the Acme grocery store at which he'd been buying *The Inquirer*. This time, the editorial was there: "To Conserve or Drill?" He went to a coffee shop and read it. It was a good, two-barreled piece, calling the new energy bill "a gussied up version of President Bush's national let-the-market-do-it, conservation-be-damned energy proposal." Spending money on the development of wind and solar power, it said, made a lot more sense than sacrificing snowy owls, bears, caribou, and the last remaining strip of undisturbed Alaskan arctic coastline.

Stuart wanted to whoop. He allowed himself a grin. William Greenland would like this. If it hadn't come too late. After the *Inquirer* visit, William hadn't been too anxious to continue the tour. He'd moped in the motel until they dragged him out to eat, and you could tell by the way he perspired and rubbed his hands down his jeans that he was close to losing the fight.

Stuart checked out the sports page to see how the Twins were doing in the series, then drove to the motel. He folded the paper so that the editorial page faced up, and went to William's door, where he got no answer to his knock. He knocked again, waited, then turned the knob and walked in.

William was stripped to the waist and was on his knees in the dim room, his dark skin glistening. His hair lay full on his damp back, not yet gathered into the workaday ponytail. The room was full of smoke. Stuart reached toward the light switch, then realized what was going on and left the room dark.

A red bandanna was spread on the dresser in front of William, and on the bandanna a small bundle of Hay River sweet grass smoldered in an ashtray. An eagle feather lay on either side of the tray. "To balance the power," William had told Stuart on their first morning together. It was a daily ritual. William was praying.

He finished, dressed, read the editorial. He looked at Stuart. *"Mussi-cho,"* he said. Thank you. He took a deep breath. "So. What we got next?"

"A Quaker high school."

"A what?"

"They don't call themselves Quakers; they're the Society of Friends," Stuart said.

William Greenland smiled. And just like that, in that subtle change of atmosphere, he won his battle; his smile broadened until his cheeks pushed his round glasses up.

One day last summer, twenty months after the stay in Philadelphia, I visited Marta. When her dog saw me, he stopped smiling and pinned me with those ice blue eyes. "Melozi," she said, and he sat beside her, his head higher than her waist. She kneaded the fur between his ears, and he looked through me as she and I talked.

Stuart was off surveying for the BLM on grizzly-infested Kayak

Island in the Gulf of Alaska, but Marta was still in the thick of the running battle over the Arctic National Wildlife Refuge—the battle of the beauty and the beset, she called it cheerfully—and I told her I was impressed that neither her enthusiasm nor her optimism appeared to have faded a shade.

"I'm glad it shows." She said she wasn't always so high-spirited about ANWR's prospects, but I had caught her at the right time. "I just got back from a trip to the refuge that was the best stress counseling I've ever had."

It had been the week before, she said, late June. Where the Aichilik River tumbled out of the Brooks Range, she had left the watercourse to climb the rocky face of a 2,000-foot hill. The river flowed north; as Marta climbed she could see it sinuating out among the spring green of the arctic coastal plain and ten miles or so across the plain to the Beaufort Sea. It took her almost an hour to pick her way up the steep, treeless slope, and when she walked out on the hill's pebbly crest, she could look ten miles out to where dark veins of water angled through the sea ice like words cracking a white page. Around her feet, a quick breeze made short, whispering swipes through the branches of a few stubby bushes of dwarf willow and bearberry. Beyond that, the world was silent. Somewhere down there was the group of photographers she had left to wander around on their own for a while, but even they weren't in evidence. Nor were there any mosquitoes, or caribou, or helicopters, or birds, or bears, or musk oxen, or foxes, or wolves. But she knew how life could teem into here and just as quickly swarm away. She had stood high like this before and watched the throngs of caribou, and the pedaling lope of wolves, and the bursting flocks. The plain below was a maze of game trails like cue marks on a stage, telling the company where to plant, where to turn. She knew that beneath and beyond her perception it was all there, all the wild world pacing in the wings. If she could read that runic folio on the far ice, she might know what the wild world should say.

She unbuttoned and slipped off her green chamois shirt so the breeze would cool and dry the T-shirt underneath. She sat on a clump of moss and sedge, clasped her knees, looked outward to take it all in carefully, and with a not quite startling recognition, realized that she was looking out at the repository of her soul. You pick the place for your soul to live, she realized; and in return it replenishes your spirit, inspires your hopes, shapes your tastes in music, and defines your Eden. It was moist out there, and lovely and vulnerable and rare.

For some moments she felt uncomfortable about thinking this way, as if she had violated the rules. She was a biologist; during the three years she'd worked here for the U.S. Fish and Wildlife Service, she had sacrificed just such subjectivity as this in order to maintain a professional objectivity. It was interesting work, at times even thrilling now that she looked back on it, but at the time it was as if she was saving the beauty for a later, private appreciation and was bound by some code of bureaucratic honor to collect the facts that would, as a result of a five-year baseline study mandated by Congress, qualify or disqualify this place as paradise.

And even that wasn't so bad until the work was corrupted. At first you worked under the assumption that of course this was paradise, and assumed that you were doing your small part to prove it so. Then came the tricklings of disbelief as the agency people began to alter data, omit data, and hide data, so that the facts you were collecting were being skewed to the side that wanted to drill for oil. At first, although the meddling was obvious, it didn't seem particularly dangerous—just tinkering with reports, mainly—the dropping of a word here and there or the modification of a phrase. The word *core* was taken out of a draft environmental impact statement so that the final report, instead of reading "core calving area" just read "calving area," so that if you read it you didn't know that the oil development would be right at the heart of the calving grounds for 180,000 animals. And instead of telling Congress that the drilling activity might eliminate 40 percent of the musk ox herd, the report was changed to say only that musk oxen might be displaced.

But then it started to get worse. While analyzing the final year of data, Marta and her co-workers were told to skip the rest of the analysis and just do the final report. And once the final report was done, the U.S. Fish and Wildlife Service didn't open its findings to public comment as was required by law but just started taking out paragraphs to which oil industry lobbyists objected. And when the House Interior Committee's Rep. George Miller wondered just how accurately these environmental impact statements were predicting things, and ordered Fish and Wildlife to assess some old ones—the ones that were done during the sixties and seventies as projections of how North Slope oil development and construction of the Alaska pipeline would affect the environment—the agency obeyed but realized after the assessment was done that some of it would be damaging to the campaign for oil exploration so tried to bury it until congressional debate on the issue was over. The biologists who worked on the assessment were ordered not to talk about it, but one of them, Pam Miller, violated the gag order, gave the report to Congressman Miller, and lost her job.

You started to feel dirty being part of it, being *used* to violate the public trust, and watching the agency twist your data so that your name lent credentials to lies.

Two years ago she left the agency, and a year ago she crossed over to the other side. She was offered the job as director of the Last Great Wilderness Project, and in that year she watched the Alaska Coalition grow to more than 200 organizations from throughout the country, and in the wake of the oil spill watched the upwelling and outpouring of public wrath against corporate deception reach a heartwarming crescendo last Halloween when Rep. Paul Johnston's House version of the giant Bush-backed energy bill—the bill that would have opened ANWR to oil explorations—went down to defeat. Even after all the public anger in the wake of the spill, the development people had almost gotten their way. They had made all those promises again, and their lobbyists had lined up plenty of votes, and things were looking so bleak for ANWR that one day Marta stood in a Senate Building rotunda and cried. What had triggered the tears and her impotent rage was a chunk of tundra that had been flown in on ice for a $16,000 display sponsored by the oil companies and the state of Alaska to show the harmony between development and arctic wildlife.

But then the oil people had cut their own throats. To Marta, it seemed that their anxiety to keep a tight lid on any activity that might be construed as questionable had backslid to paranoia. Another series of Interior Committee hearings chaired by George Miller just before the vote on Johnston's bill had revealed a bumbling series of possible oil spill cover-ups and documented cheap shots at opponents. Amid the indignation, Johnston's bill went down.

Then, after the vote, Marta had the satisfaction of seeing Johnston himself standing at the same place where the pro-development people had put that chunk of tundra, shaking his head and saying he'd never seen the voters so intense about anything in his life.

Now, eight months later, the public thought it was over. The money had dried up. Marta had spent the past six months writing fruitless grant proposals to keep the ANWR project alive, because if someone didn't watchdog all the shenanigans that were going on even as she sat here on this hill, we'd lose the place yet. The pattern was always the same: the corporation executives were contrite; they said they'd learned a lesson; they were new people, they said, more sensitive to the environment than were the good old boys; and now, in response to those terrible disasters of old, they'd developed miraculous technological capabilities that could handle any possible problem.

During the war with Iraq, they said that ANWR oil was vital to national security. Now that national security was not at risk, they were saying that ANWR oil was vital for jobs. "Massachusetts has a lot of people out of work," said the full-page ad picturing a sad-looking young couple, the wife pregnant and the husband jobless, that someone had sent Marta from the *Boston Globe* just last month. "ANWR will create 750,000 jobs—45,000 of them for Massachusetts!" State by state the ad listed the jobs: food service jobs, Styrofoam container production jobs. . . . Nowhere did it even say what the acronym ANWR stood for. Nowhere did it say that the oil companies' own geologists predicted only a one in five chance of finding any oil at all, and that even if they found the maximum amount hoped for, it would fuel American autos for only a few months.

How soon we forget.

But Marta had faith. Five years ago, when biologist and world sled dog champion Glendon Brunk had confided that he was about to give up on his dream to put together a road show that would tell the world the truth about ANWR, Marta had sent him her favorite paragraph from Goethe. And four years later, when Marta took over the project herself, the paragraph was still there, tacked to the wall over the director's desk:

> The moment one definitely commits oneself, then providence moves too. All sorts of things occur to help one that would never otherwise have occurred. A whole stream of events issues

from the decision, raising in one's favor all manner of unforeseen
incidents and meetings and material assistance which no man
could have dreamed would have come his way. Whatever you
dream, you can do; begin it. Boldness has genius, power, and
magic in it. Begin it now.

Her optimism was so unshakable that sometimes she felt it was just
blind ingenuousness. If so, it worked; it was strong and sustaining. She
knew that millions of hearts were in the right places. Honest people could
get results; you just had to help them remember that all good word wasn't
the last word.

What had this place done to deserve to die? Nothing, of course. Like
so many places that have died, if it died it would be because it had
something we wanted. Not even something we needed, just something
we wanted, and not much at that. Just a few more weeks on the freeway,
a few more miles behind the wheel.

A sudden, stiff, cold gust rocked her, made her shift her feet for
balance. She moved to sit in a pocket of quiet air where the wind washed
up over a large gray stone. As she leaned back, taking in the view, she saw
a high white curtain shimmering like an enormous wall of ice over the
Beaufort Sea, forty or fifty miles out. Marta squinted, disbelieving, trying
to reshape the white bluff into something that should be there. And then
she recognized it for what it was: *Innipkak,* the Eskimos called it—a
summer mirage so common up here that the Eskimos paid it little heed
unless, as sometimes happened, a city or mountain range rose slowly over
the northern horizon on a warm, clear day in July.

She watched, fascinated, remembering from somewhere that if the
mirage was only here or there on the horizon it foretold a shift in wind
or a change in weather, whereas if it encircled the entire sea horizon, as
it did now, the weather would continue mild and warm, and the breeze,
as it was against her right cheek now, easterly.

She half-dozed. Easterly. Her Gwich'in friend, William Greenland,
was over that way somewhere, along the Mackenzie Delta or maybe on
the shores of Great Slave Lake. She wondered briefly how his struggles
were going, and whether he had a place like this to go and feel like this.
She thought about Stuart, bushwhacking with a BLM survey crew down

along the shores of Prince William Sound. She thought about the Athabas-can fiddling festival dance where they had met. When she got through here, and he got through there, they'd go back to the cabin, the Grayling Hilton, for some time alone. It had been so long, it seemed, since that utterly silent and lovely long night. Things had been so busy. Her memory was full of noise.

Once she was an art student in Europe. And then she was an idealist, back at the books. Occasionally she would sit on the shore of Umbagog Lake in Maine, drinking Yukon Jack, playing the guitar, listening to loons, and talking with friends about Ed Abbey, not yet realizing that as a biologist she would, as do most biologists, soon be playing the games of bureaucratic funding, following the money from death knell to death knell, trying to keep one form of life after another—birds, mostly, in her case: peregrine falcons, bald eagles, ospreys, spotted owls, and the very loons she so loved listening to—from disappearing off the face of the earth.

She missed Stuart. She missed the travels with him, missed watching his honest, awkward manner with the audiences around the country that got her adrenaline pumping along with his, and the long, calming rides across open spaces. She missed the trapline cabin and the time with him alone.

But for the time being, this loneliness was enough. It felt good to air all the years out up here. It felt good to have flip-flopped careers and points of view. It felt good to be a professor's daughter from Palo Alto, turned into a champion. And it felt good to feel so oddly guilty about feeling free.

BOOK III

Termination Dust

11

Haida Way

It is as if here, finally, the dream of frontier America must face itself.
There is nowhere else to go, and it may be that deep down we are afraid
that it is already a failure so enormous that we have no words for it.
This furious industry over the face of the land is a distraction, and in
the end it will hide nothing.
                    —John Haines, "The Writer as Alaskan"

My son's godmother, Dolly Garza, prefers to see herself as a Native in a reviving, not a dying culture. She's going to revive it come hell or high water. During those years of our nonchalance, Dolly was not nonchalant. She was reascending, pulling herself up, and trying so hard to help pull up her people too that those natural tragedies that so disrupted our white lives seemed to her just the foreseeable consequences of the status quo. What had been done to the Haida and Tlingit nations for centuries had simply caught up to the water and the trees.

Correspondingly, Dolly was more pragmatic than we in her reactions to the knells we began to hear from the last of the continent's rain forests, and to the clogging of Alaskan oceans with oil. She didn't miss a beat; she just kept fixing.

And during that four-year sweep that had for the rest of us begun with an oil spill and led from anguished reaction through long months of anguished wrangling, Dolly had begun with less and ended with more, managing her days deliberately in ways that would strengthen her people and her prospects. She wasn't out to teach anyone anything, but in her handling of those years I found obvious lessons, and value in her careful stewardship of identity.

★ ★ ★

I had seen her the autumn before the spill, in the village of Craig on Prince of Wales Island, where I went whenever I could afford it to fish for steelhead and cutthroat trout. Dolly was over from Baranof Island to chair her local Native corporation's annual meeting. We'd become fast friends and confidants years before when we worked together for the university, and we still made it a point to swing by whenever one of us was in the other's neighborhood.

I found her between sessions, sitting with her uncle, Pat Gardner, in the Haida Way Lounge at a window table overlooking the waterfront. She sipped at a glass of Miller Draft while the older man palmed a white stoneware cup of coffee. She looked glum. The harbor looked dead. A few boats rocked at anchor, but there was no bustle about them. All the commercial fishermen had wrapped it up for the year. The locals had battened down the hatches, and the outsiders had headed south. Shaan-Seet Inc. had taken advantage of the lull to wedge its annual meeting between the end of salmon harvest and the beginning of winter politics.

Her dourness wasn't what I had expected. Usually she took on a glow when her relatives and all her old friends collected this way. I stood back, letting her finish a piece of conversation with Gardner.

"So who voted how?" Gardner asked her. "Who switched their vote?"

Gardner was a handsome man, graying at the temples, a strong ally of his niece on the often factionalized Shaan-Seet board of directors. As I was about to find out, Dolly had just lost her bid for a second consecutive chairmanship of the board. The vote had gone to three ballots. The twelve members split evenly on the first two, then requested the two nominees to speak to their positions. On the third ballot, Dolly lost to Jerry Mackie, seven–five.

"I don't know," she said. "I know how I voted. I better know how you voted."

Gardner grinned. "With all those women on the board, plus my vote, you should have won hands down." The directors had included nine men and three women until membership balloting the day before had replaced three of the men with Carla Yates, June Durgan, and Marjorie Young. The gender split was now fifty-fifty.

"Some women are more likely to go with a smart man."

"Maybe I should have run." Gardner watched Dolly's face as she returned his smile. Something, maybe in the smile or maybe just in the circumstance, prompted him to reach over and pat her arm. "You okay?"

"I'm fine."

"You should have won."

"Jerry's a better bullshitter."

Pat Gardner drained his coffee, then stood to leave. "Not better, just more aggressive."

"Is that it?"

"Take up boxing." He leaned over, kissed her cheek. "Knock him out next year."

Dolly stared out the window, letting her eyes flow with the gulls. The dining room in which we sat was full—many of her corporation's 350 members were in town for the meeting—and occasionally someone would wander over to say the same thing her uncle had said: she should have won.

"So otherwise how's it going?" I said.

"Well, I'm thirty-one and feel pretty much in command," she said. But, as usual when there was an interruption in the flow of her plans, she felt slightly skewed—not quite certain that her life was on precisely the right track. Not that she expected it always to be. Still, everything not being precisely right would be easier to handle if she could pinpoint what precisely was wrong. But today, as usual, the wrongness seemed to lie just outside the realm of definition, in the same old murk of being Native in a white world.

"You're just a kid," I said; "you've got a long time to figure it out."

From my perspective, Dolly knew both worlds and was rising rapidly through the ranks of Alaska's Native leadership because of her ability to function in both and bridge between the two. She was part Haida, part Tlingit, and a sliver of white. She had a master's degree in fisheries management from the University of Washington, was active in the Alaska Federation of Natives, had been selected a few years ago to join several other rising young stars for special training through the Alaska Native Leadership Program, and had been given a United Nations assignment to share the details of the Alaska Natives' successful land claims movement with other indigenous peoples from throughout the world. She worked for the University of Alaska as a biologist with specialties in marine mammal management, subsistence, and aquaculture—three issues that were, in certain circles, as politically hot as how Alaska's Natives were treating the 44 million acres of land (and the $964.5 million in cash compensation) awarded to them under the Alaska Native Claims Settlement Act of 1971.

As part of that settlement, every Alaska Native was given the opportunity to become a shareholder in two corporations: a local Native corporation plus one of the thirteen umbrella regional corporations created by the act. Thus Dolly Garza's 350-member Shaan-Seet (a Tlingit word she interpreted for me as "pass to the future") Corporation was among some 200 village corporations founded sixteen years before to conduct the land claims business.

The Natives' repossession of their ancestral lands had been both blessing and curse. The settlement act gave the corporations it created twenty years—until 1991—to come up with ways to turn enough of a buck to protect their assets. After 1991, the assets—the land and its resources—would be more tax liable, and each corporation's privately held stock would go public. To Alaska's 52,000 Natives in 1971, 846 acres and $18,548 for every Native man, woman, and child seemed like a lot of assets, and twenty years seemed like a long time. But during the past few years, with unhappy shareholders rumbling about selling out when they were allowed to, the prospect of losing Native holdings in public stock sales loomed ever larger. Some of the corporations had panicked themselves to the brink of bankruptcy with poor investments spawned by the advice of well-paid consultants eager for Native money. Others had just as naively tried to liquidate their assets to benefit shareholders in the short run, hoping to keep them happy enough to hold on to their stock.

Because in Southeast Alaska the land's primary resource was timber, the liquidation philosophy there had precipitated massive timber sales and clear-cutting operations that had left some corporations bereft of any marketable timber at all on tens of thousands of acres. Resource economist Gunnar Knapp predicted that all 550,000 acres belonging to Native corporations in Southeast Alaska would be logged well before the turn of the century.

"No village corporation has attempted to follow a 'sustained yield' approach in its timber harvesting," Knapp wrote in a 1989 report called *Native Timber Harvests in Southeast Alaska*. "Most of the village corporations will have harvested all of their merchantable timber within a ten-year period from when they began harvests, approximately one-eighth the period of time needed to produce marketable volumes of timber on second growth stands in Southeast Alaska."

Dolly's own corporation felt that a sustainable yield rotation harvest was not possible, in large part because the 23,000 acres allotted to each corporation, if divided by a regrowth cycle of sixty years for spruce and hemlock, wouldn't make enough acres available per year to attract logging bids. In addition, she told me, even the more conservative southeast corporations felt they had been forced to harvest annually despite the swings in market prices in order to generate enough cash to run the corporations that they were mandated by law to run. Administrative requirements of the settlement act had already cost her own corporation several million dollars.

The rationale for dropping every tree in a hurry was expressed in the 1984 annual report of one Native corporation, Kluckwan, Inc: "We have millions of dollars of timber on the stump and it is actually declining in value with each passing year. Even at an alternative rate of 10 per cent (which is easily obtainable for an investment of this size), we are missing out on millions in earnings as those dollars sit on the stump instead of in the bank. For this reason, we are harvesting . . . to turn our timber asset into cash assets which can meet both the immediate and long term needs of our shareholders."

High timber prices prompted some Native corporations to invest in harvesting equipment, securing the loans with a collateral of unlogged timber. But two years after the harvesting began, timber prices plummeted to less than half. Byron Mallott, president of the Southeast Alaska Native regional corporation, Sealaska, told *Anchorage Daily News* writer Hal Bernton that the value of lower-grade pulp logs had dropped so sharply that several corporations had simply left cut logs on the ground to rot. "We thought we were at the top of a mountain," said Mallott. "In fact, we were at the edge of a cliff and we all walked off together."

Instead of cutting back on their harvests, those Native corporations that had invested heavily in harvesting equipment had to log even more of the devalued high-grade timber in order to meet their debt payments. Even today, with not much of their timber left, Native corporation harvests accounted for about half of all Alaska timber harvests, even though the corporations owned less than a thirtieth of the timberland in Southeast Alaska (the 550,000 acres of Native timberland compare with 17 million acres of timberland in the Tongass National Forest).

Shaan-Seet, with much more prudent asset management than most, was one of the few village corporations that hadn't walked off that cliff with Byron Mallott. Shaan-Seet had, in fact, weathered the sink-or-swim plunge into the swift twentieth-century corporate current with relative success. The shift to corporate accountability had been traumatic, not only because most Natives weren't trained for it but also because it went against the Native grain. Until 1971, Alaska's indigenous Indians, Eskimos, and Aleuts lived what the whites call a subsistence lifestyle—one based largely on culture, tradition, wild harvests, and biological clocks. They were accustomed to dealing directly with the earth and the sea. Both the indirectness of corporate bureaucracy and the concept of a cash economy were—and in many cases remain—alien to Native culture and philosophy.

So far, Dolly Garza had been adept at hopscotching between worlds. She still went out to gather herring roe, picked and dried seaweed, and helped her mother smoke and can salmon. She tried hard to maintain her ties with the Haida culture. Yet she was relatively savvy, too, to the corporate ways of the whites. As a Shaan-Seet board member for the past six years, she had strongly supported the corporation's asset-sheltering permanent fund, which had already grown to almost $6 million, and (although she didn't yet know it) would almost double within a few years to more than $31,000 of mostly timber-earned money per shareholder.

As the board's chairman during the past year, Dolly had focused on streamlining operations and planning for long-term corporate success. "So you made a few saves, slicked a few deals, and turned a few profits," I said, and she glared at me. "That's what white people do," she said. "I'm just a careful planner."

She told me that the day before, during the general meeting when she was at the podium giving her annual and president's reports, there was a moment in which she looked out into the faces, the sea of kinship, and felt simultaneously a surge of pride in progress and despair of culture displaced. She felt it happening as she spoke, an entire people moving closer to an obligatory sophistication.

What was it she was telling them? About NOLs. Net operating losses. She was talking about selling the corporate losses in order to make money. As of last year, the federal Tax Reform Act allowed Native corporations to sell their operating losses to other corporations looking for bigger tax write-offs. During the past year, Dolly's board had negotiated the sale of Shaan-Seet's timber harvesting losses to Wall Street magnate Michael Milken's firm, Drexel Burnham Lambert, for about $10 million. Dolly was telling her audience that the Internal Revenue Service almost certainly would challenge the amount of the losses, and because it would take several years for the IRS to audit the corporation and render decisions, it would be probably five years before the Shaan-Seet shareholders would know exactly how much they'd made from the sale.

Suddenly, almost lost in her own maze of language, she'd had a moment when she feared that all her talk of accountants and legislation and corporate law was losing her audience, too. But when she looked out over the faces, she saw comprehension. And it was then, seeing her childhood neighbors, and in their faces the character of all their ancient ways, that she felt those simultaneous tides of dignity and loss.

As Dolly told me all this, unburdening herself of the busy year, her eyes followed the gulls outside until, when she was finished, her gaze steadied on some far horizon.

I watched her reflection in the window. She was pretty. "You look wistful," I said.

"Oscar," she said.

With Oscar it was off again, probably for good. She smiled at me. "What do you expect? When you're too damn busy, your love life goes to hell."

She drew a deep breath. "But you don't have to like it. Being alone. I don't want to be alone forever."

★ ★ ★

Six months later, on that Good Friday when I was helping Stu Pechek haul wood for his equinox bonfire, and Roger Kaye was flying up the Coleen River, and David Grimes was shoveling into a snowbank looking for his pickup, Dolly Garza was spending the day in a boat with her brother Pat.

The oil spill wouldn't affect her the way it did us who were more northerly and white. She was way south of Alaska's oil problems, down in the archipelago 1,100 miles southeast of the Arctic National Wildlife Refuge, 700 miles from Fairbanks, 500 from the wreck of the *Exxon Valdez*. People would talk about the spill down there, but theirs were fishing villages and logging towns. Oil was most important as it affected fish and timber, and in this case, with the herring and halibut and salmon seasons all gearing up, the talk would be about the number of fish lost in Prince William Sound, and whether the losses would be boon or bane to their own livelihoods.

But Dolly hadn't yet learned of the spill; on Good Friday she was in her little red skiff as it slapped along parallel to the Chichagof Island shoreline, just a hundred feet beyond the surf. The thirty-horse Mariner burred at a businesslike three-quarters throttle, pushing the sixteen-foot boat at about twenty-five knots. The speed was just enough to make Pat Garza nervous, but only because he didn't know the local water and wasn't at the wheel. "It was my boat," Dolly said as she told me about the day a few weeks later. "Even when I bucked a trough, he knew enough to keep quiet. If he complained, I'd speed up."

Dolly remembered the day and said she thought about it often, but not for the same reasons I did. "You tell me that it woke the white world, or at least some of the white world, from an apathy to which it had been lulled by its own greed. I think about the day because it represents how I was headed in the opposite direction from all of that. I had decided to go back, as much as I could, to our old ways—to go out and get my food myself. Not just any food, but the foods we had developed as a culture, and which had become such a part of our ways of living: the seasonal rhythms of it, and the clothing it required, and the various skills of preservation, and the menus, and the social events that were outgrowths of the seasonal ripenings. . . . All that was coming back into my life, the same as it had been coming back into our culture as a whole. We had begun to reacquaint ourselves with the past.

"And there is so much more to it even than that, because once you attach yourself directly to the earth—once you begin to draw your sustenance directly from it, rather than being twice or thrice removed from what you eat and wear—you have to pay more attention to the way you are treating it. You have to watch it closely, to make sure that others don't abuse the sources that keep you alive. As a culture, pay collective attention to the sea, to the forests, to the populations of animals and birds that provide you with furs and meat. You don't pay attention to those things only as a matter of conscience or recreation or aesthetic appreciation. You pay attention to them because they are your life. They are what you eat and what you do. And if anyone else is sneaking around messing them up, for reasons of greed or power, or even just because of an uncaring obliviousness to their value, they aren't going to take you by surprise. You know about it right away, as an individual and as a culture, and, as both, you stand right up to fight. And you know exactly what you are fighting for."

Her skiff that day was mounded high with green hemlock branches, which Pat Garza had come over from Ketchikan to help Dolly anchor in some secret spots up the coast. If it was a good year, schools of spawning herring would deposit thick, gelatinous layers of eggs on the flat hemlock needles; the Garzas would harvest a few hundred pounds of the stuff, and the family would be set for another year.

I've watched Dolly at the helm. She's small, so she always sits very erect, her head high, scouting forward as she skirts around flotsam and tangles of kelp, her shortish black hair whipping in the wind, a bow spray misting back into her face. She usually wears a fixed half smile, and I assume that on that day it was the same, because it was the kind of day she'd hoped for: no local squalls, just the milky curtains of some distant showers out among the islets of the archipelago and sunlight raying through the clouds. "I remember thinking, 'If it stays this way, we'll see rainbows toward evening when the sun drops low,' " she said. "Have you ever been out on the water among the rainbows? On Good Friday, yet. It was a day of high promise."

Just north of town and offshore from the airport runway, Dolly cut the throttle back so she could nose through a kelp forest without wrapping fronds around the propeller shaft. A few otters lolled among the bobbing stipes, cracking crabs or clams on their chests, watching the boat, lackadaisically wary. Dolly watched them, then looked overboard, down through clear water to where long banners of the big sea vegetable undulated in shadow and shafts of light.

Herring like to spawn on kelp more than on hemlock branches, and, because you can eat the kelp as well as the roe, the succulent roe-on-kelp is by far the preferable table crop. But the giant kelp—*Macrocystis pyrifera*—is at the northern edge of its range here around Chichagof Island. As soon as the herring spawned on this particular bed, there'd be a swarm of subsistence reapers out here reaching down with garden rakes and grappling hooks to pull it aboard. Because *Macrocystis* grows so sparsely this far north, however, the state would let you gather only 32 pounds per person, or 158 pounds per family.

Kozonoku kombu, the Japanese call it. When the university had sent Dolly to Japan a few years ago to research Japanese market preferences involving Alaska's five species of salmon, she incidentally found the Nippon islanders ritually addicted to herring roe. In Japan, a holiday dinner without *kozonoku kombu* is like turkey without cranberry sauce, or a potlatch without smoked salmon. At the $35 a pound paid for premium roe, the annual per family subsistence harvest in Alaska would be worth more than $5,000.

Whereas one Alaska family's subsistence allotment might satisfy a hundred Japanese, it isn't enough for the typical Haida or Tlingit household. Coastal Natives eat herring roe with just about everything. Salted or frozen it keeps for months. On kelp it is eaten mainly raw, like pickles, whereas roe on the inedible hemlock branches is dipped into boiling water, which releases the eggs in gelatinous sheets. The eggs are cooled and mixed with salads, or finger-dipped into eulachon (candlefish) grease, seal oil, soy sauce, or butter.

Dolly and Pat Garza planned to snag their 158 pounds of roe on kelp. But for their family's purposes, they'd need a quarter of a ton or so of herring roe, and they hoped to harvest the larger amount from their hemlock sets, on which the state imposed no limit.

Of course there was no surety that the swirling gray clouds of spawning fish would find any particular bundle of hemlock anchored in shallow water. Dolly Garza tried to salt the odds, though—ironically by availing herself of technology, not tradition. For the past week, she'd been attending the Department of Fish and Game's daily briefings for fishermen. As the herring spawning season approached, the management agency conducted regular aerial surveys to track schools of the eight-inch fish as they meandered shoreward from the open sea. The biologists also made regular test sets with nets to catch samples of herring, which were weighed to determine what percent of their body weight was roe. As the roe percentage went up, the briefings were more alertly attended, both by local subsistence harvesters like Dolly Garza and by commercial seiners who netted ripe but unspawned herring for export to Japan, where the sac roe was a staple but vastly less expensive item than roe on kelp.

Around Sitka, harvest success or failure among subsistence harvesters usually boiled down to who guessed right about whether the schools would move into the spawning shallows north of town or south.

And when. The timing was important. If the hemlock branches were anchored too soon, they could become coated with tidal debris that contaminated the adhesive egg clusters. And of course, if the branches were anchored too late, the fish had already come and gone.

That year, Dolly had decided—by guess, by golly, by technology, by tradition—that it was going to be north of town and within a few days. So that afternoon she turned the university's Marine Advisory Program booth over to Dana and met Pat at the city dock with a handsaw and a big roll of nylon line.

"You're sure," he said.

"Sure enough."

Pat was fairly sure the herring would spawn to the north, too, but he was, after all, a brother. "You're pretty cocky," he said.

"It's my boat."

A few miles beyond road's end, Dolly swung the skiff toward a small timbered bay with moderately steep banks. There wasn't much hemlock there, which was one of the reasons she'd picked that spot two years ago. Of all the green branches ashore, the herring would spawn only on hemlock—never on cedar or spruce. Science didn't know why that was the case, but the Natives had known it probably for aeons, and that's why there isn't much hemlock at the good spots. It's already been cut; you have to bring your own.

Dolly anchored. It was almost low tide. The herring like to spawn just seaward from the intertidal zone, so that was where they'd sink the branches, in about six feet of water.

She and Pat cut the boughs into lengths of three to six feet. They tied the ends of several branches into a bundle, tied the bundle with nylon line, and weighted it with a rock, then tied the line off to a boulder ashore. They worked easily, bantering, gossiping, sinking half a dozen bundles at this first site, then hauling in the skiff's anchor and heading another mile or so up the coast.

If they were lucky, in a few days or maybe a week, they'd be back, pulling in their half ton of roe from along this stretch of coast. They'd ship waxed crates of it to relatives in Ketchikan and Craig, and to Uncle Dennis Demmert in Fairbanks; and Dolly would send some to a friend, Aurora Kramer, up in Kotzebue. Even at that, they wouldn't eat all of it during the coming year. They wouldn't sell it; that was against the law. But it made a great trade item. A lot of Natives throughout Alaska who attended school here in Sitka—at either Sheldon Jackson College or the Native high school, Mt. Edgecumbe—developed a taste for herring roe and gladly sent things in trade for it that the Garzas couldn't get locally—caribou, for instance, or certain kinds of furs for skin sewing. Sometimes, too, they'd trade it locally for a good catch of the day. Shrimp, maybe. Or crab.

Dolly eyed the sky. The weather was holding. She didn't open the throttle yet but idled the boat forward to get through a rocky stretch. From the bow in front of her, Pat looked back at the site. The ropes were pretty well camouflaged—you didn't want to invite poaching—but he shook his head anyway.

"What's wrong?" said Dolly.

"I bet they go south."

"So take the boat south, make all the sets you want."

"Good. Now?"

"Tomorrow. Today we do what Dolly says."

"Because it's Dolly's boat."

"You got it."

★ ★ ★

A year later, Dolly's deliberate vision took another turn.

I saw only the beginnings of it, when I dropped by her second-floor Sitka office and caught her musing down on what she said she figured to be about 9 million tourists in sweatshirts. It was going to be a rare rainless day, a gift shop owner's dream; already the sun was up over the 4,000-foot peaks of The Sisters, trimming back the island's cold westerly shadow, and burning off an overnight mist. Colors were popping out along the curved thoroughfare. It was amazing how the old Tlingit village and onetime Russian seaport could transform from dull to quaint with just a little dab of sun. Down the street, where the steeple of the Russian Orthodox church got the first rays, you could tell what mood the day would be by looking to see whether the blue steeple was bleak or bright.

Dolly looked from the window to the letter in her hand and read it again. It was from Carolyn Thoroughgood, dean of graduate studies at the University of Delaware, and it was Carolyn Thoroughgood's pleasure to accept Dolly into a doctoral program in marine policy.

Delaware. She looked at the blue letterhead. *Newark?*

She stepped out into the Marine Advisory Program reception office, where her assistant, Dana Pitts, and a federal wildlife biologist from down the hall, Bill Hughes, were having coffee.

"Where's Delaware?"

"Back east," said Dana.

"But where?"

"By Connecticut, I think," said Bill.

"On the coast?"

"I think so," said Bill.

"By New York?" Dolly poured herself a cup of coffee. Dana left the room as if she'd just thought of something, and Bill shook his head and laughed. "We really should know this stuff, Dolly."

"How about Newark?" said Dolly. "I thought Newark was in New Jersey."

"It isn't?"

Dolly looked at him. "You are a very ignorant colonial boy, Bill Hughes."

Dana came back in. Somewhere she'd found a flat map of the United States, which she spread on the conference table. Bill Hughes scrunched forward to peer, then jabbed a forefinger. "Here."

"That's nowhere near Connecticut," said Dolly.

"Going to Delaware?" asked Dana.

"In August," said Dolly.

"For a conference?"

"No, for a year."

Back in her office, she stood looking out beyond the small town, across the spruce forests and the bright Pacific. This was her ancestral home; she felt in her bones the pull of its strong tides and the shapes of its thick boughs and steep mountains.

"I don't like the thought of being away for a year."

"But you've decided."

She turned from the window. "It's just a matter of getting used to the idea."

She would go as a matter of conviction, she said, which it seemed was the reason for most of what she did these days. Her seat on the board of her Native corporation, her activism with the Alaska Federation of Natives, her lobbying for the rights of indigenous peoples worldwide, her memberships on panels and boards and committees, her writings and talks on subsistence and aquaculture were all products of her belief that if her people were not part of the solution, then they would be part of the problem.

In the case of Delaware, her conviction was that a doctoral thesis in marine policy might be a good way to leverage a change in the way fish counters and politicians divvied up Alaska's seafood harvest. It was big business. Twenty-five percent of the world's renewable oceanic protein lies within the 200-mile Exclusive Economic Zone off Alaskan shores. The annual take was 200 million metric tons and $2 billion—and, right now, who got to take what was decided not on the basis of intelligent policy but as a result of political pressure applied to the biomass.

It was going to be a hard albatross to knock off the mast. Ever since the fish wars of the forties, when murder, bribery, and the abuse of tens of thousands of Native and Oriental cannery laborers finally resulted in the federal interventions that led to statehood, the allocation of Alaska's marine resources had been an annual major naval engagement. Political string yanking was fierce among the competing user groups—primarily the commercial, subsistence, and sport fishers—and every year, as the competition intensified, the bad blood got worse.

As Dolly Garza saw it, her people, Alaska, and the nation all stood to lose if fisheries politics continued to dictate the allocations. The resource managers—biologist–fish counters such as herself—recommended the divvy of salmon, halibut, herring, crab, and other maritime assets based on how much they thought was out there. But politicians decided which user group got how much, and politicians, too, could override the numbers recommended by resource managers. (For state waters—within 3 miles of shore—the allocations were decided by the state Board of Fish, which took recommendations from a system of local advisory panels. On the federal level—from 3 to 200 miles offshore—the harvest quotas were fixed by the North Pacific Fisheries Management Council.) Within the past two decades, several of Alaska's most important fisheries—king crab, red shrimp, and rockfish—had been wiped out or severely depleted by a combination of weak biology and strong politics.

Pressure to inflate the harvest allowances, as well as competition among the user groups, intensified each year. High allocations were made with regularity, almost always on the basis of the biologists' lack of proof that there weren't more fish out there than they estimated.

It had been a destructive progress. "And if it's ever going to turn *con*structive," Dolly told me, "progress will have to be on the basis of solid policies rather than fickle politics."

And what were the solid policies? How did you determine the fair share of salmon, for instance, among commercial fishermen who contributed that $2 billion a year to the economy, and sport fishermen who contributed $100 million, and subsistence users who contributed not a penny? What was the formula for balancing the value of pleasure or cultural tradition against money?

"I don't know," Dolly said. She stood a moment longer at the window, then said, "But I'm going to find out," and left the window, went to her desk, and dialed her mother in Ketchikan. She was agitated;

she pushed the speaker phone button and paced as she told her mother about the doctoral program.

"So *far*," her mother said.

"It's the only place that can teach me what I need to know."

"Delaware," said her mother. "Is that on the coast? I won't have any way of picturing where you are."

"How would you like to go with me? Just for the trip. A vacation."

After a brief silence, her mother said, "I'd have to fly back alone?"

"We can drive. I'd like to have my car back there. I need help, though; I need a copilot. You could help me find an apartment, take Amtrak back to Seattle, and the ferry home."

Her mother thought about it. "This is pretty sudden," Dolly said. "Maybe you ought to take some time and we can talk later."

But her mother had had all the time she needed, and now she said, "How far is Delaware from Atlantic City?"

In July the following year, 1991, Dolly was back in Alaska. She had written her thesis and would soon defend it before her committee. She had a plan for fair resource allocation—or at least part of a plan, and the ambition to put it to work. She was anxious on all fronts but was tired, too, she told me on the phone, and needed a break.

"I think I'll go to Ketchikan for a while," she said. "To my mother's. They'll be putting things by, and I could use some of that kind of work for a change."

Putting things by. Even before her mother opened the front door, Dolly told me later, she knew that the Garzas were smoking fish. The yard was saturated with the rich odors of smoldering alder and freshly butchered red salmon—not a ripe fishiness but the clean, meaty scent that a salmon has when it's fresh.

Five minutes later, Dolly was strapping on an apron next to her grandmother, Elizabeth Gardner, who was cutting a batch of freshly smoked fish into canning-size strips while her mother, Myrna, handled the pressure cooker and the pint and half-pint jars. Dolly's brother Pat was out on the back porch cleaning three or four dozen reds—maybe 200 pounds of fish.

It was accidental but perfect timing, Dolly dropping in for a quick visit between a Shaan-Seet committee meeting in Craig and a plane ride back to graduate school in Delaware. The flood of pungence and family memories had caught her off guard, she said, as she told me of it later. She was surprised at the acuteness of sentiment that a year of cultural deprivation in Delaware had inspired. One of her first thoughts, as she slipped back into the comfortable chattiness that had for decades risen like yeast in that small cube of womanly space between the stove and the steamy windows and the sink, was that they used to *have* to do this. They used to eat clams and cockles and fish and deer because they were poor, and now they did it for joy.

"I can't believe it. You're a godsend," said her mother.

Dolly laughed. "And I know just what God sent me for."

It was the drippy draping job, the same messy chore she and her sister had always been stuck with and never particularly enjoyed when they were kids, cutting the freshly filleted salmon into strips, soaking them in brine, then draping the strips over dowels in the smokehouse. The dowels, several across and several down, were up high to get the benefit of the rising smoke, and, because the smokehouse was such a tight space, you had to drape the dowels up near the ceiling first, then work your way down, the brine from above dripping into your hair, onto your clothes, down your neck.

She stood watching for a few moments longer, her gaze lingering first on her mother's apprehensive manipulation of the pressure cooker (all the years Dolly was growing up, Myrna Garza had refused to use such a potentially explosive contraption, holding out in favor of a hot water bath), then on Gram, who with her deft knife work was on her turf and in her glory, still kitchening for her kin through four generations.

"How is the weather in that place you're at?" said her grandmother.

"Hot and muggy."

"A good time to be here, then."

Dolly glanced out the window, down past the traffic on Tongass Avenue at the edge of the water, and across Tongass Narrows to the flashing red and white lights at the airport on Gravina Island. Through the steamed glass, it was easy to imagine Christmas. But this was a rare summer day here, crisp and clear in a town that averages almost 200 inches of rain a year.

"Was it like this in Craig?" asked her grandmother. Dolly recognized it as a hint. Elizabeth wanted to know what had gone on at the committee meeting.

"Nice, but not this nice." Dolly paused an appropriate few seconds. The meeting in Craig had been of the corporation's 1991 Committee, so named in reference to the year that Alaska's Native corporations were to lose the twenty-year tax-free status they were granted to give them time to set in order the assets they'd gained as part of the Alaska Native Claims Settlement Act of 1971. The committee business had been a bit on the frantic side lately, as its members tried to figure out how the corporation was going to pay taxes on its investment profits from the $100 million and 23,000 acres it got as part of the settlement act.

But even in the midst of its agonizing leap into the corporate fast lane, the Shaan-Seet board and the traditional village councils within its boundaries had maintained the interests of tribal elders as high priorities. Recently they'd found, in distributing dividends and benefit packages to the tribe's 317 corporate shareholders, that if the benefits were provided as monthly cash payments, the benefit amounts were subtracted from the elders' state and federal pensions.

"We talked about the benefit problem," Dolly told her grandmother. "The lawyers tell us we might be able to beat it. If you get the cash all at once, right at the end of the year, it will impact only one month of your pension rather than all twelve."

"So is that what we're going to do?"

"Maybe. We're still working on it."

Her grandmother nodded complacently. *Trustingly,* thought Dolly. She wondered at what age you stop feeling obliged to manage the affairs of your people and start letting them manage yours. Soon enough, she figured.

She stepped out the kitchen door to where her brother was cleaning the fish. The rear porch, with its eight-foot-long worktable, was only partially enclosed and had a translucent corrugated roof that transmitted a warm yellow glow. Pat prided himself on his reputation as a good fish handler. He was meticulous with them, and even more adept with the knife than was his grandmother, handily, almost artistically, splitting each salmon and filleting out the backbone and ribs with minimal loss of meat. Unavoidably some of the deep red flesh was left on each carcass, though, so he cracked the backbone in such a way that it, too, could be hung on the dowels to be smoked as a snack.

Dolly stepped up beside him and started slicing the fillets into strips for hanging. "I bet you think I'm a godsend too."

"You going to hang fish?"

"What else?"

"You're a godsend."

She cut the strips and let them slip from her hand into a five-gallon, white plastic bucket of brine and seasonings. Pat had laid some skeins of eggs from the ripe females beside the meat, and Dolly slipped those into the brine, too. They'd be canned and used in soups and salads, or stirred into scrambled chicken eggs for breakfasts. From the dozen or so ripe females he had cleaned so far, there were maybe two dozen of the one-pound skeins, which are held together by a thin membrane. Pat had removed the skeins carefully, but a few of the fish had been so ripe that the eggs had spilled out anyway and lay strewn like glistening red pearls among the meat.

Another of the plastic buckets was filled with fish that had soaked in the brine long enough, so Dolly lugged that one out through the small backyard and its tangle of salmonberries to the smokehouse. It was a small building, about four feet by eight, and only seven feet high, unlike the big outdoor racks ten or fifteen feet tall that you saw along the salmon rivers of the dry interior. Along the humid coast you couldn't dry fish outdoors, and you had to have a building small enough that the smoldering coals would keep the humidity out.

She ducked into the smokehouse and inhaled the delicious, oily tang that lingered around the blackened wood that had lined this small room for so many years. It was one of her grandmother's smokehouses—Dolly remembered three of them, side by side—over on Prince of Wales Island.

When her grandmother got too old to fill them all with her own fish, Dolly's brothers had loaded this one into a pickup and brought it on the ferry to here.

No coals yet smoldered in the fire pit. The brined fish would hang overnight to take on a good glaze before the fire was lit; otherwise, the finished product would be mealy.

Dolly moved aside the wire mesh rack that hung below the doweling to catch any falling fish. She maneuvered a small stepladder into place and wrestled the bucket onto the top of the ladder. She sighed and reached into the bucket of cold brine.

She used to feel enslaved doing this. She and her sister, trudging from smokehouse to smokehouse, sticky-haired and tacky-skinned. They put up a lot of fish back then, maybe a ton a year, because it was the main food for ten people, and they gave cases of it to widowed aunts and other elders, and traded some for furs that they used for skin sewing. There were six kids in the family, but Dolly and her sister were stuck with this, the worst of the chores, because the four brothers got to do man stuff—catch the fish, chop the wood, and take turns at the old arm-cramping can crimper.

It hadn't been all bad, though. The hanging of the fish was just the drudge-end of an annual week or ten-day Fourth of July expedition that Dolly had actually looked forward to as a girl. There had been an air of excitement about it, the boys smuggling their fireworks aboard the ferry for the trip from their mainland home in Ketchikan out to Prince of Wales Island, the aunts and uncles and cousins all funneling toward the grandparents' place, then everyone piling aboard the uncles' and cousins' seine boats and heading down the island coast to Deweyville, the elders talking on the way about old ways and old fishing holes, then the hauling of the nets and the camping on the beach and the fireworks, and then piling back aboard the seiners, all of them talking while they gutted and headed the fish during the ride back to Gram's smokehouses at Craig.

The families couldn't get through the winters without the wild food, and they handled it in such bulk that most families would have been hard-pressed to process it alone, and the elders certainly couldn't. They canned wild asparagus in the spring, and picked berries to freeze and make jams with, and harvested clams and cockles, and in addition to the five species of salmon, they brought in all the other kinds of fish—the eulachon for rendering oil, and the big slab-sided halibut, and the rockfish as bright as calico cats—and in the fall the men did the killing that they took most seriously as *killing,* taking the sloe-eyed, fall-fat deer from the mossy, spruce-dark slopes outside of town.

It brought families together and cultivated a feeling of interdependence. It took you close to the earth and close to the sea, where you handled life and death through all its colors and textures and aromas and seasons, and you came away with a sense of wholeness that you took to your table and to your trade and to your sleep.

It was something they had to do then, and she wished they would do more of it now.

They didn't have to now, of course, and because of that a lot of people would like to see the Native rights to subsistence harvests reduced or taken away. Every sockeye salmon Dolly's brother caught was a fish less for a sportsman or a few dollars less for a commercial seiner. The sportsmen didn't need to catch the fish in order to live either, of course, but they spent big bucks to do the fishing, and it was the economics of the thing that threatened the cultural value to which Dolly's people clung.

Two years ago, the state supreme court had ruled that it was unconstitutional to grant subsistence rights only to Natives, or to regulate toward a rural preference. Subsistence rights were for all or for none, the court said, and for the past two years the state had allowed them for all while the politicians scrambled to come up with a philosophy that didn't alienate the subsistence users, the sport fishers, or the commercial harvesters.

So what were the answers? In two days, Dolly would be back in her little hole of an apartment in Newark, Delaware, trying to figure out, for her doctorate, how in the affairs of state to go about dividing all the fish.

Reaching to hang a strip of flesh she paused with a chuckle, wondering just how such an ambition could have blossomed from a tortured girl in pigtails, muttering darkly in a smokehouse some twenty-odd years ago over on Prince of Wales.

Prince of Wales Island is where I saw Dolly last. She was seated at the same window table she had shared in defeat with her uncle three years ago, watching the gulls over the Craig waterfront, the breezy gray sky, the seiners rocking at dockside. When I slid into the seat opposite, she was looking across a few hundred yards of water to Fish Egg Island. She glanced at me, and back at the island, and said, "One of my great-aunts is buried over there." That's the way it is with Dolly when you see her, even after a long absence, your showing up in the flesh is just part of a continuum, a carnal version of something that's always there. "And we used to have a spring camp there for putting up fish," she said.

Her roots were here, right here; she could feel them anchored in the aeons. It is possible, she realized, to dream back through time in your native place in a way that is not possible for you elsewhere. In Delaware, whenever she looked up toward the hills on the other side of White Clay Creek, she could see nothing, either in the slow push of the stream or the lazy flow of the piedmont grass, of that countryside's movement through time. The figures of its history took no shape. But this place here, this high archipelago with its bowing, beckoning spruce and its broken ocean, this place gave you such a clarity of vision into the headwaters of your blood that you could grow your grandparents right back into their footprints on that path just there, the one down to the bay.

Dolly smiled at the vision, then shifted her woolgathering back into the dim interior of the Haida Way Lounge. It was busy; she'd be joined by a bunch of well-wishers soon.

"I look forward to the company of old friends," she said, and she said she felt very good. She felt at the top of her game. She'd have to go back to Delaware for one more semester of doctoral study, but she felt today as though the grind was already behind. A few minutes ago, over in the Commercial Building at the long table in the small room, twelve men and women had cast their scrap-of-paper ballots and she was reelected chair of the Shaan-Seet board. *That* was coming home.

She sipped from her iced Diet Coke and smiled at the reputation that had got her reelected chairman of the board three times since that tie-breaking third-ballot defeat in 'eighty-eight. No-nonsense Dolly. Efficient and to the point. Stuck to the agenda, got the work done, never tooted her own horn. Spoke up and didn't take any shit. Advocated firmly and planned decisively. And *had* a plan. After that defeat three years ago, she realized that she had to have a plan.

And as she began to chart a course, she realized that her greatest strength—or perhaps more accurately the best foundation on which to build her strengths—lay in that same ability to see through time that enabled her and all her people to summon their forebears back to the paths outside their windows. It was a vision that linked people to place to choice; and if you weighed things that way, against the test of time, you could tell pretty quickly whether something fit. The choices were not always easy, but they were always clear. You forgot about all agendas but those of your people. You forgot about today. You weighed the effects of the alternatives on the resources upon which your culture was built. You opened yourself to see into the fourth dimension of your people, so that you could sight aft and fore along the continuum to collect and project the wisdom of the ages. You carried the right things forward.

Doctor Garza, blooded brown, credentialed white, a woman of the hour. Nothing to it. Instead of five-year plans, you transacted your business by the design of the last and next millennia.

A figure in shadow at the bar end of the lounge caught her eye.

"Know him?" I said.

"It's not *him;* he's in British Columbia," she said. But something in the Tlingit bearing of this one reminded her of that one, and again her reverie shifted, this time to affairs of the heart. Just yesterday, in Vancouver, for the first time, they'd spoken of marriage. Absently, as if to arrest a blush, she picked up her frosted glass and held it to her cheek.

Leona Casey, the Shaan-Seet executive secretary, slid into a chair next to Dolly. "Congratulations," she said. And then, "It's really good to have you back."

Dolly blinked, set down her glass. "It's wonderful to be back," she said.

12

Soulcraft

"You mean, there is a senator for all this?"
    —Gary Snyder, "The Wilderness"

"If you have a passion for this place, it will carry you at some point beyond the personal to the public; and at that point, the power leaves your hands."

Rick Steiner was trying to explain to me why a feisty little man named Chuck Hamel was a hero. A worm in the side of big oil, his name had wriggled up regularly as I turned the mulch of Alaskan crisis, and now he was front-page news. In order to pluck him out, the Alyeska Pipeline Service Company had hired one of the world's largest detective agencies—the Wackenhut Corporation—to conduct an elaborate excision.

The months-long sting had involved more than a dozen agents, sham offices and personnel in Florida and Virginia, a fake environmental champion, and a seductive blond. Almost unbelievably, six of the agents assigned to the case had abruptly blown their cover, defected to their target's side, and were now telling all to California Democratic Rep. George Miller's Interior Committee. The latest testimony was almost comic, detailing how the detectives had maneuvered a child's remote-control all-terrain through the garret of an office complex in order to plant a microphone above Chuck Hamel's head.

Who was this guy Hamel, what did he have to do with Alaska, and why did big oil want to bring him down?

"It's power," said Rick. "Chuck has become very good at oil bashing in Washington. He has access to the right information, and to a lot of legislative ear. He knows the press, leaks major stories, maneuvers big oil into situations it can't manipulate. The oilmen have to play defensive ball, and they hate it."

So he was an environmental lobbyist?

"No." Rick grinned. "He hates environmental groups; says they're all money grubs, lovers and leavers, never stick to anything they start. Chuck's a bulldog, never lets go. And an ax grinder. He used to be a millionaire oil shipping magnate. He says Alyeska cheated him by pumping water into his tankers along with oil and ruined his business. I believe him. Says British Petroleum cheated him too, and says he'll sue, and sue, and watchdog these guys until he brings them down."

"Big order," I said.

Rick shrugged. "He can document costing them about $500 million so far. He proved that Alyeska wasn't treating its toxic wastewater properly and forced the company to build a new treatment plant. He broke the news that the Alaska pipeline had serious corrosion problems, and the company has had to kick off a repair program in the hundreds of millions of bucks, decades before it planned to. Just the other day he broke a story claiming that Exxon tankers were illegally dumping toxic wastewater off the coast of Florida."

"Which explains the cloak and dagger," I said.

"Begins to. There's a lot more."

"Such as why so many trails out of Alaska lead to Chuck Hamel's doorstep?"

"My trail leads there because he gets results. On this Exxon damage settlement, he's done more than all the environmental groups put together. Period. A hundred-something groups have endorsed what we're trying to do, and the weight of all that opinion has certainly helped. But not one environmental lobbyist in Washington has applied any pressure that has cost Exxon a dime."

"And Hamel has."

"Many dimes."

"And beyond his own vendetta, why would he want to help anyone else?"

"You mean a bedfellow green as me? Different motivation, but same goal. He wants restitution, we want restitution; and the only way either of us is going to get it is to nag the American conscience into doing something about Exxon. We do some of the legwork and load the gun. He pulls the trigger.

"Besides, he's a nice guy, and I think his heart's in the right place. He just doesn't have patience for anything less than ruthlessness. You play to win, and if that means you get bloody and bad, you get bloody and bad."

"So how long has he been doing this?"

"Years. Ten, maybe."

"Pays for it himself?"

"So far, but he's in serious trouble that way. Lost a house, cars. . . . He's got investments, but, good lord, his phone bill runs a couple of thousand a month. More. That's why he got suckered by the Wackenhut bunch so easily. They told him they wanted to help and had money, told him they represented the collective environmental conscience of a bunch of rich lawyers."

"And he fell for it."

"And got mad, and got even."

"How do I meet Chuck Hamel?" I said.

Rick looked puzzled. "But you have."

And as soon as I saw him, I remembered. It was that day in Valdez when David Grimes had crawled under the magistrate's table to fall asleep listening to his tape of children's chants from Papua New Guinea. Hamel had been the pugnacious little man who kept popping in and out of the oil spill cleanup headquarters. I had wondered about him—a presence perspiring, sixtyish, small and quick who had kept arranging: for a fax machine, for phone lines, for temporary living quarters, and even for a new office. But I hadn't paid much attention. For some reason, I had the impression he was a lawyer for the local fishermen's union.

"A lawyer," Chuck Hamel said. It was mid-December 1992. Hamel maneuvered around a Christmas tree that took up a third of his living room and motioned me to a beige sofa. A cut-stone coffee table in front of the sofa was strewn with loose documents, and with three-ring binders full of papers.

"I don't know what could have made me think that," I said.

"I hope it wasn't something I said."

"I'm certain it wasn't."

"You don't have to be nice," Hamel said, "you have to be a good writer. Rick says you're good."

"Rick is often nice when he doesn't have to be."

"He's also honest. Do you know Allana Sullivan?"

"No. *Atlanta?*"

"Allana." He spelled it. "She writes for *The Wall Street Journal*. Look at this; last month, front page. With a picture. *The Journal* never runs a picture. I trust Allana; she does a good, accurate piece. And I also talk to a few others I trust. Not many. Bill Coughlin, *Boston Globe?*"

"No."

"Patrick Lee, *L.A. Times?*"

"Afraid not."

"The Alaska guy, Richard Mauer?"

"I know Richard, sort of." He was with the *Anchorage Daily News*.

"He's a good man. How much of my time do you need?"

"Somewhere between five and fifty hours. Depends."

"I mean today. Can we start with three?"

"Three's fine."

"Good. You like steak?"

"Sure, but—"

"No buts. There's a great little house right down the block. We'll talk, I have to make a couple of calls, and when Kathy gets back this evening, we'll eat."

Within minutes, he was one more man telling me about what he was doing the day of the oil spill, three years before. He knew precisely, he said, which is pretty much what everyone I knew would have said. But Hamel wasn't Alaskan. He was from down at the other end of things, where people have their hands on the bungs and stopcocks that control the flow of federal decision about a place most of them have never seen. Chuck Hamel's talk of Alaska came from that southerly, spigoted perspective. You could feel the power in it, the domination.

To one who had spent a decade up in the relatively guileless outland, it was scary.

Pushing 8:00 P.M. on that March 24, he had picked up the phone, dialed, paced to a window, and looked out across the Potomac to the Capitol. Dusk always softened the place, an evening mist rising up to blue and blur the clean, hard lines of Capitol Heights, like a puff of magician's dust hanging there while the legislators did their disappearing act.

For years now, Hamel had watched across the river from this window while he talked on the phone, sometimes six or eight hours a day, waging war on the Alyeska Pipeline Service Company, which, he said, had cheated him out of a fortune. His office was in his home in Alexandria, Virginia, up a tight spiral staircase to the blue carpet, white cupboards, and white furnishings of the fourth floor, which had a wrought-iron rail at one end, where the floor looked out over the living room. When he was working Hamel seldom sat and almost never when he was on the phone. The four in his office had long cords, pacer's cords, that reached even to the bathroom down the hall.

Up in Cordova, Alaska, the phone rang three times, four. Hamel fidgeted. He worried about Riki Ott. "You're single?" he'd asked during their first telephone conversation, some months back. "In a log cabin out in the boonies in a place that gets twenty feet of snow?"

"Yes, and yes."

"Why?"

"I'm trying to write some children's books. This is a good place for it."

"You're not crazy, then?"

"I don't think so. Not yet."

Hamel had met Riki Ott through Rick Steiner, who told him that in addition to being president of the local fishermen's union, the young woman had a master's degree in oil pollution studies and a doctorate in sediment toxicology—and had been collecting sediment samples near the Alyeska pipeline terminal "with some very interesting results." Rick also told Hamel that Ott was "a real scrapper. You give her a dollar, she'll give you five hundred dollars' worth of effort." A month ago, at Hamel's

urging, she had come to Washington to testify at House Interior Committee hearings chaired by Congressman George Miller on allegations that the
pipeline service company had been intentionally discharging toxic sludge
into Prince William Sound. Hamel had invited Ott to be a houseguest
during the hearings and found her both delightful and as feisty as Rick's
report. In Miller's office one day he saw her confront Congressman Dan
Beard with the warning that a major oil spill in Prince William Sound was
not an *if* but a *when*.

Since that visit, Hamel had telephoned her every day. She was almost
family now, and one of Hamel's two or three strongest allies in his
campaign against Alyeska. In her role as union president—and because of
her terror that the 756 million gallons of oil arriving in Valdez through the
Alaska pipeline every day were a catastrophe about to happen—Ott had
persuaded the membership of the Cordova District Fishermen United to
become maritime minutemen, on call to mobilize all 600 of the community's fishing vessels to go help clean up any oil the moment it spilled.

With her local fleet convinced of the danger, Ott was now working
on John Devens, the mayor of Valdez, the pipeline terminus sixty miles
from Cordova at the head of Prince William Sound's Valdez Arm. On the
heels of a 72,000-gallon oil spill in Port Valdez by the British Petroleum
tanker *Thompson Pass,* Devens had appointed a committee of inquiry and
invited Ott to address its first meeting. "I'm calling it my *Not If but When*
speech," she had jotted on a copy faxed to Hamel that morning along with
a request for comments.

And now, after five rings, she picked up. Hamel glanced at his watch.
It was four hours earlier there, three o'clock. "So how's it going?" he said.

"I'm afraid it's not, Chuck."

"What does that mean?"

"Two feet since last night, and still snowing hard. Unless it quits in
a hurry, Stan won't be able to fly." Valdez is at road's end, Cordova sixty miles beyond. During heavy storms, no one from Cordova goes
anywhere.

"Damn!" said Hamel. "Just when we got Devens!"

"All's not lost," said Ott. "They've set me up for an audioconference
at the community college. If it hasn't cleared in a couple of hours, I'll ride
my bike down there."

257

"In the snow?"

"They're keeping the roads clear."

Hamel wasn't much relieved. "Well, it's better than nothing. It'll have to do."

They talked for a while, about the high points that Ott should cover, and about her boyfriend, Dan, who was in New Mexico, scheduled to have knee surgery tomorrow (and would be waiting for sympathy in vain. When the oil spilled, Ott would be so occupied, she'd forget to call). Then Hamel, who never said good-bye or see you later, said to Ott, "You be careful in that storm," and hung up.

He stared out across the Potomac. A full moon beamed through the mist, the reflection of it a rippling and hazy path across the water. Ironically, Mayor Devens's first choice for a speaker tonight had been an Alyeska representative, but the pipeline company had declined. Hamel had heard that Alyeska President George Nelson and the company's chief executive in Valdez, Chuck O'Donnell, were in Anchorage this very moment hosting a dinner party to congratulate their staff on successful cleanup of the *Thompson Pass* spill.

Hamel glanced down at the copy of Riki Ott's talk, which he was mildly surprised to find still in his hand. "Given the high frequency of tankers into Port Valdez, the increasing age and size of that tanker fleet, and the inability to quickly contain and clean up an oil spill in the open water of Alaska, fishermen feel that we are playing a game of Russian roulette.

"When, not if, the Big One does occur and much or all of the income from a fishing season is lost, compensation for processors, support industries, and local communities will be difficult if not impossible to obtain . . ."

The woman's conviction of impending disaster was contagious. After nine years of dueling with big oil, Hamel felt a new urgency, an ominous motion, as if things were beginning to swirl toward the mouth of a funnel. He was half eager, half afraid.

His wife, Kathy, had sensed the absence of bustle from Hamel's office. She climbed the spiral staircase and went without speaking to the pullman kitchen to put ground coffee and water in the brewer, which was set for 7:00 A.M. Then she crossed the room to Hamel and, as he slipped an arm around her, stood beside him looking out across the capital night. "The cherry blossoms are almost gone," she said.

A year later, Chuck Hamel drove from his home in Alexandria along the Potomac toward what he felt was going to be a dream come true.

He found the place easily enough—an upscale office complex in Crystal City out near the airport—and within minutes was standing outside the glass door of a corner office, appreciatively reading the corporate logo. *Ecolit,* it said, and underneath was a green earth surrounded by a white ring containing lettering, which Hamel leaned forward to read: *Treat the Earth Well.* Not particularly creative, but gratifying. Ecolit, he knew, stood for Ecological Litigation—a coalition of attorneys championing the environment. It was as if they were heaven-sent. Here he was, his ten-year fight against the Alyeska Pipeline Service Company suddenly churning into a wild tornado, a hemorrhage of oil company whistle-blowers flooding his doorstep, whistle-blowers whose corroborated stories of environmental regulation violations had cost the oil companies almost a billion dollars so far, and him running out of money, no longer able to carry the fight forward—and voilà! Out of nowhere steps Ecolit, an outfit tailor-made to tackle just the sort of wrestling match he'd been outmatched in. And to think he had never heard of Ecolit or its Dr. Wayne Jenkins until a couple of weeks ago, and them right here in the neighborhood. If they turned out to glow half as brightly as the reports he'd been getting, he would kick himself halfway from here to Sunday for not finding them sooner.

He scanned the office. The furniture was tasteful, conservatively plush. *Sierra, Wilderness,* and *Buzzworm* magazines lay in a fanned-out stack at one end of a coffee table in the reception area. Over the couch was a framed Save the Whales poster, and his gaze was just shifting toward a couple of other environmental-looking posters when around a hallway corner came tall, blond, and sexy Ricki Eidelson, smiling at him just the way she'd walked over and smiled at him and Rick Steiner in Anchorage two weeks ago. They'd been relaxing over drinks, he and Rick, at a Captain Cook Hotel lounge after a long day attending workshops at a Conference on Frontier Thinking. Ricki had seen the two of them at the conference, she said, and was looking for contacts as part of her job as a researcher for Ecolit. So they talked with her a bit; but the sheer blouse she was wearing, and the way she sort of sidled up close when she talked, made Hamel uncomfortable. Maybe he was just out of his element looking at a stranger's breasts during a conversation. Maybe. But the message in her dress and her manner seemed to him out of place at a conference on environmental issues in Alaska.

So he didn't talk to her much then, and now, watching her come toward the door to usher him in, he realized that her forwardness in Anchorage probably was due to her anxiousness about her new job, and to it being her first trip to Alaska and her unawareness that the fast lane moved a lot slower up there. If she hadn't just by chance sat directly behind him on the plane home, he would have missed out on Ecolit entirely. He probably would have come home and sunk.

But on the plane that day—it was amazing how chance can save us or sink us—she leaned forward, sad, saying she hadn't been able to make the contacts she was sent to make. Ecolit, she said, wanted to reach people whose stories would help outflank the oil companies in their bid to open oil exploration in the Arctic National Wildlife Refuge. She was a single mother of two children, she said, and now she had failed in her first assignment for Ecolit and was afraid she would lose her job.

So Hamel had given her a couple of names, and a week later he received a letter from Dr. Wayne Jenkins, staff researcher for the Ecolit Group, thanking Hamel for the names he had shared and proposing that the two men meet.

And thus the odd but sometimes pleasant and apparently serendipitous ways that doors are opened. "Chuck," she said as he walked in. "I'm so glad it turned out this way—for all of us." Her hand reached out to cup his elbow and steer him toward an office door. "Dr. Jenkins is so anxious to meet you."

The man inside the office was maybe forty, handsome, tanned, and neat—so very neat that, although it was after lunchtime, he looked as if he'd just shaved, buttoned his crisp collar, and tied a perfect overhand into his paisley tie. His hair was brown with a hint of gray, clipped fairly short and brushed back in the style of the day. His eyelids were heavy, giving him a somewhat somnolent appearance that was immediately dispelled by the quick and calculating appraisal Hamel felt from the gray eyes themselves as the two men were introduced.

Wayne Jenkins smiled. "I understand that we might be able to help each other."

"If you have the money to fight these kinds of fights," said Hamel.

"Enough, I'm sure."

Hamel shook his head. "What I want to know is where you guys have been for the past ten years."

And as Dr. Wayne Jenkins outlined what his group could do, Chuck Hamel began to feel a great falling away of accumulated pressure. Even as Jenkins talked he realized just how heavily had weighed the quickening flow of conscience-stricken oil company whistle-blowers who were trusting him, confidentially, to champion their claims. This doctor in Crystal City, Virginia, whatever kind of doctor he was, was the Emerald City wizard so far as Chuck Hamel was concerned.

But Chuck Hamel hadn't yet pulled aside the curtain. The man behind the Crystal City wizardry was not Dr. Wayne Jenkins but Wayne Black, head of covert operations for the Wackenhut detective agency. With 7,000 or 8,000 employees and net profits of more than half a billion dollars a year, George Wackenhut's company was managed mostly by former FBI agents whose staffs were in charge of surveillance and security at fifteen U.S. embassies and most of the nation's Titan missile installations, strategic petroleum reserve sites, and nuclear facilities. Wackenhut's poking, prying, and protecting was on behalf of countries more often than companies, but in important ways, oil transcends many nations, and this time, for the Alyeska Pipeline Service Company, Wackenhut was trying to stop the billion-dollar whistle-blowing by going after one man.

Like Dorothy's Wizard of Oz, Wayne Jenkins was a hope peddler and a liar. But all hope peddlers are dangerous, and Jenkins had a lot of muscle behind his curtain. The sting he had in mind would be, as Robert Hennelly of *The Village Voice* was to write eighteen months from now, a bit like hunting a gnat with a sledgehammer.

★ ★ ★

261

Hamel looked at his wife, Kathy, dressed all in black, her face clandestinely smeared with lampblack, as if she were some kind of spy or commando.

It was May 1990, two months after Hamel's meeting with Wayne Black aka Jenkins. Chuck was dressed and smeared the same way Kathy was, and he knew that the two of them—a stocky, sixty-year-old man and a willowy, fifty-year-old woman—would look absurdly funny to any friend who might happen by. But he was scared; this was serious. He hoped it wasn't deadly serious, and looking at Kathy, lovely even beneath the ridiculous costume, there was a moment when his heart caught and he almost backed out. If the most powerful corporate conglomerate in the world had, indeed, decided to do him in, what chance did he stand anyway? What was he doing placing this fragile, fiercely loyal woman in harm's way?

But the moment passed. He had been fighting these guys for so long, and with such a vengeance, that his fears lately had been just nagging echoes of the deep apprehensions with which he'd faced the corporate flak early on. The other night, though, when Muffin the apricot poodle whined and he stepped her outside for a midnight wee, he was so shocked at seeing the man rifle his trash, and then by the implications of it, that he was gripped by a fear that even the full heat of his anger had a hard time driving from his bones. Someone had stooped below the honorable to get him; these men watching him from vans and following him on his rounds were dragging the fight into terrible new dimensions. He couldn't be intimidated, though. Wouldn't. He had to control the fear, and do what he could to trace all this back to the oil interests that he figured were responsible, and find out precisely who was doing it, and why.

He checked his watch: a few minutes after eleven. "Well?" he said to Kathy.

Through the lampblack, she grinned. "Ready as I'll ever be."

They were in their bedroom on the third floor of their home in Alexandria, with the drapes drawn so that no one could see in. Chuck Hamel turned off the lights, and the two of them stepped from the room onto the mezzanine. Chuck glanced down onto the living room, where one soft night-light glowed, then led Kathy up the tight spiral staircase to his fourth-floor office. There, a thirty-five-millimeter Olympus and a video camera with battery pack were laid out on a round white table at the center of the room, both loaded and ready. Hamel moved toward them, then changed his mind and crossed to the window that overlooked the Potomac. Kathy came to stand beside him. The early-evening path of moonlight across the water was gone, but there was still an indistinct sheen from the noon-high moon, and the lights over on Capitol Hill were all aglitter. It was, as always, a stunning view.

So much had happened between here and there. For nine years— ever since he'd caught the Alyeska Pipeline Service Company pumping emulsified water into his tankers along with oil—Hamel had been hanging on to Alyeska as unshakably as a bulldog, dragging the company kicking and screaming to accountability for documented horror stories of dumping toxic sludge into Prince William Sound, spewing poisonous benzene into the skies above the sound, falsifying environmental reports to the feds and to the state Department of Environmental Conservation, lying in response to inquiries, abusing employees, and manipulating records. Painstakingly, Hamel had documented the charges through whistle-blowers within the company itself. In turn, he had fed the information to the House Committee on Interior and Insular Affairs, whose majority staff had, finally, agreed that it was time for a congressional investigation.

High time. Hamel smiled bitterly. Nine years, during which he'd lost an average of $2 million a year. The congressional committee wasn't to blame for dragging its feet, of course. Almost every ear Hamel had bent for the past decade had turned deaf. At best, he had been met with profound skepticism that the oil industry would knowingly pollute purity and bugger its own peons. And Hamel was well aware that he himself was often perceived as some in the oil industry characterize him—an extortionist with a vendetta, a pretty much wacko millionaire with eyes full of crocodile tears.

Even now that Congress was beginning to listen, the Alyeska people were maneuvering, frantically—and it appeared successfully—to delay any malfeasance hearings until after a congressional vote on the president's energy bill and its opening of the Arctic National Wildlife Refuge to exploratory drilling.

And the oil lobby did have the votes. *"They've got ANWR,"* Hamel thought, and shook his head. He believed that responsible oil development was in the national interest and didn't really care if they got ANWR eventually. But he wished he could stop them at least until they were forced to come clean. Corruption at the Valdez end of the pipeline, he knew, was fully equaled by corporate rot at the pipe's other end, 800 miles north. Hamel now had documentation that in 1988, when ARCO, Exxon, and British Petroleum executives were testifying to Congress that Prudhoe Bay was running dry, they were concealing the discovery, years earlier, of the billion-barrel Point McIntyre oil field directly under Prudhoe Bay's West End Dock. It was a concealment that Hamel figured had cost him personally tens of millions of dollars; for in 1989 Exxon, as his general partner in oil leases he partially owned under that West End Dock and elsewhere nearby, told him the wells were dry, and in a kindly gesture offered to buy him out. He sold, and a few weeks later the Point McIntyre discovery was announced.

Hamel sighed, heavily, and repeated, this time aloud, "They've got ANWR."

Kathy put her arm through his. "One step at a time," she said.

In the quiet, cavernous darkness of the garage, his heart began to pump fast. Earlier in the evening he'd parked the Lincoln across the street, facing north, the direction from which he had watched the ransackers come. He'd sent Kathy out to the car, where she sat now with her camera, in the black clothes and makeup, waiting. He doubted, again, that he should be including her in this. But she'd insisted.

The garage window was right above the spot where Hamel put his trash barrels out for collection. At four o'clock one morning he'd replaced the window with one-way glass, and it was that new glass he was standing at now, adjusting the legs on a tripod, sighting through the video camera to see where the tripod should be placed, aiming toward the lit intersection down the street.

And then there he was, half an hour early, the man dressed in black, racing around the corner full speed and directly toward the garage window. Hamel froze. He forgot that he was watching through the camera eyepiece and stood transfixed as the man moved, on the other side of the glass, to within a foot of Hamel's own face. The man thudded to a halt, raised both arms above his head . . .

He's going to kill me.

. . . and plunged his hands into the two trash barrels. He grabbed the sealed trash bags from each barrel, swung back toward the road, and sprinted toward a red sports coupe that was pulling over toward the curb, its trunk swinging open.

Hamel realized that the coupe was on the wrong side of the road. It pulled to the curb facing his own car, and its harsh white lights fixed on Kathy, sitting just as frozen as was Hamel himself, the lampblack glistening on her cheeks, the lens of the Olympus reflecting the headlights.

The driver of the coupe pulled a U-turn, paused for the man with the trash bags to dump them in the trunk and then jump into the front passenger's seat, then accelerated, tires screeching.

"Just like in the movies," thought Hamel. He saw, and recited to himself, the Virginia license plate number.

He was chagrined, deflated. He had tipped his hand without learning anything except a license number, which, when he later had it traced, turned out to belong to a little old lady over in Mount Vernon who owned not a red sports car but a four-door gray sedan.

He stepped from the garage and crossed the street to Kathy. He didn't yet know that the plate number, and the red car, and even the trash riflers themselves would pale to insignificance during the events of the coming months. It didn't feel like it right now, but he had just slipped the thin end of a wedge into an Alyeska crack. A couple of good blows and she'd split.

The Dinnertainment in Old Town Alexandria is just what it sounds like, a turn-of-the-century emporium converted to a restaurant with red-and-white checkered tablecloths and a pianist named Al Trotta, who is a three-time national ragtime champ.

On this Sunday evening, November 3, 1991, the Dinnertainment was closed to the public but open to forty or so members of a private party of strange bedfellows: Capitol Hill lobbyists, lawyers, and legislative aides;

corporate whistle-blowers; commercial fishermen; a clique of elite report-ers; and a knot of private investigators who had just blown the lid off an oil industry sting operation that got too dirty for their consciences and cahoots.

The event was to celebrate Charles Hamel's appearance this evening as the featured gadfly in a scathing *60 Minutes* report on the Alyeska Pipeline Service Company. Producer Richard Bonin was expected to portray Hamel's past decade as a one-man war that had cost Alyeska about $1 billion to eliminate environmental hazards exposed to Congress by Hamel.

To Chuck Hamel himself the gathering was not so much celebration as manifestation—a great big gong at the high noon of perfect timing: the appearances during the past week of front-page stories about him in the national press, his limelight tonight on CBS, the abrupt capitulation of the Wackenhut gumshoes who were supposed to have been bringing him to his knees, the defeat Friday of the president's energy bill, which proposed authorization of exploratory oil drilling in the Arctic National Wildlife Refuge, and the testimony scheduled tomorrow before the House Interior Committee by Hamel and the erstwhile private eyes against the Alyeska Pipeline Service Company. Everything Hamel had gadflied for the past ten years had come to this simultaneous rising up. He knew it was not the end of his story, and he was not going to get any of his $10 million in losses back this week or next, but it was a peak, and there had been few enough peaks in the last decade, certainly none as satisfying as this.

Hamel entered the restaurant beaming with goodwill and nervous energy, and with a *Wall Street Journal* bearing a front-page story on him and all the Alyeska shenanigans tucked under his arm. His wife, Kathy, steered toward Cordova's Riki Ott, but Hamel broke away and targeted a knot of reporters. He pulled the newspaper from under his arm, waved it under the nose of *The Journal*'s Allana Sullivan, and poked a finger at a highlighted phrase under Sullivan's byline and near a rare *Journal* photo-graph, this one of Hamel himself. Chuck Hamel, said the highlighted sentence, "is Rocky Balboa in a Mickey Rooney body."

"I owe you one." Hamel grinned.

Then he chummed with the other writers—Patrick Lee of the *Los Angeles Times,* who last Wednesday had broken a Hamel-generated story about an alleged ten-year conspiracy by oil companies to hide a major North Slope oil discovery in order to strengthen their argument for opening the nearby Arctic National Wildlife Refuge to drilling; Richard Mauer, whose piece had appeared just this morning on the front page of the 432-page Sunday edition of the *Anchorage Daily News,* chronicling the case of an investigator who turned double agent after becoming disgusted at what his firm was doing to Chuck Hamel; another *Daily News* reporter, Kim Ferraro, who had teamed with Mauer on much of the Hamel saga and was in town to co-cover the Interior Committee hearings that were to begin tomorrow; and William P. Coughlin, who'd been covering the Hamel affair for the *Boston Globe*. "All these stories," Hamel kept saying, "and the *timing!*"

He knew full well the timing was not coincidental. During the past weeks, as the battle over the Arctic National Wildlife Refuge built to a crescendo in the days before the congressional vote on the president's national energy bill, Hamel had carefully orchestrated his calls to the media about his claims against Alyeska and the eight oil companies that own the pipeline. He knew the oil barons wanted ANWR badly, so he'd been going for that, for the throat. He had cultivated stories so carefully that within the week preceding Friday's vote on the energy bill, major reports such as the articles by Sullivan, Lee, and Mauer appeared in virtually every metropolitan newspaper in the country. Allana Sullivan's front-pager alone, breaking as it did on Friday morning just before the House balloting, was "the straw that broke the ANWR vote," according to an American Petroleum Institute executive who telephoned Sullivan after the bill went down.

And Hamel had saved a few bullets for the coming week's congressional hearings, too—among them, allegations of oil tankers routinely dumping toxins off the Florida Keys and charges of illegal eavesdropping on telephone conversations by Wackenhut investigator Wayne Black and his electronics expert, Rick Lund. During the congressional hearings, Lund would plead the Fifth. Black, who when the sting operation first came to light was promoted to vice president in charge of all undercover operations in a show of faith by corporation President George Wackenhut, would be questioned in secret session and wouldn't say whether he pled the Fifth or not. He would, however, resign shortly after the hearings.

But that was all to be tomorrow's news. For tonight, these events and these people were enough, and Chuck Hamel wandered among them from knot to knot, grateful and satisfied.

Leaving the reporters, he scanned the guests and sensed discomfort from a group of seven who were off by themselves and looking a bit furtive. Hamel headed for their corner. He considered them an amazing, humbling company of candor in the midst of all this guile, a group of former investigators with the Wackenhut Corporation who said their concerns about improprieties and illegalities ordered by Wayne Black had turned their loyalties. Hamel hadn't dug them out; they came to him, the big former cop Gus Castillo coming first and explaining to Hamel that he was flabbergasted that some of the nation's biggest corporations and the 8,000-employee Wackenhut Corporation were "putting out so much effort against one guy, and him such a nice little underdog like yourself."

It was too much for Castillo's conscience. He quit and talked, and his capitulation inspired an exodus. With him at the Dinnertainment table were David Ramirez, who planned to testify tomorrow about what he was convinced were Wackenhut's illegal electronic surveillance methods, and four of five women who the Hamel crowd now refers to as Charlie's Angels. The four, who were involved primarily in tracing Hamel's phone calls and womaning the counterfeit Ecolit offices in which Hamel was wooed by Wayne Black, posing as Dr. Wayne Jenkins, were Ana Contreras, Sherree Rich, Adriana Caputti, and Mercedez Cruz. The fifth Angel was Ricki Jacobson, the tempting blond who, as Ricki Eidelson, had approached Hamel and Rick Steiner in an Anchorage hotel in a see-through blouse and with a soft, enthusiastic, and convincing endorsement of Dr. Jenkins and his fake group of environmental attorneys. Although she was now in Hamel's corner in terms of House committee testimony, Ms. Jacobson had deemed it prudent to hire a lawyer and not mingle.

Hamel tried to make the investigators feel comfortable with some light talk, then used a beckoning forefinger like a shepherd's crook to pull over Tom Carpenter and Louis Clark of the Government Accountability Project—a legal aid program for whistle-blowers—not only because he hoped they'd put the newcomers at ease but also because he suspected the investigators might be needing GAP's services.

"These are the heroes," Hamel told Carpenter, "the good guys. A few more like 'em, we wouldn't have any crooks."

"I don't feel like a hero," said Ana Contreras. "I feel scared and out of a job."

Carpenter nodded sympathetically. "Most of the brave people we meet—including Chuck Hamel—are just victims who have turned to fight."

Hamel left them talking and returned to his rounds, mingling with a cluster of Democratic congressmen's aides, then moving on to a table where two of his attorneys, Billie Garde (a tenacious woman who went to law school to regain custody of her children, then graduated into a national reputation as the activist-lawyer responsible for shutting down the Hanford nuclear plant), and former Alaska Attorney General Doug Baily, were leaning into an earnest discussion with their chairs pulled close. He chatted with them for a few minutes, reiterating his resolve that not even under the threat of a jail sentence for contempt would he reveal the names of the Alyeska whistle-blowers who had been providing him with documents. "But I'm not going to plead the Fifth, either," he said again for maybe the fiftieth time since the attorneys had begun to give him strategy advice for tomorrow's hearings. "There's nothing in this mess that will tend to incriminate me, and I'm not going to give anyone the illusion that there is. I'll answer their questions in detail, *all* of them, except any question about the identity of a source."

Then he moved on to one of those sources, Robert Scott, an Alyeska whistle-blower whose identity Hamel already had leaked unintentionally during those hours of conversations taped by Dr. Jenkins. Bob Scott didn't look so good. The former quality control officer for Alyeska was big and flabby and florid, a prime candidate for the heart attack he would have within two weeks, and right now his emotions were priming him for it. He'd been fired by Alyeska at age sixty-four, just shy of retirement eligibility; he looked downright scared, his worried dark eyes searching the room as though for a rescue.

So Hamel rescued him, drawing him over to a group where two men and a woman appeared relatively relaxed. Scott glanced uneasily at one of the men, who sported a ponytail. "They look like environmentalists," he said. But Hamel said, "Nah. They're fishermen."

269

The trio were from Cordova: David Grimes, Riki Ott, and Hamel's son, Chuck Junior. They were environmentalists indeed, but not the "organizational" preservationists for whom Hamel had little use. Although the Charles Hamel case had been a key to defeat of the administration's proposal to drill for oil in ANWR, you wouldn't find Hamel hobnobbing with the Washington environmental muscle.

"The big environmental organizations are big business," he told Scott. "They're in the fund-raising business, and they tackle only the issues that make big bucks. Warm fuzzies are good. And clear-cuts. Things that are visual and stirring. Professional environmentalists are the Ed McMahons of the environment. They have to do a dog and pony show or they'll lose members."

Grimes and Ott eyed each other. They didn't feel precisely the same way, but they'd known for some years that Hamel's overriding interest in the environment was a way to get to the Alyeska Pipeline Service Company. They figured that his comments right now were more for Bob Scott's benefit than for their own. Hamel was, after all, an old oilman himself; he had explained to the Cordovans many times that his stance on the environment versus development was conservatively pro-development. Industry and a clean environment could occupy the same space, he felt; but whereas many developers had a reputation for paying only lip service to that position, Hamel's track record—as evidenced by that $930 million that CBS's Richard Bonin said that Alyeska had had to spend because of Hamel's watchdogging—was deadly earnest about clean development. Grimes and Ott had talked it over before; Hamel, they suspected, was a lot more of a nature lover than he let on, even if his feeling of kinship was limited to recognition of the wildlands as a fellow victim.

"We can't hope to get meaningful participation from the major environmental groups in something as insidious as mismanagement of the Alaska pipeline," he was saying to Bob Scott right now. "Of course the environmentalists fought construction of the pipeline itself; that was the dog and pony show. But you notice they never ask for—or want—an oversight role in any of these major environmental causes they espouse. Have any of them offered to take up your cause, Bob? Help pay your bills? No way. They either win in Congress or lose, and that's the end of it. In the case of the Alaska pipeline, the pipeline management has been guilty of hundreds of infractions of environmental laws and regulations, but you never hear a peep about them from the big environmental groups. Those groups got their asses whipped on the pipeline issue in Congress and never came back. End of story."

"People? People!"

It was three-time national ragtime champ Al Trotta. He rapped on his piano for silence and quickly distributed a single sheet of lyrics to each guest. As they read and clustered around, there were some bursts of laughter. Hamel found his wife, and they read the lyrics together while Trotta ran through a few warm-up bars to the tune of "My Bonnie Lies over the Ocean." And then all forty voices—those of the six unmuzzled Wackenhut sleuths, the half-dozen writers, the Cordova fishermen, the congressional aides, the Hamel lawyers, the watchdogs from the Government Accountability Project, and the staffers from the House Interior Committee—were all raised in unison to the tune of Al Trotta's lyrics:

You loaded my tanker with water
When it was supposed to be crude.
You put my phone under surveillance,
And taking my garbage was rude.

   Chorus:
      Al-yes-ka, Al-yes-ka! You invaded my privacy.
      Al-yes-ka, Al-yes-ka! You cannot intimidate me!

The Angels will tell at the hearing
Of Wackenhut's top-secret mob.
These women are honest and fearless,
That's why they're out looking for jobs!

   Chorus

Kathy has come out of hiding,
But Castillo might never come back;

271

And whenever I open my closet
I step on some asshole named Black.

   Chorus

The wildlife that's up in Alaska
Will thank me for all of my toil.
And when all the lawsuits are over,
I'll go back to brokering oil!

   Chorus:
   Al-yes-ka, Al-yes-ka! You invaded my privacy.
   Al-yes-ka, Al-yes-ka! You cannot intimidate me.

It was time for some hors d'oeuvres and *60 Minutes*. The Hamel choir redistributed from around the piano to around the big-screen television. They seated themselves at tables and talked shop until the time arrived, the kickoff commercial was over, and Richard Bonin appeared in a brown suit and peach-colored tie in front of a large mural of the Alaska pipeline under the caption "Plugging the Leaks." Bonin began:

"When the seven major oil companies built the Trans-Alaska Pipeline fourteen years ago and began pumping oil from the North Slope to a tanker terminal in Valdez, they pledged to respect the environment and the safety of their workers.

"So when evidence began reaching Congress and the federal regulatory agencies that those promises weren't being kept, the oil companies decided to put an end to the problem by plugging the leaks—not the leaks in the pipeline, the leaks of damaging information reaching Washington.

"The Alyeska Company—a consortium of oil companies that owns and operates the pipeline—went out and hired one of the nation's largest private eye firms to conduct an elaborate, expensive, and secret undercover investigation of one man—a former oil broker by the name of Chuck Hamel."

In the Dinnertainment there was light applause, but the listeners didn't want to miss anything, so they hushed quickly. Except for David Grimes, who couldn't resist leaning to Riki Ott's ear. "This is where

Alaska winds up in the affairs of men," he said. "Not up where we live, but down here where they make television, and across the river where they make the country."

The next day Chuck Hamel was across the river testifying before the House Interior Committee when Billie Garde's knee pressed against his own. His voice faltered; then he realized what his lawyer's nudge meant. *Speak up!* Glancing from his prepared testimony up to the high, shallow U of the dais and the impassive faces of the House Interior Committee, Hamel cleared his throat. His voice wavered through a phrase, then settled into the stronger timbre.

"The more I heard, the angrier I got about what was going on," he said. "Alyeska was polluting the water by introducing toxic sludge, including cancer-causing benzene, into the pristine waters of Port Valdez and Prince William Sound. Alyeska was poisoning the Valdez fjord's air by venting extremely hazardous hydrocarbon vapors directly into the atmosphere. There was no regulatory oversight, and thus no regulatory violations. It was as if the environmental regulations of the United States did not even apply north of the Canadian border. No regulators, no oversight, no enforcement, nothing. In fact, the oil industry wasn't putting out anything but poison and lies."

Hamel felt perspiration beading and trickling under his clothes. Behind him, the room which had been bustling with comings and goings, and with murmurings and rattling sheaves of paper during the past two days of hearings, seemed conspicuously silent. Hamel knew that 100, maybe 150 people were staring at the back of his head, and it made him nervous. Everyone in the room had a copy of his prepared testimony. He was on page 5. When he reached the bottom of the page, all hundred-plus copies scuffed over to page 6.

"I desperately wanted to go on with my life, to leave the disillusionment behind, to do what other men at my age are doing—walking on beaches with their wives, enjoying the fruits of their labors. But I couldn't turn my back on those people who had turned to me for help. Personally, these were terrible, dark nights for Kathy and me; and they went on for years.

"I could never have known nor little imagined the extent of the betrayal of my trust," Hamel told the committee. "The details of the Wackenhut surveillance are now well known. Alyeska authorized the stealing of our trash, monitoring and taping of our telephone calls, concealing video cameras in hotel rooms, stealing our mail, and illegally obtaining our personal and financial information."

Yesterday, George Wackenhut, whose corporation is the country's third largest security firm, had tried to discount the testimony of his own investigators who'd stepped from the shadows to tell the congressional committee they were disgusted with Wayne Black's bag of shoddy tricks and what some of them claimed were illegal electronic surveillance methods. Wackenhut, looking like a close-cropped Uncle Sam, faced the dais with icy eyes and a voice gravelly with indignation. He looked too good to be defending garbage sifters. He looked like what on the one hand he was—a national guardian, head of a security empire.

Wackenhut's intimidating character, however, did little to ameliorate the odd, simultaneous disappearance from both Wackenhut and Alyeska files of billing reports that detailed the particulars of the Hamel investigation. And not only from the files but also from the Wackenhut computer banks in which the reports had originated. Wackenhut himself almost certainly was not privy to the disappearance, although he took an Interior Committeeman's reproach on the chin. "I'm chairman of the board," he said. "Of *course* I accept responsibility."

The man all the fingers were pointing to, and the man Hamel felt in his own mind knew the details of everything bad that had happened during the investigation, was Wayne Black. Black, Hamel felt, was a slime. He was there right now in the committee room, somewhere behind Hamel, tall, meticulously manicured, his heavy-lidded gray eyes boring into Hamel's back.

Hamel shuddered. He had friends back there, too, though, and they were a comfort. His wife, Kathy, was just behind him; he could feel her eyes fixed on him, buoying him up. And beside her was his son, Chuck Junior, and Riki Ott and David Grimes from Cordova, and some friendly reporters, and the six Wackenhut investigators who'd given up their careers to tell the truth.

Through all the years of pain, every piece of human garbage had been balanced by a human jewel. He surely never would have known about Black, for instance, if it hadn't been for Gus Castillo. Castillo, described by Richard Mauer of the *Anchorage Daily News* as a barrel of a man who "talks in short sentences like a Sergeant Joe Friday with a Spanish accent," was a former Wackenhut investigator who initially became concerned that he might be implicated in what he was convinced were illegal investigation techniques. When Castillo took his complaints to Wackenhut executives, they secretly hired him to play a double agent's role by spying on their own spies. But when Castillo presented them with what he felt was incriminating evidence and they didn't act on it, he quit, blew Black's cover by telephoning Hamel, and had since convinced more than half a dozen other former Wackenhut employees to spill more Black beans.

"They were demising this little guy," Castillo told the *Daily News*'s Mauer. Hamel had "dedicated one fifth of his life to a cause, and was such a trustful soul that he was taking these people at face value. They were doing a pretty good job on him. I felt sorry for him. I was sickened by what they were doing."

Not quite certain what Hamel's cause was, Castillo went to the library, as he said, " 'cause I don't know nothing about ANWR. When I found out what it was, and why all these big corporations are trying so hard to do in one little guy, that's when I decided to come forward."

Hamel, he said, "was flabbergasted. He didn't know what to say. He starts screaming on the phone. He was laughing, crying, about to have a nervous breakdown. I think he had to double his ration of tranquilizers."

And so now Hamel knew, and told the committee: "Alyeska successfully launched an internal witch-hunt to target everyone who had communications with me. By illicitly obtaining AT&T telephone records they identified the people who we called nationwide and people who called us, and—worst of all—violated my confidences with people who trusted me. Bob Scott was fired, lost his home, lost his retirement. Others have lost their jobs, become suspected of being sources of information and now live in fear of being monitored by their employer. All that I tried to do to help stop Alyeska's wrongdoings was being turned upside down."

Hamel's voice dropped. "I am repeatedly asked how all this makes me feel. When I first learned of the surveillance activities I was afraid for my family and friends." Billie Garde pressed his knee again, but she didn't need to, because he was about to talk louder anyway. "Next I became angry, furious that Alyeska would stoop to dishonesty, deception, and theft out of paranoia that the truth would somehow find its way to the public.

"In a classic psychological projection, Alyeska justifies its elaborate sting operation by claiming that I was in possession of stolen documents. I never picked through Alyeska's trash, broke into its offices, taped its phone calls. I never posed as one of its own. I never attempted to destroy its employees' careers, or, worse, invade its families' privacy.

"I have always done exactly as I said I was going to do—insist on responsible environmental management of the oil industry in Alaska. Today I am simply saddened and disgusted; but, in a strange way, grateful and relieved that this entire incident has come to light because it demonstrates better than I could ever do that Alyeska and its owners cannot be trusted."

It was over. The pressure on Hamel's knee relaxed.

"Thank you very much, Mr. Hamel, for your testimony," said the committee chairman, George Miller. "The committee will take a short recess for the purpose of discussion, in the anteroom."

The committee filed out; Hamel reached for a glass of water. Was such a recess usual or unusual? He glanced at Billie Garde, but she was intent on something among the big stack of papers in front of her. She was bracing herself, he knew, to help him through the grilling that was surely coming now, particularly from the committee's Republican members who had agreed to help Alaska Congressman Don Young make Hamel out to be a self-serving crackpot, if not an out-and-out, criminally bent extortionist.

He knew that George Miller would be doing his best to help keep the hearings focused on Alyeska and not on Hamel, but right now this prolonging silence felt very much like a gathering storm.

He glanced over his shoulder. Kathy's eyes smiled at him. Beside her, Chuck Junior sat erect, lips tight, eyes fierce. He met his father's glance with a firm, supporting nod.

"Lord," thought Hamel, and it seemed to him that even the still,

small voice inside him had begun to quaver. He wondered if he would be in jail before the day's end. It seemed a ludicrous thought, but he knew there was a real possibility that he would be cited in contempt of Congress. He had heard through the rumor mill that Congressman Young had stacked the committee today and was going to try to get him to reveal his sources—the whistle-blowers within Alyeska itself. There were, indeed, more conservatives in attendance than at any time heretofore during the hearings. The potential rough stuff made Hamel queasy, but revealing his sources was something he simply would not do. Those people had come to him on faith, trying to do the right thing, and he knew that if he didn't protect their confidentiality, he'd be throwing them to the wolves.

Nor would he plead the Fifth, the way slime Black did. Of course, Black probably did it for good reason. But Hamel hadn't done anything criminal; copping to the Fifth on the ground that he might incriminate himself by his testimony would be a lie. No, he'd just have to flatly refuse, and if that meant prison, then he'd be a man first and a jailbird after.

Apparently Billie Garde took his frown as a question. She shrugged with her eyebrows and leaned toward him to say something, but just then the congressmen reappeared.

"The committee will reconvene, and we thank you for sitting through the recess," said George Miller. "Are there any questions for Mr. Hamel? If there are none, uh, Mr. Hamel, let me thank you for your testimony."

Chuck Hamel heard gasps, and a woman's short bark of incredulity. He concentrated on the desk in front of him, trying not to show that he was stunned. He half-turned toward Billie Garde, but she had already risen to fend off a pressing corps of newsfolk. Hamel pushed back his chair, stood up. Somebody hugged him from behind and said, "Great job, Chuck; way to go, my friend," and he heard David Grimes saying, "I suppose this is good?"

You claw at them tooth and nail for ten years, you cost them half a billion dollars, they pound you into the poorhouse, and it comes to this? This silence?

"So it ends here, nothing accomplished," said a reporter with a microphone.

"Oh, no," he said, and even to himself he sounded dazed. "I think a lot was accomplished here. I think that what has happened here has led some honest people to do the right thing . . ."

"What's going on?" he asked himself. *"What the hell is going on?"*

"So what *was* going on?" My interviews with Chuck Hamel had run over months and then years. I had pored over so many documents, talked with so many whistle-blowing oil company, shipping, and pipeline employees, that I could almost carve the missing piece myself. Whatever it was would match the billion-piece pattern of manipulation and power brokering that has always run like a die cut throughout the international enigma of big industry, big business, and big government. "Somebody got the conservatives to back away," I said. "A trade-off?"

Chuck Hamel grinned. "More like blackmail," he said. "Call it leverage. Don Young was setting me up for the fall. He'd distributed transcripts of some tapes Wayne Black made of me sticking my foot in my mouth in the fake Ecolit offices, talking about how I was going to bring Alyeska to its knees, that sort of thing. He was going to base an interrogation of me on the tapes, but that wasn't good enough, I guess, because whoever transcribed had stuck a lot of self-implication in my mouth that wasn't there. Somebody on Miller's staff compared the script with the tapes and started discovering all these insertions."

Miller, he said, pointed them out to Young in executive session, noting that the additions were too many and too patterned to be mistakes. The chairman then said he assumed Young's staff had done the transcribing, and that if Young wanted to start pumping Chuck Hamel about his document sources, then Miller would have to start talking about doctoring evidence.

"So they took me off the hook and let me go."

"How did you find out what went on behind closed doors?"

"I hounded the staff until one of them told me."

"The one who did the nifty detecting?"

Chuck Hamel looked at me. "I heard you used to do movie scripts. You know Sissy Spacek?"

"No, I don't."

"She's an old friend, she and her husband; he's a director, just did that JFK film."

"Jack Fisk?"

"That's him. I liked her better in *Coal Miner's Daughter,* though. She did all her own singing. You know she got so good that Loretta Lynn couldn't tell her own voice when she compared the tapes."

"Chuck," I said, "what's next? Where to from here?"

"That's what I was talking about. Don't you think Sissy would make a great Kathy?"

"Come on," I said.

"Seriously!"

"So you're going to give up on Alyeska?"

His hazel eyes changed. "Oh, no. Not ever."

"This movie thing is just a breather," I said.

"Just a diversion."

"Okay; so who's going to play the die-hard champ in a Mickey Rooney body?"

"That would take character, wouldn't it," he said. "Robert Redford, of course."

13

The Voice of Silence

Stand still where you are—at the end of pavement, in a sun-break of
the forest, on the open, cloud-peopled terrace of the plains. Look deeply
into the wind-furrows of the grass, into the leaf-stilled water of pools.
Think back through the silence, of the life that was and is not here now,
of the strong pastness of things—shadows of the end and the beginning.
— John Haines, *Stories We Listened To*

One morning in August 1991, as I walked with Alaska's first poet
laureate, John Haines, out to his woodshed, we heard a mewling whimper
from somewhere down by the creek, and the sound was so plaintive and
vulnerable and full of longing that it stopped us in our tracks. It was a
porcupine, we shortly realized. We stood listening, although he said he
wasn't certain that he really wanted to hear it again. It was as if there was
something in the sound that echoed his own feelings that day, so much so
that when it first drifted to him he looked momentarily appalled, almost
as though the cry had slipped from between his own lips.

We walked on to the rear of the woodshed, where he picked up an
ax. From where it was dry under the shed roof he selected a knotless length
of birch. The wood had been splitting a little easier for the past week or
so, he said, now that the nights were cold enough to harden the resin.

He cleaved, and I carried the stovelengths to the cabin in a series of
armloads and watched him work—a tallish, spare man in wire-rimmed
glasses and the khaki pants and shirt that I was to find he favored. The only
clear sign of aging in him was a telltale deliberateness in the way he
handled his tools and moved around the precarious landscape. His brown
hair was beginning to gray but still had a healthy sheen to it and lay about
his head in an absent tossing of strong waves. He had a high forehead,
worried eyes, stern mouth, long jaw, firm chin. The effect was of both

strength and inwardness—a combination that made him appear exactly as he should: at once the woodsman and the scholar.

The sound came again. He remembered the first time he'd heard it—forty years ago?—from roughly the same place down by the creek, before he learned what it was. He'd had the vision of a small abandoned child, but then it occurred to him that maybe it was a grizzly cub, and he watched the woods anxiously until he got back to the house. Later, Fred Campbell had told him what it was, a porcupine out looking for a mate, and the next time he heard it he hunkered down in the bushes and whimpered and commiserated with the animal until it came to him. He smiled, remembering that solemnly comical black nose parting the foliage, the black, blinking eyes, the almost visibly slow wit reacting to the fact that he, John Haines, was not what the suitor was looking for in a mate.

The birch split nicely and toppled off the block. He set one split half back up to quarter it. The mosquitoes were starting to die off; it would be a good day, he said, to walk up Campbell Hill. But that asked for trouble, didn't it—to go, in the mood he was in today, up there to the maw of Fred Campbell's deserted cabin? Lately he'd been seeing his own place a hundred years from now looking pretty much just like Fred's, and he'd felt increasingly helpless to prevent the disintegration.

He quartered the chunk of birch, quartered another, halved another, quartered another. You wrenched so hard to get the right spin on your life, he said, to feel that smooth thrum of peace, and one day you woke up and it all careered around like wobbling tops, you yawing off in one direction, the one country you know in another.

He was losing the land. Just that spring, he said, he'd gone down to Wendell Berry's farm on the banks of the Kentucky River, and the two of them—fellow old champions of *place*—reaffirmed in each other as they walked among the pastures and sheep that if you didn't know where you were, you didn't know who you were. But that wasn't the problem, really. He knew about the reciprocal sustenance of self and place. The problem wasn't one of knowing, but of keeping.

His grip had slipped a few years ago on the homestead he had owned for more than a quarter of a century. It had slipped just once, but cata-strophically, and now he was paying for the mistake. He had needed money. If the damned university up here had given him the position he deserved, he wouldn't have needed money; but he did need it, and because he knew that he wasn't going to spend the long winters at the homestead anymore, he sold it. He let it go to a woman who promised to rent it back to him for as long as he wanted to keep coming back.

But now somebody wanted to buy it and parcel it up, and panic had set in. For years he didn't panic because he thought he could fix it. Handily, some friends set up a committee to buy his place and have it set aside as a historic site, and the legislature came through with $30,000 toward the purchase, but the committee fell apart politically, and the money reverted to the state. He remembered thinking, "Well, we'll have to start over and do it right this time." But the years just swept on busily by, and here we were, like Fred Campbell, jabbing a stick at the shadows.

From the stacked cordwood, he selected a few chunks of dry spruce to mix with the birch and tossed them over toward the block. He had begun to perspire; he wiped his forehead with a forearm sleeve. Apparently the noise of his ax work, or of his talk, had shut the porcupine up. Or maybe, who knows, the old fellow had found what he was looking for.

One day, he said, in the headwater hills behind the cabin about this time of year, Fred had taught him the rite of burning the quills off a porcupine, thumping the cornered animal over the head, tossing chunks of its liver to the dogs, turning the carcass in a hot fire, beating the charred quills off with a stick, the fire-eyed dogs pacing . . .

He felt too slow, perhaps, for humankind, and destined to be sacrificed no matter how sharp he'd honed his barbs of peace.

The spruce, with its knots, was harder work for less fire, but you needed it for a speedy flame.

He leaned on his ax, sleeved his brow again. "I've been having difficulty of late discerning between the pule of my own fear of mortality and the lament of the higher fear of violating a union between humanity and the land," he said. "Does that make sense?"

It did. It had been his charge to help maintain this place as it had been rightly defined by the human heart. He'd lost it. There must be something he could do. "I don't want a monument," he said. "But I need the redemption."

* * *

For years, I was apprehensive about meeting John Haines. I was intimidated—not by his literary prominence but by his fierce dedication to Alaska. He was as staunch a champion of *place* as were his close writer friends Wallace Stegner in the West and Wendell Berry down in the farm heart of America. "Place makes people; in the end it makes everything." It was the very feeling about Alaska I didn't have.

But when I finally did meet him, it wasn't Haines's devotion that scared me; it was his bitterness. I was immediately afraid that the place that he'd so loved, and that was now giving him such an unceremonious bum's rush, would take me to the same end. That was not what happened; what happened was that I finally came to understand why I needed to leave Alaska—why most of us need to leave our Alaskas—in order to gain, finally, a sense of place.

The son of a navy officer who hadn't lived in one place for more than a couple of years, Haines came to Alaska in 1947 looking for a place to belong. He found it about sixty miles south of Fairbanks on 160 acres overlooking the Tanana River. He'd traveled the dirt road to the place with an idea of homesteading it if it was right and was immediately struck by the sense of permanence imparted by the wild land.

Twenty-something years later he was known as the best serious poet Alaska had produced. He was the author of six major collections of poetry and two volumes of autobiographical essays; had received numerous awards, including two Guggenheim Fellowships, a National Endowment for the Arts Fellowship, and the Alaska Governor's Award for Excellence in the Arts; and had been named by the state legislature as Alaska's first official poet laureate.

But in spite of all the recognition that came for the poetry he wrote later, it was his early stuff that felt to me exactly right. His essays had an olfactory character to them like moose hide or aspen loam, and in his poetry he could crack a line as brittle as sixty below. "At the foot of October where the current narrows, the salmon wait, burning in the shallows," one of his poems says. "I stand alone in the smoking frost, a long hook poised, and fling the bright fish up the pebbled, icy bar to quiver and lie still, a sinking fire." And I would say yes! That's October on the river precisely! And time and again I would find that the strength of his experience corroborated what I felt: that living here needed no justification, just celebration.

So why was it that John Haines's Octobers with the fire red salmon, and his winters feeding his stiffening dogs, and his springs competing with the moles that nosed his gardens, and his summers walking up Campbell Hill to the ramshackle cabin where his nearest neighbor lived odorous, poor, and wise—why were his seasons in Alaska so much more anchored and loving of the land than my own?

I hung around him, when I could, to find out. And the next spring after that autumn day of the woodshed and the unseen porcupine, he was back, commenting, as he slid a cardboard box from the rear of his old truck, that as the sum total of his life's work it was not all that hefty. He carried it indoors, and on the cabin's only table he unpacked the contents into a respectable clutter: a dozen volumes of poetry, five of prose, a plump stack of manuscripts that hadn't yet been compiled into anything, and a stray volume of the collected poems of William Butler Yeats.

The newest book of the bunch was his memoir, *The Stars, the Snow, the Fire,* which had just come out from Graywolf Press. "But that's prose," he said. "My responsibility is as a poet." Nothing new of his poetry had been put between hard covers for almost a decade. That was what he was here to do—screen his manuscripts for a new Story Line Press collection that represented his work over the past ten years. Some of it—a few pieces particularly—he liked very much; some of it he was ambivalent about; and some of it he had created as exercise or out of a sense of obligation.

"I'm tempted to just pick the ones I like best and let it go at that," he said. He looked at the stack and sighed. "But ultimately you have to arrange the material with attention to more than affection." He let his fingers trail over the books as he talked, as if he could sort the lines by touch. The finer considerations of complement and continuity always crept in at the end, he said. There were people out there—peers and friends, scholars and critics and serious readers—who knew the progressions of his life and his efforts and his ideas; he had to select for them, too. And even they were not the most important. He was toward the end of a career; whatever structure he chose would have to bear a collective weight.

But right now the cabin was like a walk-in freezer and the light was no good. He put his gloves back on, opened the front of the barrel stove, slipped some paper and kindling and small chunks of spruce inside, opened the stovepipe damper, then struck a match and got a flame going. He watched until it took, then adjusted the stove's air vents and went about taking down the shutters, opening the place up, and working up a sweat out at the woodpile splitting birch for me to shuttle to the woodbin while the cabin heated.

When we came back in, the stove glowed red and the cabin had a dry, baked feel to it. He peeled off his steaming, damp wool and traded it for dry cotton. He dampened the stove's air vents down to slits, then sat with his feet toward the fire and picked up *The Collected Poems of W. B. Yeats*.

He browsed. "When I was a boy with never a crack in my heart," he read aloud, and again:

> *When day begins to break*
> *I count my good and bad,*
> *Being wakeful for her sake,*
> *Remembering what she had,*
> *What eagle look still shows,*
> *While up from my heart's root*
> *So great a sweetness flows*
> *I shake from head to foot.*

It was not what he was looking for. He was looking for Yeats's people; and he found them and read them again, a colonel, a drunk, a dancing girl, a grouping of stone Chinese, Kevin O'Higgins, Crazy Jane, Henry Middleton, a lady with soft eyes like funeral tapers, pearl-pale and weeping Niamh, brokenhearted Baile and brokenhearted Aillinn eating Quiet's wild heart like daily meat, and all the live and dead of Ireland under its Druid moons . . .

That was what he was looking for. He read Yeats's people because he had learned from them, and it was to them he owed much of what was new in his work of the past several years. Until a few years ago his poetry had held precious few people. Then, because he wanted to be able to take himself seriously in terms of the old bardic tradition that charges a poet with the responsibility of poetically celebrating certain important personalities and episodes, he decided to try writing an elegy in the old-fashioned and true sense, one that summed up a period and its people and places. He'd long been strong on place; almost everything he'd written had been about place, or had—as the dust jacket to one of his books said—drawn on place to illuminate the landscapes within. Influenced by the German expressionists and Spanish surrealists and particularly by the "deep image" poems of Robert Bly's emotive, romanticized landscapes, he developed a style that, as one critic said, "hopes to overwhelm the reader, not with logic but with atmosphere."

> *The knife that makes long scars*
> *in the flesh lays bare the bones—*
>
> *pale trees in the forest of blood*
> *where the birds of life and death*
> *endlessly weave their*
> *nests with straws of anguish.*

But in creating the sort of dream world in which a skinned animal's bones could leap from the wild of John Haines's everyday life into his inner self to become pale trees in a forest of blood, he never got very good at doing people. When he started on the elegiac poem, he recognized that he needed help. "I could put the place in the people; I could almost *turn* the place into people. But I had trouble doing the raw people before the place made them what they were to become."

He turned to Yeats. He hadn't read much of the great Irishman but knew that it was characteristic of him to summon this person or that, living or dead, with seemingly effortless accuracy and flair. But of course poets were country gentlemen in those days. They could spend a lot of time walking the countryside, jawing with neighbors over stone walls and watching people work. They could picnic in the shade beside trout streams. They could collect a thousand living lovers, if they were so inclined, or ten thousand ghosts. John Haines, at sixty, had to settle for the very few lovers and workers and ghosts who had peopled this wild stretch of homestead country over the past forty years, and he would have to milk them for all they were worth.

It was not that his poetry was weakly peopled. Old Fred Campbell, for instance, who had been here forever it seemed, and now gone five years, and up on the hill his old cabin

> . . . *has grown*
> *to resemble his life—*
> *a shallow cave hung*
> *with old hides, rusty*
> *traps and chains,*
> *smelling of eighty years*
> *of unwashed bedding*
> *and rotting harness.*

It was just that there were not enough of them, and because they were so few, and each so representative, he had to handle them with as much care as he possibly could; he had to do each of them justice.

Reading Yeats did help. William Butler just reached out and pulled people in, almost as though in passing. He shook them like you might an old rag, and all the homely or heroic essences of Ireland fell out onto the page. Or so it seemed. Yeats worked hard to create the illusion of artlessness, of course, but he did seem to have a relatively easy time sculpting people into his verse, and it was that gossipy, bardic, spontaneous chemistry he had with the human personality that Haines studied closely. He honed his instinct for human character, made himself trust it more, forced himself to reach out and grab for the souls, and once he had hold of them, to goad them into speaking for themselves.

> *I see him sitting there*
> *now as he used to,*
> *his starved animals gathered*

about his bony knees.
He talks to himself
of poverty, cursing softly,
jabbing a stick
at the shadows.

His early work was not known for its human portraiture. He hoped that his late work would be, and there were indications that it might. "Some of the critics are wondering whether I'm abandoning place for people," he told me. He wasn't, of course. To the contrary, these new, human images were a celebration of place through its people. Because of his conviction that place defines the human personality, he wanted the people and the places in his work to mirror one another, not to be indiscernible, but to be inseparably connected.

"To humanity," he said, "a place doesn't exist until humans have come to sniff it, touch it, sink roots into it, build in it, birth in it, love it, lie about it, kill for it, write songs about it, die in it. But what we don't often acknowledge is that neither can we humans exist without the place. The character of place defines us."

"Your friend Wallace Stegner," I said, "says that no place is a place until it has had a poet."

"Well." He frowned down at the stack that was his life's work. "For forty-five years this place has had John Haines. I'd say it was a place, all right."

There was a spring, he said, when he finally knew that he had lost the clarity of his youth. A bitterness that had been smoldering in him over the years finally set up firm, then, and he wondered whether he was still a poet.

Probably not coincidentally, it was 1989, the year of the wreck of the *Exxon Valdez*. He had, in fact, been asked to write an introduction for a collection of artists' reactions to the spill, a volume called *Season of Dead Water*. His difficulty, he supposed, stemmed from a combination of adversities: a violation of the place he loved, the accumulating bitterness at being refused a position by his home university, some deep worry about a collection of his own work he was editing, and a nagging fear that he might not be able to spark the embers of his career. A woman in his life had left about that time, too. He didn't say much about her, but to me it seemed that he deflected my few tentative questions about her with a revealing puzzlement and sadness.

At any rate, he said, there was no agony in the crisis, just a deadness—a feeling of going through the motions of a routine that had lost its vitality. At first he wasn't even aware of it. He had simply started home after wintering at the Villa Montalbo artists' retreat on the California coast. The trip would take him five weeks. (He never flew. We owe it to a place to move through it, he feels, to absorb it into ourselves as we go, and not skip over it in our hurries.)

First he drove his old blue pickup north to Port Townsend, Washington, and moved his few things into a friend's vacant house to fidget for a month until the season's first ferry run to Alaska. When he could, he worked on essays for the new University of Michigan Press collection of his work; then, the third week of April, he packed his things into the back of the truck and boarded the *M.V. Columbia*. He settled in and let the northland build up in him during the meandering, three-day run up among a thousand miles of foggy isles. In Haines, at the end of the line, he drove off the ferry for the last 560-mile leg, beginning with an icy, windswept loop up over Chilkat Pass into the Yukon Territory, then back into Alaska at its eastern boundary, and another 200 miles or so to the homestead. In the little faded utopian dream town of Delta, just 40 miles shy of the snowpacked dirt drive that led from the Richardson Highway to his own cluster of cabins and outbuildings, he pulled over at a grocery store to shop and to telephone a friend who plowed snow for hire with a blade attached to the front of his pickup. Then he drove the last hour north into the one country he knew.

Behind him—he glanced at it in his rearview mirror from time to time—the glaciated Alaska Range stretched east to west, serrated, glistening white under a pure April blue. He crossed a bridge over the Tanana River. Later, when the glaciers that fed it began to melt, the river would bloat into a milky gray torrent, but right now, between white and turquoise islands of ice, the braided channels flowed blue. April is breakup month. Most people say it is Alaska's ugliest time, with mud caking to everything, and all the snow going dirty and the trees still bare. But it's the people who churn up most of the mud, and if you get away from the towns, April feels more like the swelling of spring, the end of the long, dark white.

He was sixty-four. He wasn't sure that he could take the January cold here anymore even if he had a choice. But he did miss the winters. From the late forties through the late sixties, he'd spent most of them in a cabin above this river. Often when he was seasonally away, he recalled the utter stillness of the homestead, and then the stillness split by the ice cracking like a big-bore rifle; and sometimes at night, in silence in bed, he could hear boulders rumbling along under the ice. The strength of the elemental was in his veins back then. But later, as his reputation as a poet grew, he found it flattering to accept offers of winter residencies from universities in Ohio or New York or Wyoming or Montana or the north of England. And then he found it convenient: the residencies were anesthetic ways of aging himself out of the winter wilds; they were good excuses, and then simply excuses; and now they were the rule, and his summers here the exception.

The plow man couldn't make it out until late evening, so he had pulled as far to the side of the frost-heaved pavement as he could and walked in. At the entrance to the lane he paused and looked out across the broad flats where the ice and the braids of water flashed and twinkled in the afternoon sun. His eyes swept back and forth like a wand across the sea of dark green spruce at the far side of the river, then up the long, long hump of Molybdenum Ridge, where the snow had melted, and then up into the cirques and peaks of the high mountains, where it had not. Into the long familiar saddles that dipped and rose like ocean troughs between the 13,000-foot pinnacles of Mts. Hayes, Hess, Moffitt, and Deborah, his heart settled as comfortably as into a hammock.

The snow was crusty; water dripped from the roofs. He opened up the newer cabin, split some kindling, and started a fire. He opened the sheds and the garage, then did some shovel work up the steep trail to the studio. At the top he rested, fiddling with the solar collector and the storage batteries. He walked gingerly back down the slick trail and cleared the rain troughs along the eaves, and set out some cans to catch water for cooking and bathing. At times as he worked he was aware of himself. He was still tall, still spare, still had a full head of brown hair, and his muscles could still labor up a comfortable heat. His sweat echoed the vitality of the numberless times he had done all this before. At moments he felt young, or at least mindless in a way that is no different from how he'd felt when he sweated here when he was young. He opened the old back cabin where many of his books and manuscripts were stored, and there discovered a family of red squirrels. He did away with the young, shot the adults with a twenty-two rifle, and stopped up the hole.

The plow man came. He watched him clear the lane; then the man caught him up on some local news, which had mainly to do with how uncommonly hard the winter was; how uncommonly deep the snow. Then the plow man left and the quiet settled back in—the drip, drip from the trees and the buildings, the ticking of the melting snow, and the whisper of a mounting breeze out on the river flats. He walked out to the end of the lane to drive his pickup in, but stood there first to watch a flight of Canada geese veer to a landing on a long sandbar where the wind had scoured away the snow and was kicking up small plumes of grit. When the geese were down, he waited until the soft hootings of their excited gossip drifted up to him on the wind, then he drove the truck up the lane and unloaded his things into the cabin.

That night, over tea, he sat at the barrel-stove fire, the collected poems of William Butler Yeats in his lap. His wet gloves and damp wool socks were drying above the stove in a cage he'd built years ago out of chicken wire. He started to open the book, but just then he was distracted by a movement in the woodpile. It was only a large black ant, and for a few moments he watched it, remembering another just like it that had caught his eye and thoughts in another April, decades ago . . .

> I watch a carpenter ant crawl about on a chunk of split firewood at my feet. The wood is dry spruce from an old snag up the creek. The ant has lived there all winter in the honeycomb passages. Now he is out here in this strange, new place of warmth and passing shadows. His black skeleton glistens in the light. He feels his way along.

And suddenly he felt himself awash with all the winter residue that was absent from this spring—the sodden heap of wood dust that was left when the snow melted under the sawhorse, the accumulated mustiness of the shut-tight cabin, the bad potato at the bottom of the bin . . .

An odor, strong and sharp with ammonia, comes off the low bank where my dogs are chained to their houses. It is too wet for them on the ground; they lie on top of their houses, blinking, sleeping in the sun. . . .

All around me I see the debris of winter, long hidden by snow. The scattered woodchips, the gnawed bones; part of a moose jaw, a hoof, a lost spoon. Bits of trash, moose hair, peelings thrown out and forgotten; urine stains in the rotting snow.

This spring, the ground did not hold the winter sourness it held then. Why did that feel to him like a loss? Just because he missed those days, he supposed; as rotten as the debris of winter could be, it was the debris of his youth. But even more important than youth, he thought now, was the elemental clarity of those times.

For somehow those days in the field, those treks with the dogs over snow and grass, the long hunts, the animal killing, and the rest of it, were all part of the inmost human experience on this earth. It is rank, it smells of blood and killed meat, is compounded of fear, of danger and delight in unequal measure. To the extent that it can even be called "experience" and not by some other, forgotten name, it requires a surrender few of us are now willing to make.

His own full surrender was in those times gone. Yet even now, although he could no longer give so much of himself over to it, the sap still rose, the springwater still seeped. Shoots of fireweed and wild rhubarb still broke through. Geese flared yet to the river bars, buntings wheeled over the snow. And as for the rest of it, he could still call it back to him, and that was something. He could still work it onto the page. Certain key moments could be regained, and within those moments glowed the vitality that makes possible all art, all spiritual definition, all true relation to the world.

In September of last year he was leaving the place again, and on the last day, as we climbed the hill behind his house, he was startled by a sudden catch in his chest. After a concerned moment I realized that it was an emotional catch, not a physical one. I was embarrassed, but he readily admitted it, and said that when he was here for a long spell, summer or winter, he could make this pull almost empty-minded because it was a daily trudge, just one in an endless cycle of homestead chores, and he knew that his legs would be working against this comfortable old slope tomorrow, and for enough tomorrows after that that the end of it was beyond his concern. But now the end of it was today. "This bright, brisk day," he said. "And among all the accumulated leave-takings from this place over the past forty years, this is going to be the worst because I suspect that I might not make it back."

He quoted, "I am not old, not yet," and said it seemed like he wrote it just yesterday:

> though
> like a wind-turned birch
> spared by the axe,
> I claim this clearing
> in the one country I know.

But he was sure enough getting older now. It was still the one country he knew, and today, he said, he felt for it such a welling of love that it had rendered him weak. So much had come to *be* here: the best friends, the best work, the best women, the best years . . . and there was not time enough to craft even a single memorial from all the busy hauntings that dogged him on the last day of his rounds. The years lay about like woodyard chips; the shadows and voices of old friends drifted and murmured in the dappled woods; his women coiled in wisps of his own

September breath; and whenever he passed the silent, sealed shed where all his work was stored in dry white stacks, he heard small sounds.

It seemed impossible to be leaving. It was only for a year's residency at George Washington University. But he was sixty-seven now, and depressed and lonely, and he could feel the finality of this leave-taking in the terrifying clarity of how all the familiar fixtures of his home were suddenly standing apart from him. It was only morning; he had the whole day ahead. Yet, whenever he looked at the yard, the sawhorse, the chopping block, the mailbox, the chest-high rhubarb plant beside the door of the old cabin, he could feel himself cleaving away from them as sharply as if parted by the bite of an ax. "A day is nothing here," he said; "without tomorrow, a day is nothing."

We climbed to his writing studio at the crest of the hill. It was a small cabin, twelve feet by sixteen, and was tightly constructed and well insulated, with double-pane windows. He'd built the studio in stages between 1981 and 1984, and was pleased with the feel of it, and with what it had done for his poetry. It was made of sunny, naturally finished wood, and it was in a sunny place. The house down below was more sheltered from wind and winter, but on a mild day this was much the preferable spot. On days like today, there was no place on earth better.

He walked ahead of me up three plank steps to a small pine deck and looked out over the Tanana River Valley. Across the river to the south were Mts. Moffitt, Hayes, Hess, and Deborah. Their high slopes and summits were perpetually iced, so you couldn't read the calendar by them; but below the peaks was the long, low Molybdenum Ridge that alternately darkened and flushed and blanched to the rhythms of the year. Right now it was a blend of rich scarlet and golden orange. Within a few weeks it would be dusted white with the first low-altitude snow—termination dust, the seasonal workers called it—and you'd know that the key was about to be turned in the lock of the year.

Inside the studio, his breath still vapored, he stoked a small woodstove with a few chunks of split aspen and lit a fire. Even the homestead down below had no electricity, but up here he had rigged a solar collector and a bank of storage batteries so that he could have lights and the use of an electric typewriter. At first he'd hesitated on strictly sentimental grounds to bring electricity to his wilderness. But it had turned out all right. The electricity in this few feet of circuitry—the force that drove his words onto paper—seemed a power no less marvelous and far more personal than that which came through strangers' wires.

He connected a pair of alligator clips to a lead wire from the bank of batteries. The overhead light dilated on, and the typewriter gave a little jump.

He handed me a book of his essays, *Living off the Country*. I sat in a corner where he had placed a chair so that sunlight came over my left shoulder. He sat at the typewriter, rubbing his hands. He'd said to me once that usually he was conscious of the cold only for a few seconds, as if the acknowledgment was merely part of the ritual of shifting from the business out there to the business in here. It wouldn't take long for the stove to heat the small room, and he'd be in a trance by then anyway; sometimes he didn't even notice when the fire had died until long after the glow was gone from the ash and the iron.

An editor had asked him to do a piece on leaving Alaska. "What a hell of a time to write about that," he told me. After forty-five years, he doubted that he could really leave anyway; when it had to happen, the body might go—"sort of an out-of-heart experience—but the spirit always stays."

Anyway, he said, it wasn't leaving that was worth writing about; it was remembering. There was more solace in remembrance; leaving smacked of regret. You didn't leave a country like this; you were torn from it, ripped away. "Place makes people," he had written twenty-five years ago, when he had begun to feel solidly how this place was crafting his own life; and he reminded me again now: "in the end it makes everything."

Abruptly he looked out the southwesterly window, sat a little straighter to see a little better the piece of a view down toward the river and the far hills. I looked at him, and at the page I was reading:

As a poet I was born in a particular place, a hillside overlooking
the Tanana River in central Alaska, where I built a house and lived
for the better part of twenty-two years. . . . From the first day I

295

set foot in interior Alaska, and more specifically on Richardson Hill, I knew I was home. Something in me identified with that landscape. I had come, let's say, to the dream place.

A product of a rootless childhood, he had, over the past forty-five years, championed *place* as a vital ingredient in literature, and maybe the most vital ingredient in Alaskan literature, of which there is very little. Some good Nordic art had been made in the north, but not much in English. To Alaska people come and go. Writers write about Alaska but not often from it. The unwritten literature of the place cries for human closeness. Alaskan literature needs, he wrote,

long residence, intimacy of a sort that demands a certain daring and risk: a surrender, an abandonment, or just a sense of somehow being stuck with it.

The Alaskan writer faces a double task: to see, to feel, and to interpret the place itself, and then to relate that experience to what he knows of the world at large. Not simply to describe the place and what is in it (though valuable, this has been done many times already); but to give this material a life in imagination, a vitality beyond mere appearances. This alone allows the place to be seen and felt by an audience whose members are everywhere. It is not, in the end, Alaska, a place where a few people can live in perpetual self-congratulation, but humankind we are talking about. What we do and say here touches everywhere the common lot of people.

And now to leave?

He stared at the paper. It had been so much easier (although it didn't seem like it then) to write when the loves were fewer, and they were so comfortably at hand, and all the coming years floated ahead as clean and unrationed and charged with possibility as this white page.

The years weigh so much heavier from behind.

He knew that the words of hope would come. You always find them. But he knew, too, that where you always find hope is on the far side of despair, and first you have to work through the despair. He touched the typewriter; his fingers began to click the keys:

> There is something at once inevitable and foreboding in the changes that have taken place here in my lifetime, and the more so in recent years: this relentless filling up of open spaces, and the search for yet another space. And the question I have voiced many times repeats itself: What will happen when we at last understand that there is nowhere left to go?

He wrote on, working through the heaviness, crafting the agony, but already groping ahead with his talent toward the release at the end, so that when it came his fingers would dash through it, pushing the power of the soul and the sun onto the clean white sheet of fare-thee-well.

> With that never-to-be-forgotten sweep of river, hills, and clouds held in mind, one says goodbye one more time, not knowing when or if he will return, nor which, the place or himself, will be the most changed.

14

Leaving Alaska

Well, I'm thinking, now I'm satisfied, now I've seen it, the secret of the essence of the riddle of the Spirit of the Arctic—the flowering of life, of life wild, free, and abundant, in the midst of the hardest, cruelest land on the northern half of Earth.

—Ed Abbey, *Beyond the Wall*

For me they were all bridges, the people whose lives I searched among: Roger Kaye between the earthbound and the cloudbound; Richard Hayden between fences and frontiers; the James family between chance and no chance; Stu Pechek and Marta McWhorter between thinking and doing; Rick Steiner between defiance and compliance; David Grimes between Gaea's wounds and her healings; Dolly Garza between tradition and tomorrow; Chuck Hamel between axes and stones; John Haines between place and pain.

And all of them, always, between chaos and coherence.

My wife and nine-year-old son and I have leased a farm in western Oregon, whose February is to grass as Alaska's is to ice. From my upstairs office I look out across wide, wet meadowlands in which new green glows under thin gray clouds. Bunched in the pasturage out past the pole barn is a small flock of casual, ruminating Suffolk ewes and their new lambs, and just a few hundred yards beyond them a pair of coyotes have denned in thick brush near the crest of a low hill. The coyotes have three pups, which I've seen them drag out into the rare sun twice. I'm a bit worried, but the sheep are oblivious. The lambs are a constant commotion, gamboling and getting lost, bleating to be found, and scampering over to butt their answering mothers' teats. I can't help but think of the silent moose

I've watched, the hushed calves indefinite in the brush, the cows wary as they browse, mule ears cupped.

And the comparison inspired by the sheep is only one of a daily succession of connections from the changed to the old. Under unfamiliar skies, and along with alien neighbors, we are emerging from winter in Oregon's February rather than in Alaska's May; we listen at night to a watery horde of frogs rather than to the glacial hoot of a lone owl; and my son, who was never bothered by the sovereign baritone of wolves, comes padding down the hall at the yammering soprano of the family on the hill.

"They're laughing at me again," he says.

Occasionally these comparisons are judgmental, but usually they come more as a recognition of something lost, or as a sense of the familiar displaced. There's something not yet quite right, for instance, about that part of the old farm next door that has been ponded into a waterfowl refuge. All winter the dusky Canada geese have flocked in and out, winging past my window in the fog just after dawn, heading out to stubble, I suppose, and honking back in at dusk. It's homey, pastoral stuff, but winter, to me, is still the wrong time for geese, and although I am almost used to them now, each gabbled conversation outside my window still echoes of that island of geese that floated toward me on the Yukon, and occasionally behind the innocent goose talk I scent the memory of gunpowder and feathers on heavy river air.

The dominant differences are of season and convenience. Not long after we arrived, I was amazed in December to see a fuzz of new green under the old blades of autumn. Winter, near as I could tell, lasted without much of an identity through two and a half months. And in all this fair weather it's forty-five miles west to the coastal beaches, a leisurely, easterly hour to any of several trout streams in the Cascades, or a mild and scenic four hours to my folks' place in Brookings. All that on highways with no ice, no frost heaves; yet we seldom go. These stones' throws aren't yet real. Accustomed to the expeditionary, we are homebodies out of habit.

We do know, however—because of the fresher fruit, the longer soccer season, the well-preserved older cars, the halos that all these small western towns throw up into the night sky; and because of the sheep and

the green and the blander angle of light from the sun and the better
television reception and the coeds already wearing shorts and halter tops—
that we are back in the thick of temperate-zone living. And although it
compares in not all ways favorably with what we left, it is the right place
to be, down here where there is so much more life and so much more
wrong.

In the fall of 1993, Joan and Cody and I went back to Alaska for a
visit. We flew. I'd sworn I'd never get into a jetliner again, both because
I hate to do it and because, like the poet John Haines, I had come to
believe that we are richer for not skipping over places in our hurries.

Conscientiously, we had driven out of Alaska twice: once to scout,
once to relocate. But this time, a magazine that planned to run an Alaskan
travel piece the following spring suddenly realized that in Alaska, termination dust was already on the high peaks, and the embryos of big storms
were growing fast over northern seas. "You've got to get in and get out,"
the editor said. I had wanted back into the mainstream, forgetting that it
often is a jetstream, where windows of opportunity *fly*.

It had seemed to me in Oregon that we had moved much farther
than sixty minutes away, but within an hour out of Portland we were over
the Alaskan panhandle, watching the islands of the archipelago seem to
swim south; and two hours after that, we chirped down in Anchorage. We
rented a car, and within another hour we were out of town and up high,
thumping along a rutted highway that seemed astoundingly thin and
insubstantial in an ocean of tundra that stretched to both horizons yellow
and red.

"I would rather live here," Cody said.

Cody had become a nine-year-old soccer star. I reminded him that
in Alaska the soccer season was six weeks; in Oregon it was twenty-four.

"I know," he said. "I don't mean I want to move back, not right
now; I just mean . . ."

"We know what you mean," said my wife.

★ ★ ★

It wasn't until we were back in Alaska that I finally comprehended that we had really left. It was a realization that came in Fairbanks, when I called Roger Kaye. A woman answered. Roger had flown his plane to Fort Yukon, and she hoped he would be back within a few days. Her English was halting. Masako?

"Yes," she said tentatively.

"So did Roger get lucky and get married?"

She laughed. "Yes. I am his wife. Please, who are you?"

I told her, realizing it probably wouldn't mean much, if anything. And even more than when I'd driven, full of nostalgia, through the country with Cody and Joan, I felt the separation of myself from what I'd been. I'd never met Masako, had just listened to Roger talk about her for hours, and now here she was. I'd missed something. Between me and the place I'd tried so long to leave lay an unfamiliar year.

Stu Pechek didn't answer his phone, but I tracked down Marta McWhorter, who within minutes of hearing my voice broke into tears. One of her best friends was probably dead. Roger Kaye was in Fort Yukon, she said, because Roger Dowding had disappeared the day before while flying above the upper Sheenjek River.

I knew Dowding, had flown with him myself. He was the old man of the air above the vast Yukon River basin, the senior of the few pilots who were the lifelines between the isolated lives of the interior bush. He was the man who flew Stuart and Marta in and out of the Grayling Lake cabin, and the one who at fifty-two below had landed on the convoluted ice of the Sheenjek to save the lives of Shannon Hayden and her unborn baby, little Judi Ann, after Richard Hayden had radioed his emergency to a Japanese airliner in February 1989.

He'd flown there more than twenty years, a long time to push the adage that there are old pilots and bold pilots, but no old, bold pilots. He'd dropped one sheep hunter off along the upper Sheenjek, Marta said, and as he spiraled up into the snow flurries and clouds above the river had radioed back to the hunter that he was going to climb up through the stuff and drop over the top of the Brooks Range to check

301

on a hunter he'd left several days before along the Hulahula. It was a fifteen-minute flight.

"We'd just got back from Costa Rica with him," Marta said. "He was so happy. He'd had some bad times, and now everything was fine. We went to help him set up a new business down there, and he was so excited he couldn't sleep. We'd wake up in the middle of the night, and he'd be out looking at things in the tide pools with a flashlight."

She began to cry again. "I'd just finished helping him redo the interior of his plane," she said.

"So is Stuart up there, too?"

"No, he doesn't know. There's a halibut opener; he's at sea. I don't handle this very well, Grant. I'm supposed to be meeting planes and consoling people. . . . His girlfriend—he's finally met this perfect person— she's going to be in at midnight, and I don't know . . ."

We were staying at my sister's place, just a mile or so from Marta's. "Come on over here," I said. "It doesn't sound like the best of times to be alone."

"I'll just blubber," she said.

"That's okay. You had dinner? I'll bet not."

"I don't want dinner."

"You need to eat."

"Well," she said in a small voice, "do you have any chocolate ice cream? That sounds terrible, doesn't it?"

"We'll have some by the time you get here."

"It's just that whenever I get upset, I crave chocolate."

"That's okay. It sounds good to me, too."

"And I drink whiskey," she said.

Roger Kaye, aside from the heartache I know he must have felt at the loss of Roger Dowding, seemed to have taken his life where he had been determined to take it when I had seen him last.

On Christmas Eve 1991, he said, he'd flown up the Sheenjek River at twenty below, the cabin of his Cessna 170 filled with dark-eyed females and the scents of Japanese cooking. Roger was concentrating on the impending darkness. The river landing area he was heading for had frozen rough that year; he'd need light to avoid its ice ridges and drifts.

But he was happy. He had glanced over at Masako, who'd spent the past two days kitchening the big box of traditional dishes that were piping up a steam behind the rear seat. Masako's attention was on the landscape out the right window. She had traveled into the Alaska wilds twice before, alone and several times with him, but never this deeply into the winter cold. As Roger watched her, she leaned a bit to take in the white river directly below her shoulder, then let a fascinated gaze roam up the winding iceway to the shining Brooks Range in the north.

The mountains were salmon pink with alpenglow and streaked with charcoal shadows. The great, wide wash of it was magnificent but also denoted a quickly fading day. Roger had taken off from Fairbanks before daylight three hours ago to get to the Richard Hayden homestead before the 2:00 P.M. sunset. And it was okay now. Smoke from the Hayden homestead was in sight.

Behind him, Polly noticed that her dad had pulled back on the power. She leaned forward. "Are we there?"

He swung the nose of the plane just far enough eastward to open a view out the left window of the thin gray column rising from the Haydens' kitchen chimney a few miles ahead. The Cessna would touch down with plenty of light to spare. Roger glanced back at the twins. "See the smoke?"

They squinted. No. He swung back on course and spread his fingers for the girls to see. "Five minutes!"

Masako glanced at him. The smile on her lips was almost undetectable, but her eyes were shining. She enjoyed the Haydens; for a girl from a city of 25 million, their quietude and elbowroom seemed a balm. If the ice cream hadn't slid over next to the hot food, it could be a perfect trip.

During a lull late the next morning he'd retreated to a corner with a mug of camp coffee. He sat in shadow against the logs of the Hayden cabin wall, on the caribou hide-covered plank platform that served as both master bed and day couch. Except for the soft chatter of Susan Hayden's dog talk floating in from the kennels, his family and friends were mostly quiet, the two girls on the floor playing with five-year-old Duane and the baby, Judi Ann; Richard Hayden at the table stretching some marten skins; the older boys in their bedroom looking at a Cabela's catalog that had come in the packet of mail Roger had delivered; and Masako at the other side of the cabin with Shannon Hayden, getting a lesson in the art of woodstove cookery.

From a sheaf of papers he had carried in from the plane, he took a five-page Homestudy report that he had received the day before from the Department of Health and Social Services. He'd already scanned it—he did that immediately—and knew that it contained good news: the social worker, Harriette Guenther, had recommended that the girls be permanently placed with Roger and Masako. But Roger hadn't had time yet to peruse her analysis, and he'd been anxious since he first picked it up to learn what he looked like under the Division of Family and Youth Services microscope.

He skipped to the beginning of the meat of it, on page 2. The girls' school principal, Fredi Buffmire, it said, described Roger as distraught when he brought Lolly and Polly to her office to enroll them in Fairbanks's Pearl Creek School three days after picking them up in Bethel.

"She described the girls as 'Wild, wild, wild,' " the report said. "She stated that they were incredible and she just couldn't imagine them fitting into a classroom setting. They never stood still and made a shambles of her office."

Roger allowed himself a chuckle then read on, mildly surprised that the things that had worried him so much at first—being asked to leave stores and libraries, Polly breaking her arm at school, Masako coming to live with him and help out—were treated in the report matter-of-factly. In fact, he realized, it was the girls' apparent incorrigibility in the beginning that had given him the opportunity to look so good. If they had been little model citizens, any improvement in their demeanors might have been hard to demonstrate. Then again, if they had been little model citizens, he probably wouldn't have filed for custody in the first place.

He kept reading, gratified that the social worker had learned that after less than three months in school Principal Buffmire regarded Lolly and Polly as among the most remarkable success stories she had seen. The girls were awarded Student Achiever of the Week honors and had their pictures in the local paper. Polly, it said, "is now definitely sure to qualify for the Talented and Gifted Program. She is described as having an extremely high level of abstract thinking. Lolly seems to be artistically talented, and both girls have a now wonderful sense of humor."

He sighed and looked at the twins, who were dressing little Judi Ann now as if she were a doll. Lord. He'd thought they would never come around. He'd enrolled them in victims counseling at the Chief Andrew Isaac Medical Center. He sought out books and guidance at the Fairbanks Resource Center for Parents and Children. He continually asked questions of friends whose parenting skills he admired. He decided to work on one behavioral problem at a time and started with a ritual of getting the girls to bed and setting acceptable nighttime reading and sleeping patterns . . .

Until finally.

He watched them for a few moments more. He watched Masako, here in the wilds after giving up her ten-year career as a magazine layout artist. The report said that Masako saw her child guidance logic as partly American, partly Japanese, partly an obligation to let them express themselves with more spontaneity, freedom, and creativity than were permitted in Japan, and partly a responsibility to help instill in them a strong sense of cultural pride and expression.

Roger smiled, thinking back to that day with Lill Fickus up on the John River. He had taken the girls there to ask her advice about parenting but also to ask her—as a respected Athabascan elder—to talk to the girls about being his kids. They had told him that they wanted no part of a white man ordering them around. "This man's race is not important," she'd responded. "What is important is that he is your father. You must learn the importance of family. God gave you a white father to learn to trust and respect."

Until three months ago he had lived alone. Now, silently, he thanked these strong women. He closed the report. He collected his family, and in the low noon light they put on cross-country skis and slid out past the white and gold Cessna, which was tied down on the ice, and up the frozen river, marveling at the translucent sheen of the gelid blue overflow. In their thickly padded red snowsuits, Lolly and Polly scrambled up to top speed and aimed for a patch of slick ice.

An hour up the river they stopped and stood awhile in a silence so intense that it seemed to reverberate among the white hills, and then they skied on back, the girls sliding ahead to meet Susan, who was coming toward them with two romping sled dogs. Roger watched them and reflected: Everything that was important to him was here—this place, these friends, this family. This feeling. This freedom.

Rick Steiner went to Jakarta for a while, but now he's back in Cordova, where the grinding by humanity against nature just gets hotter, like friction building between tectonic plates. Hal Bernton, a friend of mine who writes for the *Anchorage Daily News* and knows of my interest, sent me a clip the other day of a piece he'd done on Cordova.

"Logging Sparks a Bitter Battle," says the headline; and the story chronicles how the Eyak Native corporation has begun to harvest the pristine slopes that face town and are adding insult to injury by having their logging trucks drive a circuitous, flaunting route through downtown, as many as thirty times a day. The Eyaks want to save the timber, too, says the story, "but only if the price is right. Eyak wants more than $100 million for its timber, more than 100 times the stumpage price of a 1986 Eyak timber sale."

The $100 million, of course, would come from the $1 billion oil spill settlement with Exxon. "It's a very, very difficult issue," said Eyak Corporation President Kathryn Andersen. "We would rather be mining diamonds in Africa. But we didn't get diamonds in Africa. We got trees in a national forest."

So Rick was bracing for the next round when I talked with him last. Being just back from Jakarta, he said, had helped refresh him some ways but had intensified his sense of urgency. Jakarta, he said, "is one of the most hideous places on earth. Half its people are starving. They have no handle whatsoever on population control—200 million people on a few islands—and in Jakarta mosquitoes swarming everywhere, rats literally running over your feet. I realized once that I was thirteen miles out of town and the stench was still enough to knock me over.

"But the big thing is, in terms of global survival our environmental problems pale before those in the Southern Hemisphere. Indonesia is the world's fifth largest oil producer and a major exporter of natural gas, coal, and timber. And believe me, they're going after it all. In Borneo, which is Indonesia's Alaska, smoke from the operations of more than a hundred big logging companies billows over the jungles everywhere you look, everywhere you fly.

"And all those jungles are being sold to the powers that be. Even to you and me. If you could only see what it has done. The rape by power of the third world. And the corruption; you can buy anybody. One of their economists told me privately that an estimated half of Indonesia's gross national product goes into bribery and corruption.

"I had a meeting one day with the Indonesian minister of the environment, a man named Dr. Emil Salim, who assured me in a loud voice so that all the other public officials around us could hear, that all timber harvesting would stop by the year 2000. And then behind his hand he said, 'Because by then there will be none left. I have very little hope.' "

Rick's trip to Indonesia was funded by the World Resources Institute, which also sent him to other third world countries to compare environmental crises around the world. The trip, he said, "was in hopes of finding common problems toward which we might direct common answers. And I realized as I traveled that the first part is easy and obvious. As in a word what is wrong with South America is cattle, what is wrong with North America is oil.

"Our consumerism drives our disrespect and our extirpation; and the political will to keep grubbing the world's life out by the roots is in itself rooted in our cities; and from our cities we get a flow of tithes to environmental organizations in order to appease our consciences. And all our tithing is but water across the top of the flame."

"Sounds like you're fueled for another fight," I said.

"Actually," he said, "another of the big things I realized is that the oil spill that has loomed so large in so many of our lives here was comparatively nothing. It left us with our health. We are incredibly healthy. We

307

have a comparatively incredible health care system. We are incredibly stable. And we are, comparatively, incredibly honest.

"On the one hand, when you see all that is about to happen, you are caught up by the Cassandra syndrome, in which the world is perpetually on the brink of disaster. It's empowering, in a way; it sets you free; it sets your rage free, to do whatever you think you have to do to fight the apocalypse. But it scares me, and I don't like it.

"I find myself wanting to work a different way. I want to help redefine our notions of prosperity. I want to see what I can do to inspire people to believe that to benefit the whole is to benefit themselves.

"I don't mean that I want to spend my time arranging chairs on the deck of a sinking *Titanic*. I mean that I want to spend more of my time trying to change the premises on which we base our lives. I don't know that we can unlearn our frontier mentality in a generation. But we can unteach it to our children; you can unteach it to Cody.

"And where we haven't learned the art of the long view, maybe he can. And maybe in the process he can help humanity find its place. We have defined practically everything else, but as a species we've never, in all our sentience, been able to define the kind of world in which we want to live."

The last time I talked with David Grimes, he phoned from Santa Cruz, California, to tell me he wouldn't be able to swing by like he'd thought he would. Yes, he still owned the *Orca II,* and still sailed the sound. But he was leaving more often now and was thinking about moving on.

To do what, he didn't know. Maybe write, maybe compose music; something, at any rate, to help earth heal. "I know the direction," he said; "I don't know the destination."

It was October 1992. He told me about a walk he'd taken that morning down to the beach. It was early, about six, and drizzly; the morning sun had not yet burned off the coastal summer fog. He liked that time best, because in the camouflaging fog and in the absence of surfers and traffic and metropolitan roar he found it easier to imagine the place as it had been until some Franciscan cartographer named the mission and its little inflowing river after two distant saints. Before Cruz and Lorenzo, this river mouth had been no less wild than an estuary in Alaska. Brown bears chased salmon and steelhead through the shallows, right here, where the San Lorenzo washed only a foot or two deep over the dark gray sand of Santa Cruz beach into the Pacific. The bears were gone, of course, and David hadn't seen salmon here, but he knew the steelhead still came. There were none right now because the tide was at ebb, but just a few days ago he'd stood here and watched dozens of mercury-bright *Oncorhynchus mykiss* porpoise into the current on a flood tide. And later he'd floated the little river down from a state park ten miles upstream and seen the dark fish holding in pools, and for all the ten miles a broken line of glazed orange eggs lay stranded along the high-water mark ashore.

He'd stood watching the clear river spill into the gray Pacific, then slipped off his sandals, sat, and leaned against a boardwalk piling. Way above him, a delivery truck clunked over the heavy planks of the Santa Cruz boardwalk. He found it amusing and vaguely ironic that this river, this small artery of the earth, continued busily to feed the sea beneath the feet of some tens of thousands of summer tourists who flocked to the roller coaster and the cotton candy booths of the arcade thirty feet overhead.

He was newly in love. Her name was Betsy; she was a student of Chinese medicine, and he was certainly in a mood to be healed. That had been almost the entire message of these past few years, hadn't it—humanity, heal thyself? Given his disposition toward a philosophy in which healing relies on harmony among the body, the spirit, and the earth, it seemed to him not only natural but probably ordained that he and Betsy should meet. They were, after all, walking the same path.

It was David's habit to begin each day ceremoniously. It didn't have to be much; when we were on his boat he would go topside to bow to a day or to the boat itself, or to a delight or an idea. Some mornings he would take a purifying plunge into the cold, glassy water, or row to a beach to build a small fire and waft sage smoke into his lungs, Athabascan style, to purge away the staleness of sleep. The point of whatever he did was to strip oneself if only for a moment of all human clutter, and to face the earth, the elemental, one to one. He appreciated the aboriginal logic of having these ceremonies early in the morning, when there wasn't much clutter to strip.

Today, meditating here at the oceanic womb of the earth, his trib-
ute was to women. His actions weren't so much of ceremony as of
acknowledgment: a simple clutching of sand at the ocean's edge, feeling
the unmistakable pulse of the feminine as he pressed the sea from the
wet dune. In the toss and sigh of the surf he recognized, as the writer
Ursula Le Guin had described them, the foam women tumbling in to lie
"at the longest reach of the waves, rounded and curded, shaking and
trembling. . . ."

To them, then; to the foam women, and to all the other women of
his life. To the woman of his present, who was certainly enough, but who
was not all, and who was not the reason he'd been unable to sleep last
night. The sleeplessness was because he was troubled by a worry that he
might be fashioning an alliance that might exclude, or at the very least
hurt, two very important others: Brenda, the woman who had been his
balm; and Beth, the woman who had been his escape.

He leaned his head back against the piling. Amid the gray and green
swell that the ocean created behind his closed eyes, he re-created Brenda,
her own eyes glistening large and brown from a face with the olive tone
and high cheekbones that hinted firmly of its Cherokee heritage. Brenda
was a wartime romance. She went to Cordova to be associate director of
the state's oil spill office and in the chaos soon found herself sought and
seeking. Today, looking back, David pictured himself and her as small
children huddling in a storm. They were no longer lovers, but they were
fast friends. Would they be fast friends after she learned of Betsy?

And then there was Beth, of course, with whom it would be even
more difficult. Not that David flattered himself with his worry. Maybe
Beth would be devastated, maybe she wouldn't. Maybe she could accom-
modate a new love in his life, maybe she couldn't. He just didn't want to
hurt her, and he didn't want to lose her. She had been, in Ireland, such
a refuge. Even the thought of her came with a sort of quietude. At night,
even though she was 10,000 miles away, he both quickened and quietened
himself with memory of the equine fall of her long brown hair, and the
deerlike repose of her green eyes.

He thought of the road from the beach at Clew Bay, and all the
ghosts of Eire along it, getting inside him, making him feel their songs,
and him sitting beside the road on stones next to a bramblebush singing

of Beth. It had been a year ago, almost exactly. *Samhein*. Halloween. Bewitched, he had transformed into a bard.

In Santa Cruz he stirred and looked out under the lifting fog, over the Pacific. But then, all Irishmen are bards, he thought. All women are loves, all loves are songs, all songs are ghosts.

He stood and took a last brief look at the clear ripplings of the San Lorenzo. He pictured the water separating from the land, spreading away from where he stood, weaving among the isles of the archipelagos north, and washing in to replenish the wounded waters of Prince William Sound. It came to him that all beaches are points of departure, and all rivers are saints.

The Richard Hayden family remains intact, in the wilderness, in the Sheenjek River valley below the peaks among which Roger Dowding died. At sixteen, pretty Susan made a foray into the world, as she called it when I was visiting, and took up with a notorious carouser in Fairbanks. She collected whatever hurts were necessary to convince her that her better options lay in the wildlands she knew. She went home, and I've heard that she and her brother Daniel have moved into one of the line cabins. Under the watchful eye of a father some 70 miles of trail away, they have at once both family and independence, as they roam a continent's farthest hills, to tend 150 miles of trapline alone.

Don Peter, my guide along the Yukon, resigned from his directorship of the Alaska Native Human Resource Development Program for the University of Alaska. A woman who'd worked with him told me that he resigned under pressure. "If he hadn't, several of us would have sued him for harassment, sexual and otherwise."

I don't know that story. I'd never found Don Peter particularly agreeable as an administrator, but he'd been a companionable man of the bush and had introduced me to what I saw as an alien and tragic river world.

I haven't followed that world, haven't heard what has become of Ramona and Eddie James. In Don Peter's retreat to the village in which he remains a prominent Native leader, I sense something that smacks of the same old us-and-them-ism that is obvious to all who live in Alaska, and is only bureaucratically denied.

I telephoned Don one day, to try to get a feel for what might have happened, and when I brought it up, he snorted. "The bastards," he said. "They don't understand Indians, so they get rid of them. That's all there was to it. That's all there ever is."

Dolly Garza still neither makes nor tolerates excuses—for her culture or any other. She enforces progress.

Chuck Hamel grinds his ax.

It's getting sharper. In 1993 he sued the Alyeska Pipeline Service Company and the giant private-eye firm Wackenhut. Just before Christmas—after federal judge Stanley Sporkin warned Alyeska lawyers that he was about to rule that the two companies' spyjinks against Hamel were illegal—the case was settled out of court. As part of the agreement, Chuck can't say how much he got, but sources close to the case say that Alyeska and its owners, including Exxon, British Petroleum, and Atlantic Richfield, spent between $10 and $20 million to defend the suit. Chuck Hamel, they guess, got between $5 and $10 million.

In the spring of '94, he was gearing up to go after Exxon for the value of a North Slope oil lease he says the company cheated him out of by lying about its value. His price tag this time: a reported $125 million.

In May of 1992, John Haines wrote me from George Washington University. "I am in a state of near collapse," he wrote. "I just cannot take this life anymore."

But he took it, and went back to Alaska for another season, and on July 29 he wrote me from there:

> Being back here now makes for a specially acute sense of having come back to something that is finished, over with. And I can't say that it is a good feeling, far from it. Alaska for me now

has another feeling altogether different from the one it gave me when I first arrived. Partly it is subjective, but it is more than that. It's hard to see a decent future for things here, and Fairbanks seems more of a travesty than ever. Maybe I've been spoiled by a *real* city, with bookstores and decent places to eat; but also the people make a difference, and there seem now fewer of them here than ever—I mean the sort one can talk to.

But I have not been able to decide on what to do about it, and have had too little time for that yet. I am cleaning up what I can, making the best of it while there is still some summer left. I had hope and energy last summer that I haven't now, and that is what makes the real difference.

It's true that when I left here last summer I did not know if I would come back to live and rather suspected I would not. Nothing was clear, except that things might after all be coming to an end for me in Alaska. A complicated matter, as I'm sure you know, and has to do with, among other things, the expiration of a hope, both personal and social and political. Also, I am older.

Where to go is the question. Missoula is still a decent small city, and I would not mind moving back there if there was even a small chance of teaching at UM.

I only know I can't stay here. I feel the isolation all too keenly; which is to say that I seem to have outgrown this place, finally. A little late, perhaps, but it seems not to be a matter under anyone's control; it happens.

So John left Alaska again, for yet another residency, the latest in Alabama. Someone wrote to me and asked me if I would consider being a charter sponsor of a Save the John Haines Homestead Committee, which planned to lobby for legislation that would do just that. I said of course; and they have sent me a packet of material on letterhead that includes along the lefthand margin the names of myself and the twenty-four other committee members.

I should recognize all of them, probably, but don't. Those I do recognize are exceptional company: the poets Hayden Carruth and Molly

Peacock and William Stafford; writers William Kittredge, Ed Hoagland, and N. Scott Momaday; humanists and lovers of place from across the country.

It's a list that does not speak to an expiration of hope. I am sure that John will recognize that, and will emerge from this spiraling funk we friends of his have seen in him over the past few years, and will do whatever it takes to answer the question, Where to next?

In going, you look around to see who's staying, and you judge your exodus at least in part by the company you leave behind. When I began to sift among my friends for clues to what was pressing me to leave Alaska, and to measure the rest of humanity against their strength and community, I saw that we are malevolent in our greed; that we are addicted to comfort gained at the expense of place; and that to maintain the luxuries to which we have become accustomed, we slave securely for powers that will work us and bury us. We watch our champions benignly; and they become our heroes at great expense to themselves and little to us. We mistake an absence of military war for peace. As have so many other slaves of so many other times, we misinterpret tyranny as security and apathy as powerlessness. And as Abraham Lincoln said about the necessity of getting rid of that sickness, "We must touch this country once again with the better angels of our nature."

I like Rick Steiner's belief that we must redefine our notions. It diverts us from expiration of hope and toward the possibility of reaching the far side of despair.

I like it here. I like coaching a long season of soccer, and I like dependably brief nights, and snow that doesn't stick. In spite of all the new arguments about who's going to spend what holiday with whom, I like being close to kin. I like fishing with my brothers. I like fishing in December.

I like the light. Kim Heacox, the wildlands photographer for whom Alaska is a geography of hope, reminds me that photography, by definition, is writing with light. I have only recently recognized that inasmuch as *all* lifely energies are the phenomena of sunbeams transformed, each of us writes the world that same way: effulgently, through the lenses of ourselves.

We humans, in fact, are so basically creatures of light that we define our natures by it—or by its lack. Our moods are sunny or black, our minds bright or dim. If we don't understand, we're in the dark; but when we begin to comprehend, the light goes on, we get a glimmer. At our best, we are each other's sunshines, and in that state our eyes gleam, our faces beam, our voices glow, our conversations shed light; we are bright, radiant, and lustrous, with occasional flashes of inspiration, streaks of brilliance, and blazes of glory: the better angels of our nature.

But I am not finished with Alaska. Its light, although not as winterly kind, is, after all, exquisite. Besides, leaving at once opens the portal to a new beginning and the portal to a return; it never finishes anything . . .

And the world cannot be discovered by a journey of miles, no matter how long, but only by a spiritual journey of one inch, very arduous and humbling and joyful, by which we arrive at the ground at our feet, and learn to be home.

—Wendell Berry, *The Unforeseen Wilderness*

ARCTIC
OCEAN

Barrow

Arctic Circle

BROOKS RANGE

Arctic Circle

Nome

Yukon River

Fa

ALASKA

ALASKA RA

De

Anchorage

BERING SEA

Kodiak
Island

PACIFIC OCEAN